Social Problems, Women Empowerment, Population Issues and Diversity of India

Second Edition

For UPSC & State Civil Services Examinations

Bitasta Das
Centre for Contemporary Studies,
Indian Institute of Science, Bengaluru

About The Author

Dr Bitasta Das is Instructor-Undergraduate Programme, at the Centre for Contemporary Studies, Indian Institute of Science, Bengaluru. She has a Ph.D in Cultural Studies from Manipal University, Karnataka on Ethnic Issues of India. Her interests are in the areas of Nationalism, Post Colonialism, Ethnicity, Folk Arts and North East India. She teaches two courses on culture and folk arts to the undergraduate students of Indian Institute of Science.

Centre for Contemporary Studies, Indian Institute of Science, Bengaluru

The Centre for Contemporary Studies is a relatively new experiment at the Indian Institute of Science, Bengaluru. The aim of the centre is to create useful and meaningful interaction between different disciplines. Besides organising one-off lectures, workshops and seminars, the centre biennially offers a one-semester course- "The Production of Knowledge". All the events are open for the public. The centre has also recently embarked on conducting and teaching the Humanities component of the institute's Undergraduate Programme.

Social Problems, Women Empowerment, Population Issues and Diversity of India

Second Edition

For UPSC & State Civil Services Examinations

Bitasta Das
Centre for Contemporary Studies,
Indian Institute of Science, Bengaluru

G. K. PUBLICATIONS (P) LTD.

Title : Social Problems, Women Empowerment, Population Issues and Diversity of India (Second Edition)

Language : English

Authors : Bitasta Das

Typeset & Published by :

Career Launcher Infrastructure (P) Ltd.

A-45, Mohan Cooperative Industrial Area, Near Mohan Estate Metro Station, New Delhi - 110044

Marketed by :

G.K. Publications (P) Ltd.

Plot No. 9A, Sector-27A, Mathura Road, Faridabad, Haryana-121003

ISBN : **978-93-5681-120-1**

Printer's Details : Printed in India, New Delhi.

For product information :

Visit ***www.gkpublications.com*** or email to ***gkp@gkpublications.com***

Dedicated to
the resilient spirit of
India...

Acknowledgements

This book owes a lot to many people and their constant support and encouragement. Foremost is Prof. Raghavendra Gadagkar, Chairman, Centre for Contemporary Studies (CCS), Indian Institute of Science (IISc), Bengaluru. He has been less of an employer and more a mentor to me in all these years. He inspires me every single day by his dedication to work and unflinching strive towards excellence. CCS has been my intellectual home since I started working here in 2011 and I will forever remain grateful to Prof. Gadagkar for creating this space where established scholars can find their mooring and researchers like me can delve deep into their areas of interest.

My esteemed colleagues at CCS have taught me discipline and sincerity towards research and writing. I thank Prof. Rajan Gurukkal, Dr. Uday Balakrishnan, Amrita Shah, Prof. Srinivasan Raghavendran and Prof. S.V. Srinivas for building a conducive atmosphere of learning and sharing.

A special note of thanks to Dr. Uday Balakrishnan, he has been instrumental in my writing this book. Geetha Gadagkar and Dr. Debjani Banerjee have guided me during my academic and personal challenges. I thank them for their trust and the constant encouragement.

Words can never be enough for thanking my parents! Therefore, I will not attempt to thank them. They have been my backbone and my never ending source of love and support. They are my first teachers and have taught me the values of accepting diversity and respecting people. The broad outlook and attitude they have inculcated in me have been the basic tools by which I have understood issues and examined problems. The most important lesson they have taught is that I do not have any constraint against fulfilling my dreams.

My sisters Bipasha, Bikalpa, Bidisha and Bidita are the happy factors of my life. Everything would have been meaningless without their company. Thank you sisters for walking together in the journey of life like pearls in a string. I thank my brothers-in-law, Tilak, Amar, Partha and Joutishman for bringing even more joy to the family and everyday life. Rig, thank you for turning our lives innocent again!

None of my professional or personal accomplishment will be complete without acknowledging the one person who holds my entire world together-Vikram. Thank you for the guidance, goodness and cheer, beyond good and bad times. Above all, thank you for being there for me always... just like the sky above my head and earth beneath my feet.

Finally, this book would not have materialised without the unstinted support of the entire editorial team of GK Publications Pvt. Ltd. Special thanks to Mr Kannath Prakash who constantly interacted with me during the entire process of creation of this book.

Dr Bitasta Das
Bengaluru

Preface to the Second Edition

The second, revised edition of this book is updated with the latest statistical data and information at relevant places in the book. This book will be helpful for aspirants of the UPSC and state civil services examinations. A thorough reading of this book will enable aspirants to equip themselves with the theoretical knowledge and factual information to answer the questions asked in General Studies Papers II & III of the UPSC main examination. The topics covered relate to social issues like population, women's empowerment, child development, poverty alleviation, urbanization, social evils like drug addiction, alcoholism etc.

Some of the updated information given in this edition is as follows:

- Updates on population situation in India such as fertility rates, child mortality etc.
- Trends in urbanization in India; housing and sanitation issues
- Welfare schemes of the government especially after 2014
- De-globalisation and its impact
- Welfare programmes for women and children

We are hopeful that this updated edition with latest data would be a valuable tool for aspirants preparing for the UPSC and state civil services examinations.

We wish all readers the best in their endeavours.

The Publishers

Preface to the First Edition

This book titled *Social Problems, Women Empowerment, Population Issues & Diversity of India* emerges from my curiosity to understand the enigma that we know as India. India is a vast and diverse country, embodying a long history and multifarious culture. Indian society today is an epitome of a colourful mixture of tradition and modernity where science and technology co-exist with ritualistic beliefs and practices.

This book is an attempt to carefully map and dissect the issues that stares starkly at our face and that which hamper the unity and progress of India. Our aim has been to encompass the key problems of contemporary Indian society—the age-old as well as the modern issues ensued by the changing politico-cultural environment. The book also draws from the extensive research done by scholars and experts in discrete fields that constitute the Indian society. This has been done in order to provide and facilitate an in-depth knowledge to the readers to grapple and understand India holistically.

We must bear in mind that India is a dynamic society and its elements are fluid and ever evolving. If we attempt to interpret the elements as frozen and unassailable, we will fail to appreciate the very essence of this country. Being the home for criss-crossed, multi-religious, multi-linguistic, multi-ethnic communities, it is but explicable that disputes would arise time and again. Indian society in its long history of existence have faced many such challenges; sometimes fleeting and sometimes prolonged. It is undeniably because of the will and intent of the Indian masses to remain together that India has sustained itself as a society despite the challenges.

This book is specifically designed for the candidates attempting competitive exams to contextually and coherently comprehend in a gist, the challenges of contemporary India.

Dr Bitasta Das

CONTENTS

1

DIVERSITY OF INDIA

"Creativity stems from diversity."

INTRODUCTION

Mark Twain had said, "India is the cradle of human race, the birthplace of human speech, the mother of history, the grandmother of legend, and the great grandmother of tradition. Our most valuable and most instructive materials in the history of man are treasured up in India only!"

India, as we know today, has emerged as a result of numerous integration and disintegration that took place during a long period in history. To understand the characteristics of contemporary India, we need to understand its history which has bestowed the diversified essence to the nation.

Excavations of sites belonging to the Harappan era show that the people lived in brick houses in towns with excellent drainage. One of the oldest scriptures in the world is the four volume Vedas that many regard as the repository of national thoughts that anticipated some of the modern scientific discoveries. Despite formidable barriers in the form of the mighty Himalayas and oceans, India also received a succession of foreigners, many of them carrying swords and guns. But nearly all of them stayed on. Out of these waves of immigration has emerged the composite culture of India and made it a land of unity in diversity. India became a land of assimilation and learning, a land of change and continuity. According to the one school of thought, the Aryans were among the first to arrive in India, which was inhabited by the Dravidians. Others who came here included Greeks, Persians, Mughals, and even British, Portuguese, and French. Over the years there have been many major ruling dynasties like the Shakas, the Kushans, the Maurayas, and the Guptas. Nearly every major religion in the world is represented in India. It is also the land of Lord Buddha, Lord Mahavira, and Guru Nanak Dev, the founders of Buddhism, Jainism, and Sikhism.

EARLY HISTORY

The Early Empires

Whereas human settlement in India dates back to roughly 400,000 to 200,000 B.C., urbanisation and trade appear to have begun in the Indus River Valley around 3000 B.C. with the Harappan civilisation. From this period numerous empires ruled various portions of South Asia, often assimilating a rich array of peoples and each adding its own contribution to an increasingly rich tapestry of cultures, ideas, and technologies.

Among the most influential early empires were the Aryans, who migrated from Persia to northwestern India around 2000 B.C. and brought a new pantheon of anthropomorphic gods, an early form of Sanskrit language, a tiered social system essentially based on ethnicity and occupation, and religious texts that are an important part of living Hindu traditions.

From 326 B.C. to around 200 B.C., the Mauryan Empire emerged as India's first imperial power and ruled its areas with a highly centralized and hierarchical administration. For the next few hundred years, North and South India experienced a succession of ruling powers. From 320 A.D. to 550

Among the most influential early empires were the Aryans, who migrated from Persia to northwestern India around 2000 B.C. and brought a new pantheon of anthropomorphic gods, an early form of Sanskrit language, a tiered social system essentially based on ethnicity and occupation, and religious texts that are an important part of living Hindu traditions.

A.D., most of North India was ruled by the Gupta Empire, which in contrast to the Mauryan Empire, maintained a decentralized form of government, using numerous regional and local officials to govern vast territories with an array of local political, economic, and social arrangements. As under the Aryans, Gupta authority was religiously legitimized, and it was in this period called the Classical Age that the multiple components of Hindu culture became crystallized into a more unified system of thought.

From the disintegration of the Gupta Empire to the mid-thirteenth century, various regional kingdoms emerged, and conflicts among them often led to their defeat but rarely to their total annihilation. As a result, no highly centralized government emerged in South India, and South Indian villages and districts enjoyed much greater local autonomy than those in North India. During this period, South India engaged in flourishing trade with Arabs and Southeast Asia, which facilitated the diffusion of Indian mathematical concepts to the Middle East and Indian art, literature, and social customs to Southeast Asia.

Islamic influence in South Asia emerged around 711 as Arabs conquered part of Sindh (now in Pakistan), and by the tenth century, Punjab came under the control of Turkish ruler Mahmud of Ghazni. By the thirteenth century, much of India had been periodically conquered, but rarely held for long, by a steady succession of Turkish rulers collectively referred to as the Delhi Sultanate or Mughal emperors. The most prominent Mughal ruler was the astute and religiously tolerant Akbar, who ruled from 1556 to 1605. Akbar oversaw substantial political and geographic consolidation by using locally established warriors and powerful zamindar landlords to control local populations and collect revenues. But over time, the administrative capacities of later Mughal rulers suffered from bloated and excessively corrupt bureaucracies and huge, unwieldy armies.

DIVISIONS OF INDIA'S ANCIENT HISTORY

The ancient period in the Indian history can be broadly categorized into the following heads: Pre-historic Period, Early Historic Era, and Golden Age.

Pre-historic Period

This age of the Indian history is mainly sub-divided into two parts, which are discussed below:

Stone Age

The period starts from the age of Homo erectus and continues till the starting of the Indus Valley Civilisation. Homo erectus remains including crafted tools found near the Narmada Valley prove that the central part of India was inhabited during the period dating back in between the past 5,00,000 years and 2,00,000 years. The oldest archaeological site was found near the river valley of the Soan River, which is a site of Palaeolithic Hominid. The Neolithic Age featured by extensive settlements followed the Mesolithic Age. The findings of Mehrgarh, dating back to 7000 B.C. near Balochistan in Pakistan represents the early South Asian Neolithic culture. This culture even gets reflected from the remains of the civilisation of Indus Valley, which was the earliest urban civilisation of India.

Bronze Age

The earlier part of the Indus Valley Civilisation, which is even known as the Mohenjo-daro–Harappa Civilisation dating back to 3300 B.C. marks

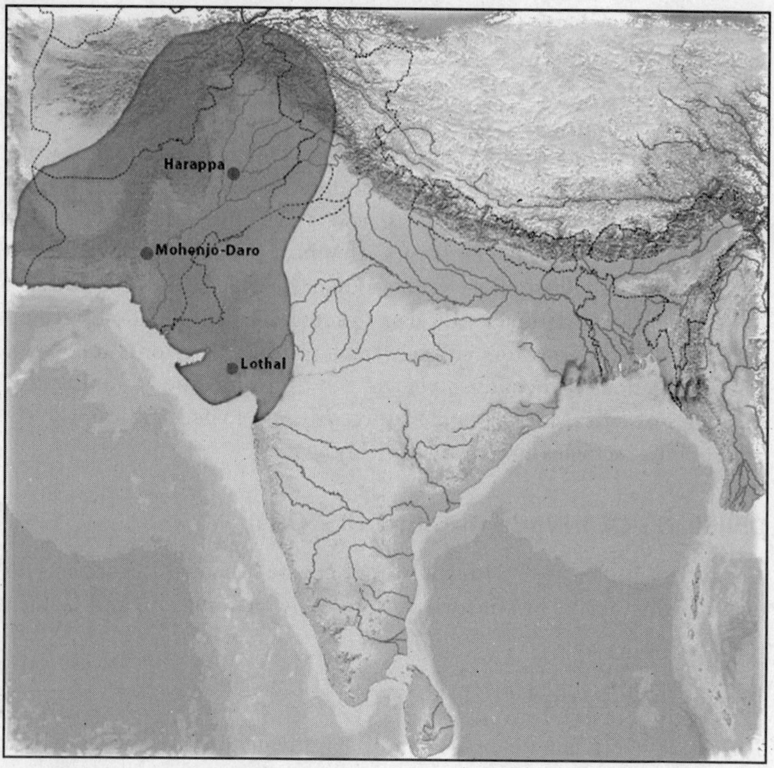

Map 1 *Pre-historic Age Map of India*

the beginning of the Bronze Age. Originating from the banks of the river Indus and its tributaries, primarily, the civilisation was located in the present day Gujarat, Haryana, Rajasthan, and Punjab states of India and some parts of Pakistan. The archeological findings of this civilisation prove the handcrafted and metallurgical techniques developed by the Harappans who were the inhabitants of that region. The civilisation of Mohenjo-daro and Harappa reached its matured stage during the period in between 2600 B.C. to 1900 B.C. Known for its improved brick multi-storied establishments and modernised drainage system, the civilisation includes some famous urban centers in India like Dholavira, Kalibangan, Lothal, Rakhigarhi, and Rupar. (Refer to Map 1 for a view of pre-historic India.)

Early Historic Era

Following are the different sub-divisions of India's early historic period (refer to Map 2).

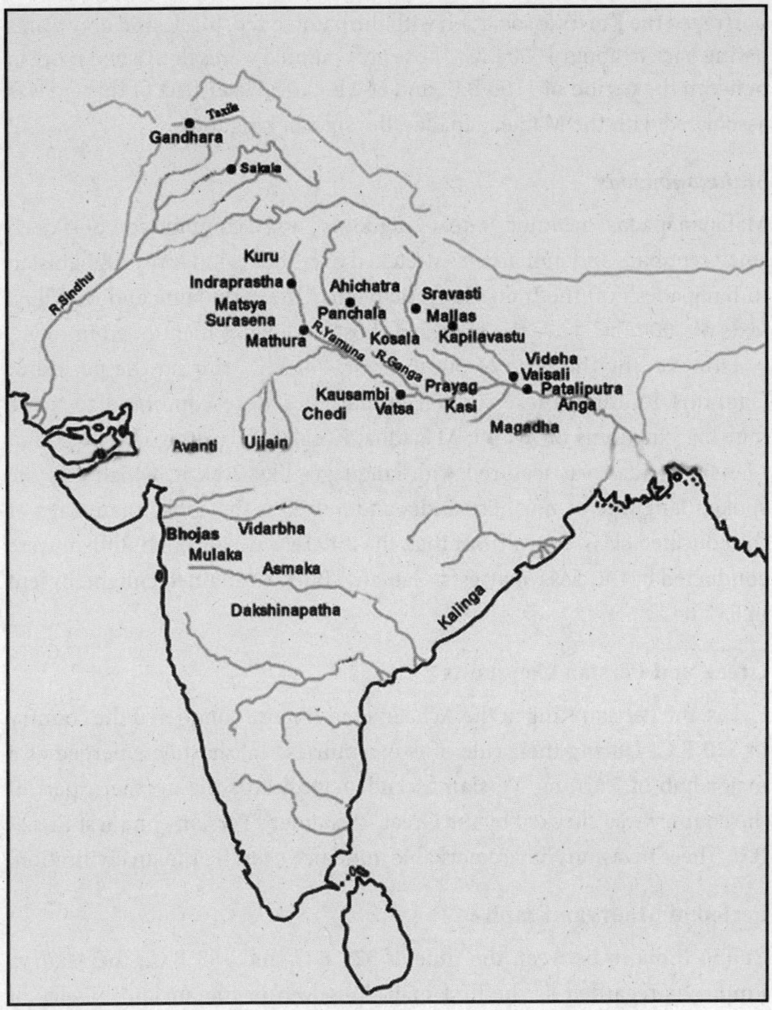

Map 2 *Ancient India (500 B.C.)*

Vedic Period

Lasting from around 1500 B.C. to 500 B.C., this historical period gained its name from the sacred text of Hindus, the Vedas. Vedic civilisation marked the foundation of the Hindu religion and its association with Indian culture. The Rig-Vedic period witnessed the social as well as agricultural development of the Aryan society. It was during this early historical time that the *Ramayana* and the *Mahabharata*, the two great Sanskrit epics came into existence. The starting of the Iron Age in India's northwestern side portrayed the Kuru's association with the painted red, black, and grey wares dating back to about 1000 B.C. Those grey painted wares flourished more in between the period of 1100 B.C. and 600 B.C. The later part of this era was associated with the Mahajanapadas, the sixteen kingdoms.

Mahajanapadas

Mahajanapadas, meaning "Great kingdoms", was a combination of sixteen small republics and monarchies stretched over the region from Afghanistan to Bangladesh on the Indo-Gangetic plains. The early Jaina and Buddhist texts of 1000 B.C. have the names of those Janapadas mentioned in them.

However, by the time of 500 B.C. or 400 B.C., during the period of Gautama Buddha, these sixteen monarchies were combined to make four big kingdoms of Avanti, Magadha, Kosala, and Vatsa. This period of Mahajanapadas was featured with languages like Prakrit, which was the spoken language of northern India and Sanskrit, the spoken language of the educated class. Apart from that, the different rituals of Hinduism were conducted by the class of priests. Gautama Buddha attained enlightenment in 537 B.C.

Greek and Persian Conquests

Cyrus, the Persian King of the Achaemenid Empire conquered the country in 530 B.C. During their rule of two centuries, Takshashila emerged as a major hub of learning. Persian ascendancy towards the northern part of the country was checked by the Great Alexander's Persian conquest in 327 B.C. These invasions had remarkable influence over the Indian civilisation.

Period of Mauryan Empire

Ruling India in between the time of 322 B.C. and 185 B.C., the Maurya Empire is regarded as the first main kingdom in the ancient history of India which was geographically extensive as well as politically powerful. Founded in Magadha by Chandragupta Maurya, the empire had military strength as well. However, the empire flourished most during the 37 years' rule of Ashoka the Great from 268 B.C. to 232 B.C. Apart from an efficient and modern socio-economic society, this period of Indian history even witnessed the massive development of slavery. The Ashokan inscriptions and the *Arthashastra* written by Kautilya are the main written records of this period.

The Golden Age

The Golden Age in the ancient history of India included the rule of the following dynasties:

Satavahana Empire

The decline of the Maurya dynasty marked the emergence of the Satavahanas. Established by King Simuka, this dynasty was spread over a huge area of western as well as southern part of the country. Though this empire ruled India from 50 B.C. to 250 A.D., it earned its fame during the reign of Satakarni I. Besides the flourishing of Buddhism, their rule was featured with great works of art as well as architecture. Many Buddhist Chaityas, Stupas, and Viharas were constructed in the country during this period.

Kushan Empire

Among the several kingdoms emerging during the period in between 185 B.C. and 300 A.D., the Kushans were the biggest. It was during this period that India witnessed a rise in the country's foreign trade, art, and culture. Originating from Turkistan in China, the Kushans established their empires

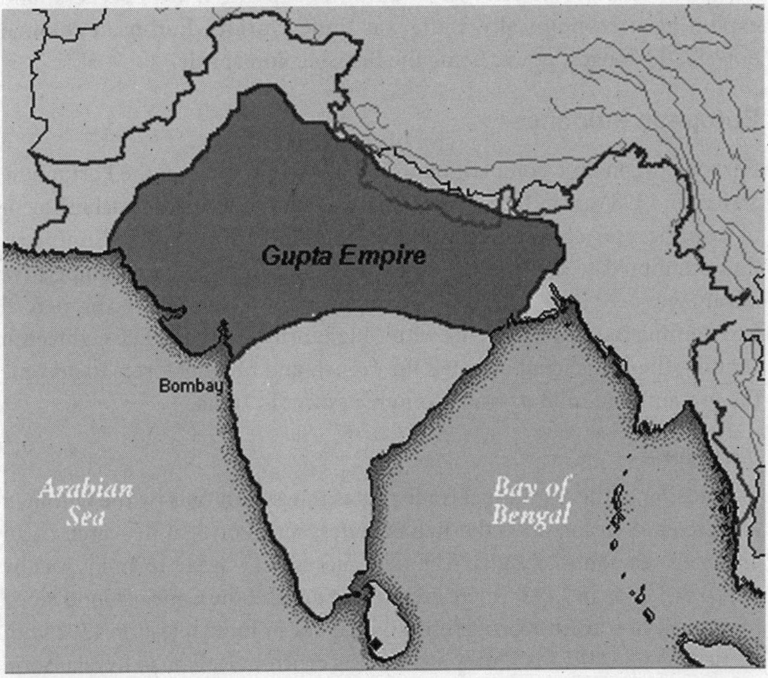

Map 3 *Gupta Empire*

in Peshawar and Taxila. Numerous foreigners migrated to India during the period from 200 B.C. to 100 A.D. Kanishka who was the third emperor of this dynasty made the empire flourish the most.

Gupta Dynasty

Being one of the largest empires in the world, which had military and political strength, the rule of the Gupta Empire is said to be India's Golden Age (refer to Map 3). Though the empire was established by Srigupta I, a Magadhan ruler, Chandragupta laid the foundation of this great dynasty as well as combated foreign invasions. Some of the other prominent rulers of this dynasty were Samudragupta, Chandragupta II, Kumargupta I, and Skandagupta. In spite of his heroic efforts, it was during the time of Skandagupta that the Gupta dynasty failed to survive the repeated Hun invasions.

COLONIALISM AND INDEPENDENCE

Colonialism is defined as the policy or practice of acquiring full or partial political control over another country, occupying it with settlers, and exploiting it economically. India was under various European colonial powers, the longest power being the British colonial rule.

European Influence

European economic competition in India began soon after the Portuguese arrived in 1498, and by the early 1600s, it was manifested in the establishment of commercial companies, such as England's East India Company, that attempted to capture the spice trade. In order to gain competitive advantages over each other, European powers also engaged in commercial and administrative alignments with Mughal rulers. By the late eighteenth century, the British had defeated the French and Mughal forces to become the pre-eminent military and economic power in India.

Portuguese

The closing of the traditional trade routes in western Asia by the Ottoman Empire, and rivalry with the Italian states, sent Portugal in search of an alternate sea route to India. The first successful voyage to India was by Vasco da Gama in 1498, when after sailing around the Cape of Good Hope he arrived in Calicut. Portuguese colonial era in India began in 1502 with the setting up of the first European trading centre at Kollam in Kerala. Soon the city of Goa was also captured.

The Portuguese established a chain of outposts along India's west coast and on the island of Ceylon (now Sri Lanka) in the early 16th century. They built the St. Angelo Fort at Kannur to guard their possessions in North Malabar. Goa was their prized possession and the seat of Portugal's viceroy. Portugal's northern province included settlements at Daman, Diu, Chaul, Baçaim, Salsette, and Mumbai. The rest of the northern province, with the exception of Daman and Diu, was lost to the Maratha Empire in the early 18th century. The less inhabited areas of southern Bombay were given by Portugal to England in the form of dowry, marking the beginning of the English presence in India.

Dutch

The Dutch East India Company established trading posts on different parts along the Indian coast. For some while, they controlled the Malabar southwest coast, the Coromandel southeastern coast, and Surat. The Dutch later became less involved in India after they had the Dutch East Indies (now Indonesia) as their prized possession.

French

The first trade establishment of French was in Pondicherry on the Coromandel Coast in southeastern India in 1674. Subsequent French settlements were Chandernagore in Bengal, northeastern India in 1688, Yanam in Andhra Pradesh in 1723, Mahe in 1725, and Karaikal in 1739. The French were constantly in conflict with the Dutch and later on mainly with the British in India. After some initial French successes, the British decisively defeated the French in Bengal in the Battle of Plassey in 1757 and in the southeast in 1761 in the Battle of Wandiwash, after which the British East India Company was the supreme military and political power in southern India as well as in Bengal.

Danish

Denmark was one of the colonial powers to set foot in India. It established trading outposts in Tranquebar, Tamil Nadu (1620), Serampore, West Bengal (1755), Calicut, Kerala (1752), and the Nicobar Islands (1750s). At one time, the main Danish and Swedish East Asia companies together imported more tea to Europe than the British did. Their outposts lost economic and strategic importance, and Tranquebar, the last Danish outpost, was sold to the British in 1845.

British Influence

Though India had waves of European influence at different points in time, it was the British colonial rule that was the longest and impacted the Indians in every sphere of life.

Slowly but surely, the entire Indian subcontinent came under the British rule (refer to Map 4). By mid nineteenth century, the British introduced the railways, telegraph, and postal service in India. This was a move to establish their rule permanently in India. The first railway line was from Howrah in Calcutta to Raniganj in Bihar. The introduction of telegraph and postal services simplified communication all over the country. The British passed many Acts that were met with dissatisfaction and resentment by the Indians. As a result, the Indians formed large groups and revolted against the British. Each movement was brutally crushed by the British forces. Leaders like Mahatma Gandhi, Jawaharlal Nehru, Lala Rajpat Rai, Subhash Chandra Bose, etc. arose and openly condemned the British. They were people's leaders who inspired the masses not to be afraid of the forces. Finally, after 200 years of British rule, India gained independence from them on 15th August, 1947. Many innocent lives were sacrificed for this achievement and India was also separated from Pakistan. The partition of India and Pakistan spread incidents of brutality and horror in both the countries. But due to the effort of the leaders and the ever sacrificing masses, India was able to gain freedom from the British and progress till the present times.

Independence Movement

India attained Independence on 15th August 1947, after a great political and social struggle. The British had ruled over India for a considerable period of time. Their initial intentions were to carry out trade in India, but in due course of time they developed political and administrative ambitions.

The Evolution of the Indian Independence Movement

The British East India Company had gained much control over the internal affairs of India. The spirit of nationalism in India gained ground in the middle of the 19th century. It was strengthened by the formation of the Indian National Congress in 1885. The authoritative and indifferent attitude of the British towards the Indian sentiments led to the national movement gaining momentum. National leaders, like Mahatma Gandhi, Pandit Jawaharlal Nehru, Vallabhbhai Patel, and many others fought for political and administrative rights of the people. The British were ruthless in their dealings with those who fought for the rights of the Indians. The divide and rule policy of the British led to the division between the Hindus and the Muslims and the formation of the Muslim League.

Extremists' Views Among the Indian National Congress Members

During the early 20th century, the spirit of nationalism received an impetus by growing extreme views among some of the Indian National Congress members. They did not favour the moderate stance taken by some of national leaders, and criticised the British for their overbearing and autocratic attitude towards the Indians.

The Role of Mahatma Gandhi

By 1920s, the national movement had become very aggressive. Mahatma Gandhi began several movements against the British, one of the most important being the Non-cooperation Movement (1920–1922 A.D.). This was followed by the Civil Disobedience Movement. The movement for independence continued through the 1930s, but it gained much ground during the Second World War. The Indian National Congress cooperated with the British in war efforts. It was hoped that the British would leave India after the Second World War. But the British did not relent. Then Mahatma Gandhi began the "Quit India Movement" in 1942. The British eventually realised that they had to leave India for good.

The Rise of the Muslim League

The Muslim League sought a separate nation for them—Pakistan. The League was concerned that independent India would have Hindus at the helm of its affairs, although it was planned that power would be divided between the Hindus and Muslims. This was the proposal by the Cabinet Mission, yet, senior leader of the Muslim League Mohammad Ali Jinnah did not agree to it. The League favoured direct action, which led to Hindu–Muslim riots. In March 1947, Lord Mountbatten had come to India and favoured partition of Punjab and Bengal despite the civil war. Gandhi did not favour partition and suggested that Jinnah should become the leader of united India. But many nationalist leaders did not favour this. Eventually, the British Parliament passed the Indian Independence Act, which led to the formation of India and Pakistan.

India is a now a sovereign republic and is a force to reckon with in world politics. It is the largest democracy in the world. It has retained its secular identity despite communal flare-ups.

CONTEMPORARY INDIA

India as a nation was born from the struggle against the colonial yoke. The challenge was to integrate the diverse people within one physical unit through the national sentiment, to stand against the British rule, and attain independence. India as a nation was consolidated at this critical juncture.

Emergence of New States

Independent India, using the boundaries drawn by The Government of India Act 1935 as the starting point, introduced federal structure to its Constitution. There were officially 565 princely states, including 210 "states". Only 21 major ones had actual state governments, and among them only four were large (Hyderabad, Mysore (now Mysuru), Baroda (now Vadodara), and Jammu and Kashmir). They acceded to one or other of the two new independent nations of India and Pakistan between 1947 and 1949. In addition, there were several colonial enclaves controlled by France

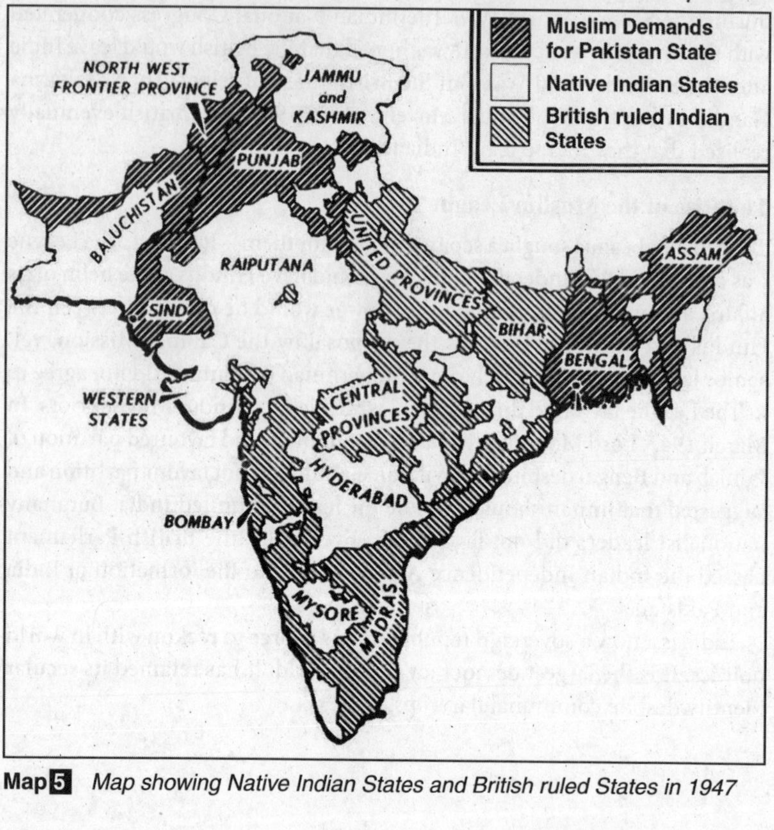

Map 5 *Map showing Native Indian States and British ruled States in 1947*

and Portugal. The political integration of these territories into India was a declared objective of the Indian National Congress, which the Government of India pursued over the next decade. Through a combination of factors, Sardar Vallabhbhai Patel and V. P. Menon convinced the rulers of the various princely states to accede to India. Having secured their accession, they then proceeded to secure and extend the central government's authority over these states and transform their administrations, until by 1956, there was little difference between the territories that had formerly been part of British India and those that had been part of princely states. Simultaneously, the Government of India, through a combination of diplomatic and military means, acquired de facto and de jure control over the remaining colonial enclaves, which too were integrated into India.

New Social and Political Developments

In 1956, States Reorganisation Act redrew the original borders along linguistic lines. Since then, there have been a few more border rearrangements. The Indian federal system was meant to divide power, with a 'Concurrent list' enumerating shared powers such as civil and criminal law, and planning; a 'State list' enumerating state power such as education, agriculture, and welfare; and a 'Union list' enumerating the centre's powers from defence and foreign affairs to income taxation, banking, and so on, and with all residual powers reverting to the centre as well. In addition to the huge powers allotted to the centre through the union list, the most vital is the power bestowed upon the Parliament to create new states, to alter boundaries of existing states, and even abolish a state by ordinary legislative procedure without recourse to constitutional amendment. Also, under emergency powers, the Constitution allows the federal government to convert itself to a unitary one. Even when the Parliament is not functioning under emergency conditions, it can make laws with respect to any matter falling in the state list for a temporary period. With the exception of Emergency period from 1975 to 1977, India has maintained a democratic political system. Building on the British-established education system, India developed an educational infrastructure that has trained one of the world's largest scientific and technical populations. Using Green Revolution agricultural technologies, the country has become self-sufficient in food production. Moreover, a combination of socialist planning and free enterprise from the 1950s to the 1970s led to substantial industrialisation with the goal of making India economically self-sufficient.

In the 1980s and 1990s, socialist economic planning and import substitution industries were slowly replaced by liberalisation measures.

A large middle class emerged, information technology developed into an important economic sector, and at times economic growth has been impressive. India has also become somewhat influential in international political and economic matters and appears set to continue those trends.

The Road Ahead: Challenges

In spite of India's march towards progress, numerous problems remain, however, such as substantial poverty, large income gaps between wealthy and poor, a large mass of people who lack the skills to participate in the new economy, and numerous insurgencies that threaten the nation's territorial integrity. Some social issues remain unresolved, and the rise of Hindu nationalism has become a particularly contentious topic in both Indian society and politics. Furthermore, some observers believe that the nation is facing difficulties in the political capacity to address these problems. Intense multiparty political competition over numerous economic and social issues has resulted in often-fragile coalitions of political parties, and no single political party has held a parliamentary majority since 1989. The government changed nine times from December 1989 to the elections in May 2004 in which the Indian National Congress returned to power under Prime Minister Manmohan Singh. Thus, increasing pluralism of political parties, growing diversity in interest-group representation, and substantial ideological divisions among parties are significant obstacles in policy implementation.

This trend, however, changed in the two consecutive elections in 2014 and 2019 when a sweeping and single majority was achieved by the BJP (Bhartiya Janta Party). There are also instances of fundamentalism and short-circuiting of the parliamentary procedures of decision-making and discussion due to the absolute majority.

Environment—Current Issues

India faces many issues on the environmental front such as, Deforestation, Soil erosion, Overgrazing, Desertification, Air pollution from industrial effluents and vehicle emissions, Water pollution from raw sewage, and runoff of agricultural pesticides. Tap water is not potable throughout the country. Huge and growing population is overstraining natural resources.

The IPCC Sixth Assessment Report reiterates the dire consequences of this human-induced breach for the Indian subcontinent: increased dry spells, intensification of extreme rainfall by more than 20 per cent, and an exponential surge in heatwaves and cyclonic events. India is the seventh-most vulnerable country with respect to climate extremes (Germanwatch 2020). Climate action needs to be scaled up both at the sub-national and district levels to mitigate the impact of extreme events.

GEOGRAPHICAL DIVERSITY OF INDIA

The Indian Subcontinent

The Mountains

Physically, the massive country is divided into four relatively well defined regions—the Himalayan mountains, the Gangetic river plains, the southern (Deccan) plateau, and the islands of Lakshadweep and Andaman and Nicobar. The Himalayas in the far north include some of the highest peaks in the world. The highest mountain in the Indian Himalayas is Khangchenjunga (8,586 m) which is located in Sikkim on the border with Nepal. To the south of the main Himalayan lays the Lesser Himalaya, rising to 3,600–4,600 m, and represented by the Pir Panjal in Kashmir and Dhauladhar in Himachal Pradesh. Further south, flanking the Indo-Gangetic Plain, are the Siwaliks which rise to 900–1,500 m.

The Plains

The northern plains of India stretch from Assam in the east to the Punjab in the west (a distance of 2,400 km), and extends to south to terminate in the saline swamplands of the Rann of Kachchh (Kutch), in the state of Gujarat. Some of the largest rivers in India including the Ganga (Ganges), Ghaghara, Brahmaputra, and the Yamuna flow across this region. The delta area of these rivers is located at the head of the Bay of Bengal, partly in the Indian state of west Bengal but mostly in Bangladesh. The plains are remarkably homogenous topographically. The agriculturally productive alluvial silts and clays of the Ganga-Brahmaputra delta in north-eastern India, for example, contrast strongly with the comparatively sterile sands of the Thar desert which is located at the western extremity of the Indian part of the plains in the state of Rajasthan.

Wetlands

India has a rich variety of wetland habitats. The total area of wetlands (excluding rivers) in India is 18.4% of the country, 70% of which comprises areas under paddy cultivation. India adds 11 more wetlands to the list of

Ramsar sites to make total 75 Ramsar sites covering an area of 13,26,677 ha in the country in the 75th year of Independence (2022). Tamil Nadu has the maximum no. of Ramsar sites (14 nos), followed by UP which has 10 nos. of Ramsar sites. India is one of the Contracting Parties to Ramsar Convention, signed in Ramsar, Iran, in 1971. India signed it on 1st Feb 1982. During 1982 to 2013, a total of 26 sites were added to the list of Ramsar sites, however, during 2014 to 2022, the country has added 49 new wetlands to the list of Ramsar sites.

Montreux Record under the Ramsar Convention is a register of wetland sites on the List of Wetlands of International Importance where changes in ecological character have occurred, are occurring, or are likely to occur as a result of technological developments, pollution or other human interference. It is maintained as part of the Ramsar List. Currently, two wetlands of India are in Montreux record: Keoladeo National Park (Rajasthan) and Loktak Lake (Manipur). Chilika lake (Odisha) was placed in the record but was later removed from it.

Forests

India possesses a great diversity of its natural ecosystems. The panorama of Indian forests ranges from evergreen tropical rain forests in the Andaman and Nicobar Islands, the Western Ghats and the northeastern states, to dry alpine scrub high in the Himalayas to the north. Between the two extremes, the country has semi-evergreen rain forests, deciduous monsoon forests, thorn forests, subtropical pine forests in the lower montane zone, and temperate montane forests.

The main areas of tropical forest are found in the Andaman and Nicobar Islands, the Western Ghats, which fringe the Arabian Sea coastline of peninsular India, and the greater Assam region in the northeast. Small remnants of rain forest are found in Odisha state. Semi evergreen rain forest is more extensive than the evergreen formation partly because evergreen forests tend to degrade to semi-evergreen with human interference. There are substantial differences in both the flora and fauna between the three major rain forest regions.

The Western Ghats Monsoon forests occur both on the western (coastal) margins of the ghats and on the eastern side where there is less rainfall. These forests contain several tree species of great commercial significance (e.g. Indian rosewood *Dalbergia latifolia, Malabar Kino Pterocarpus marsupium*, teak, and *Terminalia crenulata*), but they have now been cleared from many areas. In the rain forests there is an enormous number of tree species.

The tropical vegetation of northeast India (which includes the states of Assam, Nagaland, Manipur, Mizoram, Tripura, and Meghalaya as well as the plain regions of Arunachal Pradesh) typically occurs at elevations up to 900 m. It embraces evergreen and semi-evergreen rain forests, moist deciduous monsoon forests, riparian forests, swamps, and grasslands. Evergreen rain forests are found in the Assam Valley, the foothills of the eastern Himalayas, and the lower parts of the Naga Hills, Meghalaya, Mizoram, and Manipur where the rainfall exceeds 2,300 mm per annum.

The Andaman and Nicobar islands have tropical evergreen rain forests and tropical semi-evergreen rainforests as well as tropical monsoon moist monsoon forests. The tropical evergreen rain forest is only slightly less grand in stature and rich in species than on the mainland.

Marine Environment

The nearshore coastal waters of India are extremely rich fishing grounds. The total commercial marine catch for India has stabilised over the last ten years at between 1.4 and 1.6 million tonnes. Coral reefs occur along only a few sections of the mainland, principally the Gulf of Kutch, off the southern mainland coast, and around a number of islands opposite Sri Lanka. This general absence is due largely to the presence of major river systems and the sedimentary regime on the continental shelf. Elsewhere, corals are also found in Andaman and Nicobar, and Lakshadweep island groups although their diversity is reported to be lower than in southeast India.

Indian coral reefs have a wide range of resources which are of commercial value. Exploitation of corals, coral debris, and coral sands is widespread on the Gulf of Mannar and Gulf of Kutch reefs, while ornamental shells, chanks, and pearl oysters are the basis of an important reef industry in the south of India. Commercial exploitation of aquarium fishes from Indian coral reefs has gained importance only recently and as yet no organised effort has been made to exploit these resources. Reef fisheries are generally at the subsistence level and yields are unrecorded.

Other notable marine areas are seagrass beds, which although not directly exploited are valuable as habitats for commercially harvested species, particularly prawns, and mangrove stands. In the Gulf of Mannar, the green tiger prawn *Penaeus semisulcatus* is extensively harvested for the export market.

Five species of marine turtle occur in Indian waters: Green turtle (*Chelonia mydas*), Loggerhead Caretta caretta, Olive Ridley (*Lepidochelys olivacea*), Hawksbill Eretmochelys imbricate, and Leatherback Dermochelys coriacea. Most of the marine turtle populations found in the Indian region are in decline. The principal reason for the decrease in numbers is deliberate human predation. Turtles are netted and speared along the entire Indian coast. In southeast India, the annual catch is estimated at 4,000–5,000 animals, with C. mydas accounting for about 70% of the harvest. In the Gulf of Mannar, turtles are still reasonably common near seagrass beds where shrimp trawlers operate.

BIODIVERSITY OF INDIA

Species Diversity

India contains a great wealth of biological diversity in its forests, its wetlands, and in its marine areas. This richness is shown in absolute numbers of species and the proportion they represent of the world total (see Table below).

Table Comparison Between the Number of Species in India and the World

Group	Number of species in India (SI)	Number of species in the world (SW)	SI/SW (%)
Mammals	350	4,629	7.6
Birds	1,224	9,702	12.6
Reptiles	408	6,550	6.2
Amphibians	197	4,522	4.4
Fishes	2,546	21,730	11.7
Flowering Plants	15,000	2,50,000	6.0

Western Ghats

The Western Ghats, also known as the Sahyadri Hills, are well known for its rich flora and fauna. It is considered as one of the 25 most biodiverse hotspots in the world. The Western Ghats extend from the Satpura Range in the north, go south past Goa, through Karnataka and into Kerala and Tamil Nadu and end at Kanyakumari embracing the Indian ocean. The major hill range starting from the north is called Sahyadri in northern Maharashtra and Sahya Parvatam in Kerala. The Niligiri ranges southeast of Mysuru in Karnataka, meet the Shevaroys (Servarayan range) and Tirumala range farther east, linking the Western Ghats to the Eastern Ghats. In the south the range is known as the Nilagiri Malai in Tamil Nadu.

Eastern Ghats

The Eastern Ghats, also called the Purva Ghat or Mahendra Parvata are a discontinuous range of mountains along India's eastern coast. The Eastern Ghats run from West Bengal state in the north, through Odisha and Andhra Pradesh to Tamil Nadu in the south, passing some parts of Karnataka. They are eroded and cut through by the four major rivers of peninsular India, known as the Godavari, Mahanadi, Krishna, and Kaveri. The mountain ranges run parallel to the Bay of Bengal. The Deccan Plateau lies to the west of the range, between the Eastern Ghats and Western Ghats. The coastal plains, including the Coromandel Coast region, lie between the Eastern Ghats and the Bay of Bengal. The Eastern Ghats are not as high as the Western Ghats. The Eastern Ghats form a discontinuous crest on the eastern periphery of the plateau. They are represented by an irregular line of hills, such as the Nallamalais, Velikondas, Palkondas, and the Pachaimalais. These hills are often referred to as the northern hills in the northern sector, Cuddapah ranges in the middle, and the Tamil Nadu hills in the south.

The Coastal Plains and the Islands

The plateau is flanked by coastal plains of varied width extending from Kutch to Odisha. There are striking differences between the eastern and the western coastal plains; with notable exception of Gujarat, the west coast has narrow alluvial margin interspersed by hilly terrain. It has indentation except in the south where the beautiful lagoons introduce an element of diversity.

The eastern coast on the other hand has a wide plain with well developed deltas of the major rivers. The climatic transition between the southwest monsoon regime of the north and the northeast monsoon regime of the south has given rise to interesting differences in the alluvial features in the two different stretches of the east coastal plain.

River System of India

India has seven major rivers (Indus, Brahmaputra, Narmada, Tapi, Godavari, Krishna, and Mahanadi). These rivers along with their numerous tributaries make up the river system of India (see Map 6). Most of the rivers pour their waters into the Bay of Bengal. The rivers may be classified as follows:

a. The Himalayan
b. The Deccan
c. The Coastal
d. The rivers of the inland drainage basin

The Himalayan Rivers

The Himalayan rivers are generally snow-fed and flow throughout the year. During the monsoon months (June to September), the Himalayas receive very heavy rainfall and the rivers carry the maximum amount of water, causing frequent floods. Three major rivers that originate from the Himalaya are Ganga, Brahmaputra, and Indus, along with the five smaller rivers: Beas, Jhelum, Sutlej, Ravi, and Chenab.

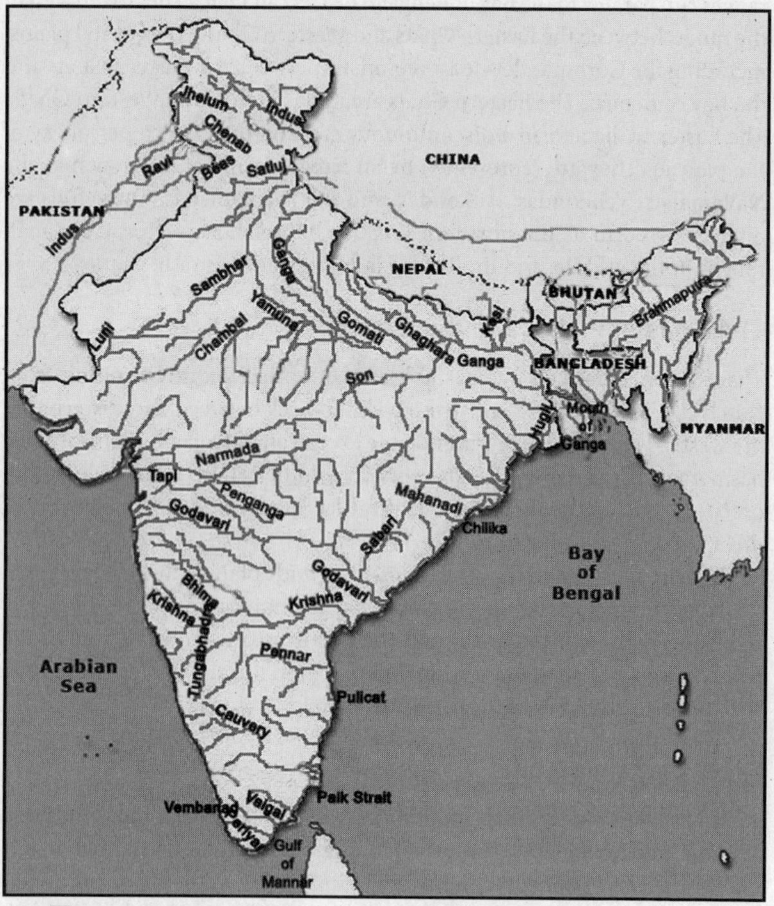

Map 6 *Map of India showing the major Indian rivers*

The Deccan Rivers

The Deccan rivers are generally rain-fed and, therefore, fluctuate greatly in volume. A very large number of them are non-perennial. Godavari, Krishna, Cauvery, Mahanadi, Narmada, Tapti, Indravati, Tungabhadra, and Bhima are the main Deccan rivers.

The Coastal Rivers

The coastal rivers, especially on the west coast, are short and have limited catchment areas. Most of these are non-perennial as well. The rivers on the inland drainage basin are few and ephemeral.

The Rivers of the Inland Drainage Basin

The rivers of the inland drainage basin drain towards individual basins or salt lakes like the Sambhar or are lost in the sands, having no outlet to the sea.

CULTURAL DIVERSITY OF INDIA

Introduction

The National list of communities brought out by Archaeological Survey of India elucidates that there are 2,205 different communities living in India. Indian population is polygenetic and is an amazing amalgamation of various races and cultures.

The people of India are believed to be composed of 6 main racial stock:

1. Negrito
2. Proto—Australoids or Austrics
3. Mongoloids
4. Mediterranean or Dravidian
5. Western Brachycephals
6. Nordic Aryans

The Six Racial Stocks

Negroids

The Negritos or the Brachycephalic (broad headed) from Africa were the earliest people to have come to India. They have survived in their original habitat in Andaman and Nicobar Islands. The Jarawas, Onges, Sentinelese, and the Great Andamanese are some of the examples. Some hill tribes like Irulas, Kodars, Paniyans, and Kurumbas are found in some patches in southern part of mainland India.

Pro-Australoids or Austrics

These groups were the next to come to India after the Negritos. They are people with wavy hair lavishly distributed all over their brown bodies, long headed with low foreheads and prominent eye ridges, noses with low and broad roots, thick jaws, large palates and teeth, and small chins. The Austrics of India represent a race of medium height, dark complexion with long heads, and rather flat noses but otherwise of regular features.

The Austrics laid the foundation of the Indian civilisation. They cultivated rice and vegetables and made sugar from sugarcane. Now these people are found in some parts of India, Myanmar, and the islands of South East Asia. Their languages have survived in the central and eastern India.

Mongoloids

These people are found in the northeastern part of India in the states of Assam, Nagaland, Mizoram, Meghalaya, Arunachal Pradesh, Manipur, and Tripura. They are also found in northern parts of West Bengal, Sikkim, and Ladakh. Generally, they are people with yellow complexion, oblique eyes, high cheekbones, sparse hair, and medium height.

Dravidians

These are the people of south India. They have been believed to come before the Aryans. They have different sub-groups like the Paleo-Mediterranean, the true Mediterranean, and the Oriental Mediterranean. They appear to be people of the same stock as the peoples of Asia Minor and Crete and pre-Hellenic Aegean's of Greece. They are reputed to have built up the city civilisation of the Indus valley, whose remains have been found at Mohenjo-daro and Harappa and other Indus cities.

Western Bracycephals

These include the Alpinoids, Dinarics, and Armenoids. The Parsis and Kodavas also fall in this category. They are the broad headed people living mainly on the western side of the country such as the Ganga Valley and the delta, parts of Kashmir, Kathiawar, Gujarat, Maharashtra and Karnataka.

Nordics or the Indo-Aryans

This group were the last one to immigrate to India. They came to India somewhere between 2000 and 1500 B.C. They are now mainly found in the northern and central part of India.

2

CONCEPT OF SOCIAL PROBLEMS

"I cannot change the world, but I can cast a stone across the waters to create many ripples."
—Mother Teresa

INTRODUCTION

India emerged as an independent nation-state on 15th August 1947, after a long struggle against the British colonial yoke. The country is a Sovereign, Socialist, Secular, Democratic Republic with a parliamentary system of government. Though India has shown tremendous growth in all spheres of national life in the years after independence, yet many problems plague the everyday social life; the problems, many a time, are interrelated. Poverty, Population, Pollution, Illiteracy, Corruption, Inequality, Gender discrimination, Terrorism, Communalism, Lack of Infrastructure, Unemployment, Regionalism, Casteism, Alcoholism, Drugs Abuse, Violence against Women are the major ones.

CONCEPT OF SOCIAL PROBLEMS

Contemporary Indian society is flecked with numerous issues that are labelled as social problems. Some of them are age-old, and some are of recent origin that have erupted owing to the change in global socio-political order.

A social problem, in general, is the condition which is not ideal and disrupts the balance of a society. A dictionary of sociology defines social problems as, "any undesirable condition or situation that is judged by an influential number of persons within a community to be intolerable and to require group action toward constructive reform" (Theodorson and Theodorson, 1969:392). Another widely used definition specifies that "no condition, no matter how dramatic or shocking to someone else, is a social problem *unless* and *until* the values of a considerable number of people define it as a problem" (Horton and Leslie, 1970:5). *Some of the other definitions of social problems given by sociologists are:*

- **Horton and Leslie:** It is often defined as the condition which many people consider undesirable and wish to correct.

- **Lindbergh:** It is any deviant behaviour in a disapproved direction of such a degree that it exceeds the tolerance limit of the community.
- **L.K. Frank:** It is defined as any difficulty of misbehaviour of a fairly large number of persons which we wish to remove or correct.
- **Fuler and Mayer:** A social problem starts with the awakening of people in a given locality, with the realisation of certain cherished values that are threatened by the conditions which have become acute.

Emergence of Sociology as A Discipline

Sociology has emerged as a discipline which systematically studies social behaviour or society, including its origins, development, organisation, networks, and institutions and problems. The American Sociological Association defines Sociology as "the study of social life, social change, and the social causes and consequences of human behaviour". To a sociologist, a social problem is an issue that negatively affects a person's state of being in a society.

To understand social problems, sociologists look "from outside" at individuals rather than looking them "from inside", to examine the thoughts, cause, and action. This is due to the fact that for the sociologist, many problems that appear as personal are actually social problems, because personal experience in one way or another is influenced by social forces. Prominent American sociologist C. Wright Mills uses the term "sociological imagination" to refer to this ability to see the impact of social forces on individuals, especially on their private lives. He argues that people must understand how extraneous factors contribute to individual situations. To understand this, we must apply sociological imagination—the ability to look beyond the individual as the only cause of action and see how society influences a person's outcome. Mills noted that this macro (large-scale) point of view helps us understand how history and societal organisations influence people. We often see social issues from our personal viewpoints, interpreting actions at face value, i.e. a micro (small-scale) view. Using only a micro point of view is detrimental to a holistic and genuine understanding of the world. It can negatively influence our understanding of events while applying sociological imagination, and considering that an individual might act and respond because of a number of reasons. As Mills argued, the goal of sociology is to move beyond our own perceptions and toward a sociological imagination. Without connecting what we know about society to the individual, we run the risk of wrongly placing blame and misconstruing the way we interpret events.

The shift then is to look at social problems in relation to other aspects of society like economy, culture, or religion. The sociological imagination is stimulated by a willingness to view the social world from the perspective of others. It involves moving from thinking about the individual and his problems, and focusing on social, economic, and historical circumstances that produce the problem. Sociological study is not the same as our everyday "common sense."

CHARACTERISTICS, CAUSES, AND TYPES OF SOCIAL PROBLEMS

Social problems are serious to the extent that they undesirably alter the existing order of the society. *On the basis of the aforesaid discussion, we can identify the following characteristics of social problems*:

Characteristics of Social Problems

- All social problems are situations which have injurious consequences for society.
- All social problems are deviations from the "ideal" situation.
- All social problems have some common basis of origin.
- All social problems are social and political in origin.
- All social problems are caused by pathological social conditions.
- All social problems are interconnected.
- All social problems are social in their results—they affect all sections of society.
- The responsibility for social problems is social—they require a collective approach for their solution.
- Social problems occur in all societies (Ahuja, 2002:5).

A social problem does not exist for a society unless it is recognised by that society to exist. In not being aware of a social problem, a society does not perceive it, address it, discuss it, or do anything for eradicating it. So the crucial point is, identification of a particular issue by the society as a problem. History changes the definition of social problems. The issues that society considered major in the past are often not that important in the present. For example, at one point in time a major concern in the United States was horse theft—obviously, this is no longer an issue. For example *sati*, child labour, illiteracy, child marriage, slavery, and religious conversion were not considered a malady in Indian history. But today, all of these are undesirable in contemporary India.

Causes of Social Problems

The causes of social problems may be three-fold but cannot be treated in isolation:

(i) Individual (ii) Cultural (iii) Structural. The social evils that are plaguing our society today could hardly be catalogued. They are very uncountable in the true sense of the assertion. Prominent among them are: juvenile delinquency; child abuse; escalating crime waves such as armed robbery; arson; fraud; drug peddling; currency trafficking; bribery and corruption; embezzlement of public funds; student and youth unrest; cultural violence; religious intolerance; boundary disputes; stark dishonesty; election rigging; coups and counter coups; lack of commitment to duty; examination malpractices; filthy and gross indiscipline; result racketeering; disrespect for other species; gross economic inequality; poverty; disease and hunger; widespread illiteracy; lack of gainful employment opportunities; open injustice; ostentatious spending; abuse of authority; hoarding of essential commodities; cheating and exploitation of the masses; discrimination and ethnic jingoism; inordinate ambition; cultism; lack of realisation of human potential; narrow education resulting in ill-informed citizens; civil wars; famine; drought and unchecked desertification; and human trafficking and child labour.

Three Factors that Result in Social Problems

James H. Reinhardt (1952:7–12) has recounted three factors in the development of social problems:

(1) Differentiation and Multiplication of Interests and Functions

The principle that the greater the number of parts in a machine or an organism, the greater the probability of maladjustment among the parts holds good for human societies too, where there is increased opportunity for the collision of interests of various individuals, groups, institutions, and systems. Untouchability, communal riots, and political crimes are the social problems which is the result of the clash of interests of different castes and classes.

(2) Accelerating Frequency of Social Change or Growth of Civilisation

This has been made possible due to the multiplication of scientific and mechanical innovations. For example, the invention of machines has destroyed many old forms of employment resulting in the migration of millions of people, and has given rise to class conflicts. It is thus the structural and functional maladjustments arising from revolutionary inventions which create many social problems.

(3) Man's Developed Insight to Make a Scientific Analysis

Ever since man has developed his social insight of looking into the working of nature, issues which were formerly regarded as simple are now perceived as the result of various kinds of natural conditions which influence man and society.

Types of Social Problems

Social problems are of diverse nature. However, these diverse social problems can be broadly grouped under four categories:

Economic Factors

These problems arise due to imbalance in economic distribution such as poverty, unemployment, etc.

Cultural Factors

Problems that arise from established beliefs, values, traditions, laws, and languages of a nation or society fall under this category such as dowry, child marriage, juvenile delinquency, etc.

Biological Factors

The problems that arise due to natural calamities, infectious diseases, famine, etc.

Psychological factors

Problems that arise from ill mental and neurological health fall under this category.

Case (1964:34) has enumerated four types of social problems on the basis of their origin:

(i) Problems that are rooted in some aspect of the physical environment.
(ii) Problems that are inherent in the nature or distribution of the population involved.
(iii) Problems that result from poor social organisation.
(iv) Problems that evolve from a conflict of cultural values within the society.

Fuller and Myers (1941:367) have enlisted three types of problems:

(i) *Physical problems:* Though these are problems for the society, but their causes are not based on value conflicts, for example, floods and famines;
(ii) *Ameliorative problems:* There is consensus about the effects of these problems but there are differences pertaining to their solutions, for example, crime, poverty, and AIDS; and

(iii) *Moral problems:* There is no consensus pertaining to the nature or causes of these problems, for example, gambling, alcoholism, drug abuse, and divorce.

REACTIONS TO SOCIAL PROBLEMS

Different people react differently to social problems. *The differences may be explained in terms of the following four factors:*

(i) An Attitude of Unconcern

Many people and the State at times, remain indifferent to a problem, thinking that it does not affect them. At times, their own individual problems like family tensions and job pressures keep them so engaged that they do not find time to be interested in what affects others. It is only when their own interests are involved that they become agitated and start taking interest in the problem. The indifference and passivity of the State only add to the problem further.

(ii) Fatalism

Some people are so fatalistic that they attribute everything to destiny. Issues like poverty and unemployment are also explained in terms of misfortune and past karma. They, therefore, suffer the misfortune quietly and wait for some miracle to happen.

(iii) Vested Interests

Some people take no interest in the existing problems because they stand to gain so long as the problem exists. Motivated by self-interest, they describe the problem as insoluble and talk about its eradication as a waste of time.

(iv) Absence of Expert Knowledge

Some people, though deeply concerned about the problem, do not take much interest in it believing that its solution is impossible unless people change their attitudes and values. As the changes must be initiated by a change in outlook, they remain unconcerned about finding alternative possibilities of treatment. Dowry is one such problem in our society.

THE THREE MAJOR PARADIGMS OF SOCIOLOGY

Introduction

The issues that we define as social problems are complex in nature, and because of the increase in globalisation and media outlets, they do not remain confined to one institution or geographic area. For this reason, sociologists must look carefully at a problem to see all its parts. So, how do we begin to approach thinking about social problems? Historically, sociologists use either macro or micro paradigms, the theoretical frameworks through which scientists study the world. These include three major paradigms that we'll be focusing on in this text: functionalism, conflict theory, and symbolic interactionism. Sociologists from each school of thought analyse similar issues, but the manner in which they reach conclusions differs. Let's explore each of these paradigms a little further.

Three Major Paradigms

(a) Functionalism

Functionalism is a theoretical framework that defines society as a system of interrelated parts. Because functionalism focuses on the entire social system and not just the individual, it is considered a macro approach to sociological study. If something happens to one component of a social structure, the other components will automatically step in to help restore balance. Think about an automatic HVAC (heating, ventilating, and air-conditioning) system. Some warehouses manufacture products that must be stored at a certain temperature and humidity. If the temperature and humidity outside goes up or down, so do the conditions inside the warehouse. But if an HVAC system has been installed, it can be switched on to maintain a stable temperature and humidity level. Social structures operate in the same manner. If problems occur, society automatically acts in ways to offset these issues. Functionalism treats society as relatively secure—everything that occurs has a purpose in the preservation of stability. Functionalists believe that the best way to understand society as a whole is to understand how social institutions (such as family, education, and the economy) are interrelated. Each institution has an impact, no matter how small it may seem; because everything is connected, a butterfly effect occurs. Here's an example: When the economy does poorly, it doesn't just affect your wallet. Companies fold, jobs are lost, families go hungry, and children do poorly in school. Because society's balance is reliant on each of its components, functionalism suggests that all social structures must agree on values and norms. These values and norms create society's rules and laws, thus regulating the relationships between institutions.

Let's take a quick look at a few prominent functionalists from history and their beliefs.

Prominent functionalists

- *Herbert Spencer (1820–1903):* Society can be considered a living organism in which some are more apt to deal with social dynamics and, therefore, adapt better to changes in the environment.
- *Emile Durkheim (1858–1917):* Social integration and social control hold society together. People view themselves as unified wholes, which helps them stay within the boundaries of their social structure's rules and laws.
- *Talcott Parsons (1902–1779):* Society is a grand interrelated system in which each individual is instrumental in keeping the system functional. If one individual falters, society as a whole will suffer.
- *Robert Merton (1910–2003):* Every action in society has manifest functions (factors that lead to an expected consequence) and latent functions (factors that lead to an unforeseen or unexpected consequence).

(b) Conflict Theory

Conflict theory is a theoretical framework that views society as being in a constant struggle over a limited amount of resources. Similar to functionalism, this theory also uses a macro approach because it deals with the interaction of multiple groups fighting to gain power. For example, conflict theorists would examine how and why the rift between the rich and the poor affects the quality of education, health care, and living conditions of those groups. The wealthy can afford better housing and tend to live near people of the same status. Because of this, the values of these homes increase, and the poor who originally lived there are forced into separate areas. It is no surprise that individuals who can afford to live in more expensive neighbourhoods can also afford better schools for their children, thereby increasing the chances that their offspring will also be more successful. Conflict theorists suggest that once inequality begins to take root, those at the top are unlikely to push for social change. This is because the elite set standards and rules that benefit themselves, not the individuals or groups below them. These standards also help keep the wealthy and powerful in prominent positions. Conflict theory can be applied to many institutions, not just social class. Conflict theorists apply their principles to age, gender, race, religion... any social construct in which inequality can be viewed as a social problem.

Take a look at the list below to see the different ways in which conflict theorists approach this paradigm:

Conflict Theorists

- *Harriet Martineau (1802–1876):* A society's actions are often quite different from the values expressed by that society. For example, despite boasts of freedom and democracy in the United States, only men had the right to vote until 1920.

- *Karl Marx (1818–1883):* Capitalism breeds conflict between the rich and the poor. The pursuit of wealth corrupts society and will ultimately destroy it. Economic power should not lie in the hands of the elite few, but in the hands of all people.
- *W. E. B. Du Bois (1868–1963):* Social equality is impossible to achieve in corrupt social systems. The past strongly influences the present, such as the connection between past and present discrimination against African Americans and all disadvantaged groups.
- *John Bellamy Foster (1953–Present):* Social unrest is a result of unequal distribution of power and wealth. Capitalism cannot continue as is; the process of seeking short-term rewards and avoiding long-term consequences must be stopped if society is to continue.

(c) Symbolic Interactionism

Symbolic interactionism is a theoretical framework that focuses on how individual interactions between people influence their behaviour and how these interactions can impact society. Unlike functionalism and conflict theory, this paradigm is a micro approach because it deals with individuals, not groups or institutions. Symbolic interactionists analyse how social interactions influence, create, and sustain human relationships. They believe that symbols such as body language, words, gestures, and images affect communication. Humans interact with one another according to the meanings of these symbols. How did you first learn your name? Early on in your life your parents called you something, and you learned to respond to it. Now if someone calls you by another name, you're unlikely to even move your head. Why? Because somewhere in your mind, you use this symbol to help form your sense of self. It is this identity that you carry with you your entire life and use in interactions with others to create a social world. We also learn the meaning behind symbols within social contexts. For example, a photo of Chinese revolutionary Mao Zedong probably has little or no meaning to you, whereas a picture of Mahatma Gandhi might bring forth thoughts of freedom and rebellion. Despite both men being revolutionary leaders, your cultural context influences how you view each photo.

Symbolic Interactionists

- *George Herbert Mead (1863–1931):* Society is made up of symbols that teach us to understand the world. We use these symbols to develop a sense of self, or identity. We then take this identity into the world to interact with other identities to create society.

- *Herbert Blumer (1900–1987):* An individual's behaviour depends on the meanings we've already created through experience and interaction. We use an interpretive process to handle and alter these meanings.
- *Erving Goffman (1922–1982):* Social interactions are the building blocks of society. Individuals alter their behaviour constantly, requiring a complex series of actions and reactions.
- *Howard Becker (1928–Present):* Social interactions can lead to self-fulfilling prophecies that limit a person's outcomes. We place labels on people in society; individuals then feel as though they must embody those labels.

Understanding the three paradigms can be confusing, especially when applying them to complicated social problems. Use the table as a reference to help you remember the basic ideas behind each theory. Often, the types of questions sociologists ask give clues to their school of thought.

The Three Paradigms—How are They Interrelated?

Often, the lines between micro and macro analysis blur. Most sociologists follow in the footsteps of Max Weber, a famous social scientist who in many ways defied being put into any one of these categories. Like conflict theorists, Weber asserted that social class is one of the most important influences in the outcome of our lives. Power disparities between the classes often dictate who succeeds in a society and who does not. However, he also took a more functionalist approach, arguing that society at its most

CORE QUESTIONS OF THE THREE PARADIGMS			
	Functionalists	**Conflict Theorists**	**Symbolic Interactionists**
Approach to Analysis	**Macro**	**Macro**	**Micro**
Core Questions	1. What are the components of society? 2. How do these components relate to each other? 3. What keeps society in balance? 4. What are the expected and unexpected consequences of an event?	1. How are wealth, power, opportunities, and resources divided within society? 2. How do individuals or groups maintain their wealth and power? 3. Which groups thrive in society and why?	1. What influence do individuals have on the creation of a social structure? 2. In what manner does social interaction impact human relationships? 3. Do individuals alter their behaviour depending on setting? If so, why?

efficient will naturally run like a bureaucracy: One leader presides over a group of smaller organisations that all share a common goal. At the same time, Weber incorporated symbolic interaction into his theories, noting that values influence people's goals and behaviours. Weber understood that sociologists aren't naturally immune to personal biases, and he urged his colleagues to separate their private values from their professional work. Like Weber, modern sociologists often find themselves taking on the roles of functionalist, conflict theorist, and symbolic interactionist interchangeably to best analyse today's social problems.

Emerging Paradigms

Other paradigms exist, apart from the major three. Let's take a look at some of the more modern approaches to sociological theory.

Feminist Theory

Feminist theory is a female-centered, interdisciplinary approach that seeks to demonstrate how women fit into the social world. Feminists often ask questions such as, "Why is the social world the way that it is?" and "Can we change the social world to make it a fair place for all people?" Feminists are also interested in how race, ethnicity, social class, and age interact with gender to determine the outcomes for individuals.

There are three prominent feminist theories:

- *Gender-inequality theories:* Women's experiences of the social world are not equal to those of men. Such theories focus on sexist patterns that limit women's opportunities for work, education, and other social needs.
- *Theories of gender oppression:* Men purposefully maintain control over women through discrimination and the use of power; this leads to oppression.
- *Structural oppression theories:* Women's oppression is rooted in capitalism; patriarchies keep women on the margins of the social world.

Exchange Theory

Exchange theorists suggest that our social experiences consist of a series of costs and rewards. People inherently seek to maximise their rewards and minimise their costs, resulting in social action. Exchange theory often appeals to thinkers on a micro level—for example, why do we choose one mate over another? If you're dating someone and the effort you're exerting makes the relationship feel like the cost is higher than the reward, you're likely to end the relationship. But exchange theory also has a macro point of view. For example, do you suppose it's in the best interest of a country to export all manufacturing jobs to other nations that can provide cheaper labour? In calculating the value of the exchange, we must consider not only the short-term reward (the immediate profit, in this case), but also the potential long-term costs (economic collapse when transportation of goods is interrupted, for example).

Environmental Theory

Environmental theory is the most recent paradigm to emerge in sociology. This theory combines social thought and ecological principles to discover how environmental policies influence society, and how attitudes toward the environment have changed over time. Environmental theorists often attempt to understand how societies adjust to ecological changes. For example, how many people can live in a specific area? This amount is known as carrying capacity. Often we believe that humans are an exception to the ecological limits of carrying capacity. However, for environmental sociologists, humans are merely one type of organism sharing the same ecological space with other organisms. How do societies adapt to these limits? If they fail to adapt, will they continue to survive? These types of questions are at the centre of environmental theory.

METHODS OF STUDYING SOCIAL PROBLEMS

Quantitative and Qualitative Methods

Introduction

There are two categories of research that sociologists use. Neither of them is necessarily linked to functionalism, conflict theory, or symbolic interactionism. There are no set rules about which methods must be applied to each of the theories, but sociologists have found that each framework uses data in different ways. Quantitative and qualitative data are the foundation for these differences.

Quantitative Methods

The term quantitative data refers to data based on numbers and that used for macro analysis. Physicians often ask their patients to rate their pain on a scale of 1 to 10. The patient's response would be an example of this type of data. Another type of quantitative data is research numbers, such as the number of recent arrests involving domestic violence. Methods of quantitative analysis include participant observation, case studies, and ethnographies.

Triangulation

Triangulation is the process of using multiple methods to study a phenomenon. For example, perhaps you want to study the influence of after-school recreation on high school students. First, you'd want to look at quantitative data such as the number of students who are and aren't involved in after-school activities. Then, you'd conduct a qualitative study that looks into what these students do during their free time and how the activity, or lack thereof, influences their education and grades. The idea is that if you can't gather the information you need from one type of data, the others will help fill in the gaps.

Qualitative Methods

Qualitative data may include interviews, pictures, photos, or any other type of information that comes to the researcher in a non-numerical form. These data tend to be used for microanalysis. A good example is content analysis, a type of research in which sociologists look for common words or themes in newspapers, books, or structured interviews. Methods of qualitative analysis include cross-sectional, comparative, and longitudinal studies, as well as surveys and experiments.

Sociologists often frame their thinking by borrowing ideas from the three major paradigms. Similarly, sociologists sometimes use both qualitative and quantitative methods to collect data from different angles, providing a larger picture of an issue or event (See Box)

SOLVING SOCIAL PROBLEMS

Although C. Wright Mills identified the relationship between a personal trouble and a public issue more than 50 years ago, less has been said about the transformation of an issue to a solution. Mills leads us in the right direction by identifying the relationship between public issues and social institutions. By continuing to use our sociological imagination and recognising the role of larger social, cultural, and structural forces, we can identify appropriate measures to address these social problems. Let's consider homelessness. It does not arise out of mysterious or special circumstances; it emerges out of familiar life experiences. The loss of a job, the illness of a family member, domestic violence, or divorce could make a family more susceptible to homelessness. Without informal social support, a savings account, or suitable and adequate employment—and with the increasing cost of healthcare and the lack of affordable housing—a family's economic and emotional resources can quickly be tapped out. What would it take to prevent homelessness in these situations? The answers are not based in each individual or each family; rather, the long-term solutions are structural solutions such as affordable healthcare, livable wages, and affordable low-income housing. In the US, President Franklin Roosevelt proposed sweeping social reforms during his New Deal in 1935, and President Johnson declared the War on Poverty in 1964. Solutions require social action—in the form of social policy, advocacy, and innovation—to address problems at their structural or individual levels. Social innovation may take the form of a policy, a programme, or advocacy that features an untested or unique approach. Innovation usually starts at the community level, but it can grow into a national or international programme. The concept of "partnership housing" was developed by Millard and Linda Fuller in 1965, partnering those in need of adequate shelter with community volunteers to build simple interest-free houses. In India, recent initiative 'Swachch Bharat', 'Digital India', 'Make in India' etc are also unique social innovations that can transform Indian society in a big way.

3

POPULATION AND ITS ASSOCIATED PROBLEMS

"We control the growth of every other species, except our own."

INTRODUCTION

India like most countries of the world, has evolved from conditions of high mortality due to famines, accidents, illness, infections, and war and from the time when high levels of fertility was essential for survival of offspring. Over the years, enhancement in areas of diseases prevention, cure and vagaries of nature, and better care for women and infants, it has witnessed significant increase in life expectancy along with a steep fall in mortality.

ASPECTS OF POPULATION IN INDIA

Size and Growth

India is the country with the second largest population after China. These two countries lead the top of the most populous countries by a considerable margin. In terms of surface area, this is remarkable, as 400 people live in one square kilometer. For comparison: in Germany, this is only slightly more than half, in the USA not even one tenth.

At the same time, India is a country with extreme urbanization. Only a few people live in the desert and mountain regions, while in the cities there are sometimes more than 25,000 inhabitants per square kilometer. In Berlin, the figure is just 4000. 60% of the inhabitants live in the few large cities along the fertile parts of the country. With 40 cities with over a million inhabitants, India is the country with the most large metropolises after China.

At the beginning of the 18th century, India had just 137 million inhabitants. This number rose to about 255 million within 100 years and fluctuated by 20% up and down during the 18th century. Only since the beginning of the 20th century has population growth increased dramatically, but has been losing some momentum for about 50 years. It is assumed that India will even overtake China by the year 2023 and will then be the most populous country on earth.

Although life expectancy in India, at around 68 years, is considerably lower than in countries such as Germany (81 years) or the USA (79 years), the birth rate is significantly higher. In the early 70s, every woman gave birth to an average of 5 children. It is declining only slowly and is now just over 2 children per woman (Germany: 1.6). One third of India's population is now under 15 years old. The average age is just 26 years.

Population growth is the result of the birth rate, the mortality rate and the migration rate. Take the example of the year 2020: The population in India increased by about 13,587,000 inhabitants. In the same year, the death rate was 7.3 per 1000 people (~ 9,976,000 deaths) and the birth rate was 17.4 per 1000 people (~ 23,826,000 births). As a result, around 263,000 inhabitants have migrated to other countries.

Over the past 10 years, the number of average deaths per year was 9,552,447 in India. The number of births was 24,552,358 annually.

1 of every 6 people on the planet live in India, and between the 2001 and 2011 censuses, the country grew by 17.7%, adding 181.5 million people. The country has doubled in size in just 40 years, and is expected to unseat

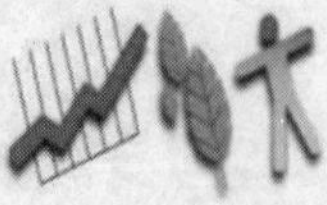

Population growth in India

CENSUS OF INDIA 2011

- India is presently the second most populous country of the world with over
- The current population growth rate being 1%, implies India will be adding over 13 million people in the current year. The life expectancy is 69.42 years, and the death rate is 7.3 per thousand.
- India's current population estimated to be 1.412 billion people being almost 17.7% of the world's population
- India is expected to surpass China as the world's most populous nation by 2024 and is expected to reach a total population of 1.5 billion by 2030 (UN's World Population Prospects, 2022)
- Although the fertility rate has been falling in India, yet the birth rate is much higher than the death rate compared to other countries.
- India's population remains young, with more than one-fourth aged under 15 years and less than an eighth over 60.
- As per the National Family Health Survey (NFHS) 5, over half the population (52%) is below 30, compared to 55.5% in NFHS-4.

China as the world's most populated country in 2023. India's current yearly growth rate is 0.91%.

In Mumbai, the population density is 21,000 people per square kilometer (54,000/square mile). Delhi, India's second most populous city was home to 11,034,555 people according to 2011 data, and its metro area contains 21,753,486 people. Growth in Delhi is even more rapid than Mumbai's, and it is likely that it will overtake Mumbai to become the largest city in India within a decade. India's largest state is Uttar Pradesh which, with a population of 199,581,520 in 2011, is larger than most countries in the world. If it were a country in its own right, it would be the fifth largest in the world, falling just behind China, India, the United States and Indonesia.

Determinants of Population Change

The main causes which are generally identified for the high population in India are listed here:

a) *The birth rate is still higher than the death rate:* India has been successful in declining the death rate. On the other hand, it has not been able to control the high birth rates. The fertility rate due to the population policies and other measures has been falling, still it is much higher compared to other countries. Various social causes are at the root of overpopulation in India.

b) *Early marriage and universal marriage system:* Though legally the marriageable age of a girl is 18 years, the concept of early marriage still prevails and getting married at an young age prolongs the child bearing age. Also, in India, marriage and child bearing are sacrosanct obligations and a universal practice, and almost every woman is married at the reproductive age.

c) *Poverty and illiteracy:* Underprivileged families have a presumption that more the number of members in the family, more will be the hands to earn income. Some feel that more children are needed to look after them in their old age. Also, malnutrition can be the cause of death of their children and hence the need for more children. Many parts of India still lag behind the use of contraceptives and birth control methods. Many of them are not willing to discuss or are totally unaware about them.

d) *Age old cultural norm:* Sons are believed to be the bread earners, the carriers of lineage, and the source of salvation for their parents. Many families give birth to multiple children in the hope of a male child.

e) *Illegal migration:* Finally, the fact that illegal migration is continuously taking place from lesser developed neighbouring countries is leading to increased population density.

Implications of the Size and Growth of Population

The impact of overpopulation is varied and has far reaching consequences in many areas of life.

Ecological Consequences

Global population growth and the destructive consumption habits of high-wealth countries put pressure on biodiversity and human communities, exacerbating food and water shortages, reducing resilience in the face of climate change, and making it harder for vulnerable groups to rise out of intergenerational poverty.

Population growth and natural resources are intricately linked and play a role in climate disruption and farmers' ability to adapt to climate change especially in developing countries with rapid demographic changes and economies mostly dependent on natural resources.

Land carrying capacity shows the amount of land, which is able to support human life, not only as agricultural land but also for settlement and another socio-economic activity. Based on that definition, it can be stated that the factors of decline in land carrying capacity are influenced by factors of population pressure rate on agricultural land.

As human numbers further increase, the potential for irreversible changes of far-reaching magnitude also increases. Indicators of severe environmental stress include the growing loss of biodiversity, increasing greenhouse gas emissions, increasing deforestation worldwide, stratospheric ozone depletion, acid rain, loss of topsoil, and shortages of water, food, and fuelwood in many parts of the world.

Some of the major ecological adverse effects reported in India include:

- Severe pressure on the forests, due to both the rate and the nature of resources used. The per capita forest biomass in the country is only about 6 tons as against the global average of 82 tons.
- Adverse effect on species diversity
- Conversion of habitat to land use such as agriculture, urban development, and forestry operation. Some 70–80% of fresh water marshes and lakes in the Gangetic flood plains have been lost in the last 50 years.
- Tropical deforestation and destruction of mangroves for commercial needs and fuel wood. The country's mangrove areas have reduced from 700,000 ha to 453,000 ha in the last 50 years.
- Intense grazing by domestic livestock
- Poaching and illegal harvesting of wildlife

- Increase in agricultural area, high use of chemical fertilizers pesticides and weedicides, water stagnation, soil erosion, soil salinity, and low productivity
- High level of biomass burning causing large-scale indoor pollution
- Encroachment on habitat for rail and road construction, thereby fragmenting the habitat.
- Increase in commercial activities such as mining and unsustainable resource extraction
- Degradation of coastal and other aquatic ecosystems from domestic sewage, pesticides, fertilizers, and industrial effluents
- Over fishing in water bodies and introduction of weeds and exotic species
- Diversion of water for domestic, industrial, and agricultural uses leading to increased river pollution and decrease in self-cleaning properties of rivers
- Increasing water requirement leading to tapping deeper aquifers which have high content of arsenic or fluoride resulting in health problems
- Disturbance from increased recreational activity and tourism causing pollution of natural ecosystems with wastes left behind by people

Urbanisation

India's urban population has doubled from 109 million to 218 million during the last two decades. As a consequence, cities are facing the problem of expanding urban slums. Cities and towns have become the location of social change and rapid economic development. Urbanisation is associated with improved access to education, employment, and health care; these result in increase in age at marriage, reduction in family size, and improvement in health indices. As people have moved towards and into cities, information has flowed outward. Better communication and transportation now link urban and rural areas both economically and socially creating an urban–rural continuum of communities with improvement in some aspects of lifestyle of both. The ever increasing reach of mass media has made information readily available.

However, the rapid growth of urban population also poses some serious challenges. Urban population growth has outpaced the development of basic minimum services— housing, water supply, sewerage, and solid waste disposal; increasing waste generation at home, offices, and industries, coupled with poor waste disposal facilities result in rapid environmental deterioration. Increasing automobiles add to air pollution. All these have adverse effect on ecology and health. Poverty persists in urban and peri-urban areas; awareness about the glaring inequities in close urban setting may lead to social unrest.

Rural Population and Their Development

Over 70% of India's population still lives in rural areas. There are substantial differences between the states in the proportion of rural and urban population (varying from almost 90% in Assam and Bihar to 61% in Maharashtra). Agriculture is the largest and one of the most important sectors of the rural economy and contributes both to economic growth and employment. Its contribution to the Gross Domestic Product has declined over the last five decades but agriculture still remains the source of livelihood for over 70% of the country's population. A large proportion of the rural workforce is small and consists of marginal farmers and landless agricultural labourers. There is substantial under employment among these people; both wages and productivity are low. These in turn result in poverty; it is estimated that 320 million people are still living below the poverty line in rural India.

Though poverty has declined over the last three decades, the number of rural poor has in fact increased due to the population growth. Poor tend to have larger families which puts enormous burden on their meagre resources, and prevent them from breaking out of the shackles of poverty. In States like Tamil Nadu where replacement level of fertility has been attained, population

---

Urban population growth has outpaced the development of basic minimum services— housing, water supply, sewerage, and solid waste disposal; increasing waste generation at home, offices, and industries, coupled with poor waste disposal facilities result in rapid environmental deterioration.

---

growth rates are much lower than in many other States; but the population density is high and so there is a pressure on land. In States like Rajasthan, Uttar Pradesh, Bihar, and Madhya Pradesh, population is growing rapidly, resulting in increasing pressure on land and resulting in land fragmentation. Low productivity of small land holders leads to poverty, low energy intake, and under nutrition, and this, in turn, prevents the development, thus, creating a vicious circle. In most of the states, non-farm employment in rural areas has not grown very much and cannot absorb the growing labour force. Those who are getting educated specially beyond the primary level, may not wish to do manual agricultural work. They would like better opportunities and more remunerative employment. In this context, it is imperative that programmes for skill development, vocational training, and technical education are taken up on a large scale in order to generate productive employment in rural areas. The entire gamut of existing poverty alleviation and employment generation programmes may have to be restructured to meet the newly emerging types of demand for employment.

The world is becoming less rural. Not only was the point at which more than 50% of the world's population is urban passed in 2007, but it is expected that between 2015 and 2030 the world's rural population will peak, at about 3.3 billion, and then decline. The developing world still remains, however, more rural than urban, albeit narrowly so. Urbanization has risen from 20% in 1960 to 46% in 2014.

Rural areas differ demographically from urban areas in developing countries in four ways:

- Mortality tends to be higher in rural than urban areas, largely owing to high mortality of children under age five. This stems from many rural households having lower incomes, poorer nutrition, less clean water and sanitation, and fewer medical services than their urban counterparts. This comparison, however, may only be valid at the mean: informal urban settlements often suffer all the health disadvantages that rural areas experience, and sometimes worse;
- Fertility in rural areas also tends to be higher than in urban areas. That again may be a function of lower incomes; but may also be associated with agriculture, since it is easier for mothers to combine child-raising with farm work compared to say, working in a factory – and the children can help on the farm from an early age;
- The combination of higher mortality and fertility delays the demographic transition in rural areas so that rates of natural population growth in rural areas are usually higher than those in urban areas; and,
- Most rural areas experience out-migration to urban areas, so that the population of cities grows faster than the rural population, despite the underlying more rapid increases in rural areas.

Development of rural areas and ensuring sustainable urbanization are required to go parallel to ensure that the challenges emerging from the rising population and the associated demands and pressure are sufficiently handled.

Water Supply

One of the consequences of overpopulation is the pressure that is put on available water resources in order to serve a growing population. Approximately fifty percent of the world's population will be living in regions around the globe that are considered "water-stressed", a term defined as when the demand for water exceeds the amount that is available, either due to lack of it, or poor quality, by the year 2030 (compared to fifteen percent currently). Since 1990, the global population increased by an average of eighty million people, which heightens the world demand for freshwater by about sixty-four billion cubic meters of water per year (United Nations World Report). This increasingly high demand for water will also affect food production in water-stressed areas such as the Middle East, India, China, and the southwestern United States.

Growths in regional and global population will also lead to increased cases of water pollution. According to the Composite Water Management Index released by the NITI Ayog, India is experiencing a very significant water challenge, approximately 820 million people of India - living in twelve river basins across the country have per capita water availability close to or lower than 1000m3 – the official threshold for water scarcity as per the Falkenmark Index.

Increased population pressure and climate change will, in some cases, lead to the use of raw waters that may be more difficult to treat, and to increase the need for water reuse. Seawater desalination will also increase. All of these will lead to more challenging treatment requirements, and will also favour the increased use of membrane processes.

Food Security

Technological innovations in agriculture and increase in area under cultivation have ensured that so far, food production has kept pace with the population growth. Evolution of global and national food security systems has improved access to food. It is estimated that the global population will grow to 9 billion by 2050 and the food production will double; improvement in purchasing power and changing dietary habits (shift to animal products) may further add to the requirement of food grains. Thus, in the next five decades, the food and nutrition security could become critical in many parts of the world, especially in the developing countries and pockets of poverty in the developed countries.

FERTILITY AND MORTALITY

Measurements of Fertility

Definitions

$$\text{Crude birth rate (CBR)} = \frac{\text{Number of live births during the year}}{\text{Mid-year population}} \times 1000$$

$$\text{Age-specific fertility rate (ASFR)} = \frac{\text{Number of live births in a particular age group}}{\text{Mid-year female population of the same age group}} \times 1000$$

$$\text{General fertility rate (GFR)} = \frac{\text{Number of live births in a year}}{\text{Mid-year female population in the age group (15–49) years}} \times 1000$$

Total fertility rate (TFR) is defined as the number of children who would be born per woman (or per 1000 women) if she/they were to pass through the child-bearing years.

Gross reproduction rate (GRR) is the average number of daughters that would be born to a woman (or a group of women) is she/they survived atleast to the age of 45 and conformed to the age-specific fertility rate of a given year.

$$\text{Age-specific marital fertility rate (ASMFR)} = \frac{\text{Number of live births in a particular age group}}{\text{Mid-year married female population of the same age group}} \times 1000$$

$$\text{General marital fertility rate (GMFR)} = \frac{\text{Number of live births in a year}}{\text{Mid-year married female population in the age group (15–49) year}} \times 1000$$

$$\text{Crude death rate (CDR)} = \frac{\text{Number of deaths during the year}}{\text{Mid-year population}} \times 1000$$

Measurements of Mortality

Definitions

$$\text{Age-specific mortality rate (ASMR)} = \frac{\text{Number of deaths in a particular age group}}{\text{Mid-year population of the same age group}} \times 1000$$

$$\text{Infant mortality rate (IMR)} = \frac{\text{Number of infant deaths during the year}}{\text{Number of live births during the year}} \times 1000$$

Infant mortality rate comprises of two parts, viz. neo-natal mortality rate and post neo-natal mortality rate. The neo-natal mortality rate also comprises of two parts, viz. early neo-natal mortality rate and late neo-natal mortality rate. These are defined as:

$$\text{Neo-natal mortality rate (NMR)} = \frac{\text{Number of infant deaths of < than 29 days during the year}}{\text{Number of live births during the year}} \times 1000$$

$$\text{Early neo-natal mortality rate} = \frac{\text{Number of infant deaths of < than 7 days during the year}}{\text{Number of live births during the year}} \times 1000$$

$$\text{Still birth rate (SBR)} = \frac{\text{Number of still births during the year}}{\text{Number of live births and still births during the year}} \times 1000$$

$$\text{Maternal Mortality Ratio (MMR)} = \frac{\text{Number of maternal deaths to women (15-49 years)}}{\text{Number of live births to women (15-49 years)}} \times 1000$$

Levels and Trends of Fertility in India

India's Total Fertility Rate (TFR) has declined from 2.2 to 2.0 as per the fifth National Family Health Survey (NFHS-5). There are now only five states that have a TFR above the replacement level of fertility of 2.1 children per woman: Bihar (2.98), Meghalaya (2.91), Uttar Pradesh (2.35), Jharkhand (2.26), and Manipur (2.17).

The total fertility rate is 2 children per woman, which declined from 2.2 children in 2015- 16 and is currently below the replacement level of fertility of 2.1 children per woman. Women in rural areas have higher fertility, on average, than women in urban areas (TFR of 2.1 versus 1.6 children).

Between 1992-93 and 2019-21, the TFR declined from 3.4 children to 2.0 children (a decrease of 1.4 children). The TFR among women in rural areas has declined from 3.7 children in 1992-93 to 2.1 children in 2019-21. The corresponding decline among women in urban areas was from 2.7 children in 1992-93 to 1.6 children in 2019-21.

The report further found that the number of children per woman declines with women's level of schooling. Women with no schooling have an average of 2.8 children, compared with 1.8 children for women with 12 or more years of schooling.

Women in the lowest wealth quintile have an average of 1.0 more children than women in the highest wealth quintile (TFR of 2.6 children versus 1.6 children). The TFR varies from a low of 1.4 children per woman among Buddhists/Neo-Buddhists to a high of 2.4 children per woman among Muslims.

The NFHS-5 report also revealed that the Overall Contraceptive Prevalence Rate has increased substantially from 54% to 67%. "Use of modern methods of contraceptives has increased in almost all States/UTs. Unmet needs for family planning have witnessed a significant decline from 13% to 9%. The unmet need for spacing, which remained a major issue in India in the past has come down to less than 10%," according to the report.

The NFHS-5 also mentioned that institutional births have increased substantially from 79% to 89%. Even in rural areas, around 87% births are delivered in institutions and the same is 94% in urban areas.

Levels and Trends of Mortality in India

Between 2019 and 2021, 35 children below the age of one died for every 1,000 children born, 15 per cent fewer than the 41 infant deaths per 1,000 live births in 2015-16, shows the latest health data from India's national survey.

India's average neonatal mortality rate (NMR) — deaths in the first 28 days of life for every 1,000 births — fell from nearly 30 deaths in 2015-16 to 25 deaths in 2019-21. The greatest improvement (based on the percentage change) was in Sikkim, while the highest increase was in Tripura.

Infant mortality rate (IMR) is not only a result of medical factors, such as health infrastructure, antenatal care, maternal health, postnatal care, immunisations, and the overall preventive health system, but also of deeper social problems, such as malnutrition and sanitation.

Although India's average IMR — infant deaths before one year for every 1,000 live births — has fallen, it has increased in some states. Sikkim, Puducherry, Kerala, and Goa have among the lowest rates of neonatal, infant, and child mortality rates.

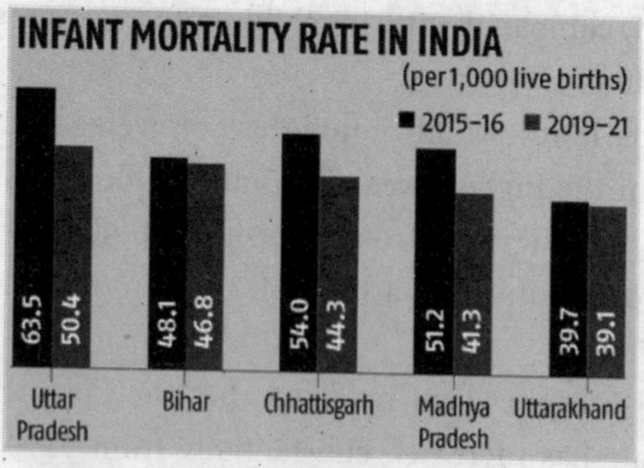

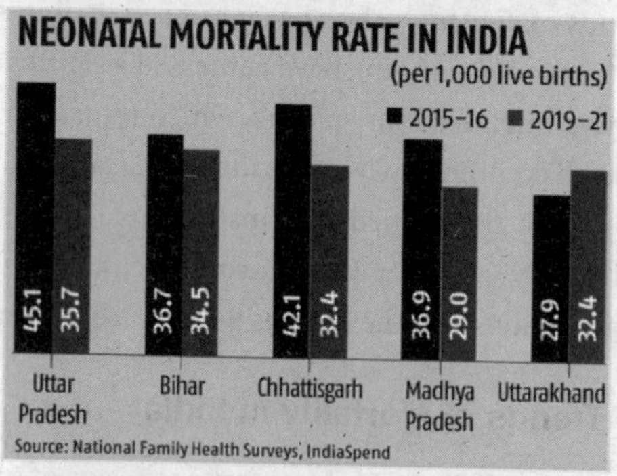

The fifth National Family Health Survey (NFHS-5) has valuable data on IMR and neonatal mortality.

The data from NFHS-5 for 22 states and Union Territories, that were collected between June 1, 2019, and January 30, 2020, were released in December 2020. The second phase of the survey was conducted between January 2, 2020, and April 30, 2021, and its data released on November 24.

Implications of the Levels of Mortality

The major causes of infant mortality in India as per the SRS reports (2010-13) are: prematurity & low birth weight (35.9 percent), pneumonia (16.9 percent), birth asphyxia & birth trauma (9.9 percent), other noncommunicable diseases (7.9 percent), diarrheal diseases (6.7 percent), known or ill-defined causes (4.6 percent), congenital anomalies (4.6 percent), acute bacterial sepsis and severe infections (4.2 percent), injuries (2.1 percent), and fever of unknown origin (1.7 percent).

As per the World Health Organization, the IMR in India – Asia's third largest economy, after China and Japan – is better only than Pakistan (57) and Myanmar (35), its immediate neighbors. Smaller and less prosperous countries like Sri Lanka (6), Bangladesh (24), and even tiny Nepal (24) and Bhutan (23), have lower infant mortality rates than India.

Currently, India ranks among the highly vulnerable countries for IMR also because it is the world's second-most populous country, with a population of 1.37 billion people.

Health professionals say that focusing on better nutrition for mothers, upgrading the national medical infrastructure that has taken a hit due to the pandemic, and public sensitization campaigns to educate mothers about childbirth can go a long way in helping augment India's infant health outcomes.

Activists opine that along with economic growth, improvement in health and social services is foundational to address the national IMR. When improved access to better healthcare and good nutrition improve child survival, there is no compulsion to produce many children to compensate for possible child deaths and seek security for support in old age, they say.

Implications of the Levels of Fertility

In an analysis of change in the level of fertility between 1970–72 and 1989–91, the various socio-economic variables (female literacy, urbanisation, infant mortality, percentage of male workers engaged in non-farm activities) in the 16 major states showed no statistically significant association, except for female literacy. However, the values for Kerala seem to contribute a great deal to the association. Otherwise, one essentially observes two clusters of states. One of the clusters includes the four large North Indian states (Bihar, Madhya Pradesh, Rajasthan, and Uttar Pradesh) with both a high TFR and low female literacy and the second cluster having moderate levels of both TFR and female literacy.

The sharp decline in the level of fertility in Tamil Nadu without anything like the high level of literacy and low levels of infant and child mortality observed in Kerala, attests to the difficulty of identifying preconditions for fertility decline. Fertility has declined by more than 50% and reached almost three-fourths of the way towards a replacement level of fertility in at least three districts of Gujarat state where the IMR continues to be high and female literacy rates are much lower than even in Tamil Nadu. These findings do not imply that universal literacy and low infant and child mortality are not worthwhile goals for a society to pursue or that societies can divert resources from the pursuit of these objectives to other issues. They do confirm, however, that it is difficult or impossible to specify the threshold levels of progress in social goals or modernisation that would usher in a sharp fertility decline.

In several discussions, Kerala's experience is cited as a model to suggest that universal female literacy, low infant mortality, and a high status of women, summarised as social development, would help to accelerate fertility transition. However, the important role of international migration to the Gulf countries as a means of escaping the poverty trap and the associated rise in the aspirations of living desired for the family and the children is often underestimated.

In several discussions, Kerala's experience is cited as a model to suggest that universal female literacy, low infant mortality, and a high status of women, summarised as social development, would help to accelerate fertility transition.

Likewise, the history of matriarchal tradition in Kerala is often cited as indicating the high status enjoyed by Kerala women. However, the evidence on the subject is by no means clear. The key word at the International Conference on Population and Development (ICPD) at Cairo was empowerment of women. However, the concept of empowerment is difficult to translate. The NPP 2000 has stressed the need for ending discrimination against girls during childhood and early adolescence and against women during the childbearing period in order to improve their health and nutrition. Legal action is certainly not enough. Many laws enacted by our progressive legislatures continue to be violated with impunity in large parts of India.

The implication of Fertility Trends

Longer lives and fertility far below the replacement level of 2.1 births per woman are leading to rapid population aging in many countries. Many observers are concerned that aging will adversely affect public finances and standards of living. Analysis of newly available National Transfer Accounts data for 40 countries shows that fertility well above replacement would typically be most beneficial for government budgets.

However, fertility near replacement would be most beneficial for standards of living when the analysis includes the effects of age structure on families as well as governments. And fertility below replacement would maximize per capita consumption when the cost of providing capital for a growing labor force is taken into account. Although low fertility will indeed challenge government programs and very low fertility undermines living standards, it is found that moderately low fertility and population decline favor the broader material standard of living.

Determinants of Declining Mortality

The main reasons responsible for the decline in mortality rate are as under.

1. *Decline in epidemics:* In India, systematic efforts are being made to reduce the incidence of epidemics like plague, malaria, etc.
2. *Urbanisation of population:* Majority of population has migrated to towns. In 2011 Census, about 31% of the total population was in towns as compared to 28% in 1991. Moreover, development of medical and sanitary conditions has also reduced the death rate.
3. *Late marriages:* The late marriages have been encouraged in the country. Laws regarding marriages have been vigorously enforced.
4. *More medical facilities:* Medical facilities in the country are going on to develop rapidly.
5. *Spread of education:* The literacy ratio in the country has been increasing at an equal interval. People have more resources and better facilities to nourish their children.
6. *Change in habits:* Habits of the people are also changing. Now they have more care for their health which has led to a decline in death rate.
7. *Decline in social evils:* In India, various social evils like caste system, superstition, etc. are steadily being rooted out. This has also led to the decline in the death rate.
8. *Balanced diet:* People are getting better and balanced diet.

Table Population Growth, Crude Birth and Death Rates & Sex-ratio : Census 1901-2011.

Year	Population (in million)	Percentage Decadal	Average annual exponential growth rate (percent)	Crude Birth Rate	Crude Death Rate	Sex Ratio (females per 10000 males)
1901	238.4	-	-	45.8	44.4	972
1911	252.1	5.75	(+) 0.56	49.2	42.6	964
1921	251.3	-0.31	(+) 0.03	48.1	47.2	955
1931	279.0	11.00	(+) 1.04	46.4	36.3	950
1941	318.7	14.22	(+) 1.33	45.2	31.2	945
1951	361.1	13.31	(+) 1.25	39.9	27.4	946
1961	439.2	21.51	(+) 1.95	41.7	22.8	941
1971	548.2	24.80	(+) 2.2	41.2	19.0	930
1981	683.3	24.66	(+) 2.22	37.2	15.0	934
1991	846.4	23.87	(+) 2.14	32.5	11.4	927
2001	1028.7	21.54	(+) 1.97	24.8	8.9	933
2011	1210.2	17.64	(+) 1.64			940

Source : Census of India

AGE AND SEX STRUCTURE

The age-sex structure of a population refers to the number of females and males in different age groups. A population pyramid is used to show the age-sex structure of the population. The shape of the population pyramid reflects the characteristics of the population. The left side shows the percentage of males while the right side shows the percentage of women in each age group.

The importance of age and sex extends considerably beyond demography, however. The division of labor in traditional societies is based almost entirely on age and sex. In fact, age and sex differences of one form or another are found in all known human societies

For expanding population, the age-sex pyramid is a triangular-shaped pyramid with a wide base and is typical of less developed countries. These have larger populations in lower age groups due to high birth rates.

Age-sex pyramid is bell-shaped and tapered towards the top for countries with constant populations. This shows birth and death rates are almost equal leading to a near-constant population.

Countries with declining population have a narrow base and a tapered top showing low birth and death rates. The population growth in developed countries is usually zero or negative.

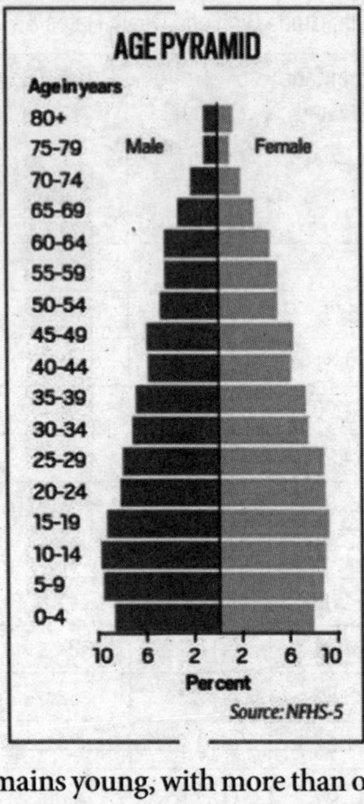

India's population remains young, with more than one-fourth aged under 15 years and less than an eighth over 60. There has been only a slight dip in the

young population's share in the last five years between the National Family Health Survey-NFHS-4 (2015-16) and NFHS-5 (2019-21). The under-15 population has declined by 2 percentage points, from 29% to 27%, while the over-60 population has increased by as many points, from 10% to 12%.

Over half the population (52%) is below 30, compared to 55.5% in NFHS-4. The NFHS divides the population into 5-year age groups from 0-4 years to 75-79, while those over 80 are counted in a single age group.

The age pyramid shows India's population is young, which, NFHS-5 notes, is typical of developing countries with low life expectancy. The pyramid also shows that fertility has decreased considerably in the last 5 years, it says.

The dependency ratio, which is the ratio of economically active to economically inactive persons, is dependent on age composition. India has one of the largest proportions of population in the younger age groups in the world. 31.2% of the population of the country has been in the age group 0–14 years. Census 2001 data on marital status of persons show that out of over a billion population of the country, 513 million (49.8%) have reported as 'Never married', mainly due to high proportion of young people. The 'Married' constitute about 45.6% of the total population.

SEX RATIO IN INDIA AND ITS DETERMINANTS

India's artificially wide ratio of baby boys to baby girls – which arose in the 1970s from the use of prenatal diagnostic technology to facilitate sex-selective abortions – now appears to be narrowing, according to newly released data from the country's National Family Health Survey (NFHS-5).

India's sex ratio at birth has been moving toward balance in recent years

Sex ratio at brith, or the number of male births per 100 female births

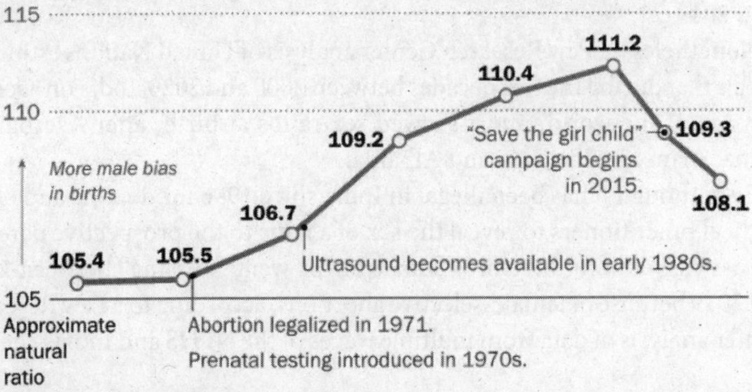

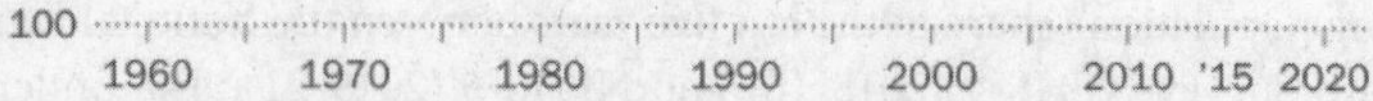

Notes: The sex ratio at birth is about 105 boys per 100 girls. Numbers in this chart generally describe the sex ratio of births in the previous five years, except for the 2001 and 2011 numbers, which are from the census and are based on a question introduced in 2001 measuring the sex of babies born in the previous year.

Sources: Census of India, 2001 and 2011. National Family Health Survey. 2015-16 and 2019-21; United Nations, Department of Economic and Social Affairs, Population Division,
'World Population Prospects 2019'
'India's Sex Ratio at Birth Begins to Normalize'

Pew Research Center

The new data suggests that Indian families are becoming less likely to use abortions to ensure the birth of sons rather than daughters. This follows years of government efforts to curb sex selection – including a ban on prenatal sex tests and a massive advertising campaign urging parents to "save the girl child" – and coincides with broader social changes such as rising education and wealth.

Abortion was legalized in the country in 1971. Once prenatal testing allowed Indian families to learn the sex of a fetus during pregnancy, sex selection took off. The sex ratio at birth widened rapidly from about 105 boys per 100 girls before 1970, to 108 boys per 100 girls in the early 1980s; it reached 110 in the 1990s and remained at that level for roughly 20 years.

From a large imbalance of about 111 boys per 100 girls in India's 2011 census, the sex ratio at birth appears to have normalized slightly over the last decade, narrowing to about 109 in the 2015-16 wave of the National Family Health Survey and to 108 boys in the latest wave of the NFHS, conducted from 2019-21.

Nonetheless, a Pew Research Center analysis of United Nations estimates reveals that during the two decades between 2000 and 2020, India on average had one of the world's most skewed sex ratios at birth, after Azerbaijan, China, Armenia, Vietnam and Albania.

Even though it has been illegal in India since 1996 for doctors and other medical practitioners to reveal the sex of a fetus to the prospective parents, at least 9.0 million (0.9 crore) female births went "missing" between 2000 and 2019 because of female-selective abortions, according to a Pew Research Center analysis of data from multiple waves of the NFHS and India's census.

To put the recent decline in sex selection into perspective, the average annual number of baby girls "missing" in India fell from about 480,000 (4.8 lakh) in 2010 to 410,000 (4.1 lakh) in 2019, the Center's analysis finds.

CONCEPTS OF FAMILY PLANNING AND FAMILY WELFARE

India was the first countries to initiate a government policy of promoting a family planning programme in 1952. The programme, which began somewhat timidly, has been a major effort at social engineering in a democratic polity with an unusually high level of heterogeneity. *A study of the various documents, relating to and preceding the formulation of successive Five Year Plans of India, has highlighted the following points:*

1. The Indian concern with population growth and the need to influence the behaviour of the people with respect to fertility was entirely indigenous. While influenced by the exposure of Indian leadership to western intellectuals, there was no extraneous pressure on the Indian authorities to adopt any particular approach in the late 1940s or early 1950s.
2. The Indian family planning programme has certainly not been a 'dismal failure'. The contrary statements are based on the use of a wrong yardstick, focused solely on the lack of change in the rate of population growth during successive decades. The latter outcome is a result of the simultaneous operation of two processes of decline in the death rate as well as the birth rate that have neutralised each other. If the change in the average number of children born to women in reproductive ages is used to assess the performance of the family planning programme, India has done reasonably well.
3. Despite the promising performance so far, it seems unlikely that India will soon attain the goal of a replacement level of fertility of 2.1 per cent. Some major changes, introduced in the management and approach of the family welfare programmes, augur well, but they are yet to be effectively implemented. There is a large momentum of growth built into the young age distribution of the Indian population. Also, the four large North Indian states with a population of 336 million in 1991 (40% of the total) continue to have a very high fertility, despite the decline that has occurred even there. As a result, the progress towards replacement level of fertility is likely to be slower than desired.
4. The task ahead demands a concerted effort for a substantial improvement in rural infrastructure and levels of health, literacy, and education. Also, the large army of health workers, entrusted with the responsibility of 'motivating' millions of rural couples to regulate family size faces an

uphill task. If they are to become counsellors of the people, they need to be encouraged and trained to broaden their concerns to include the delivery of a whole package of high quality services to their clients, instead of promoting only particular methods of contraception, such as sterilisation.

EVOLUTION OF INDIA'S POPULATION POLICY

It is important to reflect on the antecedents of the first steps taken by the Planning Commission during 1951–52. Unlike in the case of several other developing countries, the Indian concern about the relatively high level of fertility or the number of children born to Indian women rather than the rate of population growth, reflected a genuine desire to improve the living standards of the people. It was not imposed from abroad. The Indian leadership had been exposed to the development in western countries and did not want India to lag behind. During the 1920s and 1930s, some pioneers had set up family planning clinics in Poona and Bangalore (now Bengaluru). In the 1940s, the Bhore Committee on Health Survey and Development (1946) and the subcommittee on population set up by the National Planning Committee (1940) favoured the involvement of the government in the promotion of family planning. Not surprisingly, therefore, the memorandum submitted by the Family Planning Association of India, set up in 1949 under the president-ship of Lady Dhanvanti Rama Rau, elicited a favourable response from the Planning Commission.

The Health Panel, chaired by Health Minister Rajkumari Amrit Kaur, had appointed a subcommittee on population growth and family planning. R.A. Gopalswami, the Census Commissioner in charge of the first Census of independent India, was its convener. There were differences of opinion. The health minister insisted that 'no contraceptives should be used'. But Prime Minister Jawaharlal Nehru supported a more flexible approach and also the idea of state action to promote family planning. It was because of the report of this subcommittee that in 1952 India became the first developing country in the world to adopt a policy of governmental efforts to promote a reduction in the number of children born to Indian couples.

Simultaneously, there was considerable effort to initiate varied programmes to lower the level of morbidity and malnutrition and to raise life expectancy at birth from the then low value of around 32 years. Thus, the early concept of population policy covered both mortality and fertility and did not exclusively focus on fertility. There was also recognition of the need to improve the quality of life of the people by lowering the burden of disease or morbidity, promoting universal primary education, and eradicating illiteracy, exploitation, and poverty.

There were references to an urgent need to slow down the pace of rural–urban migration and the growth of major cities where it was proving difficult and expensive to provide basic amenities to people. However, these statements did not constitute a 'policy' on population distribution or urbanisation. This was not really surprising because prior to the 1961 Census, the database relating to migration was scanty. Reports of even the 25 'city surveys' commissioned by the Research Programmes Committee of the Planning Commission in the 1950s became available later.

The effective date of the adoption and implementation of a clear family planning programme is often put at 1966, when the 'extension approach' to the promotion of family planning throughout the country replaced the earlier clinic-oriented approach. The earlier approach seeking to set up a large number of family planning clinics was based on the experiences of concerned social workers and professionals in urban areas who were trying to initiate a major programme of social engineering without any precedents to follow.

A separate Department of Family Planning was set up in the Ministry of Health during the Fourth Five Year Plan period. Around the same time, a 'time-bound' target of reducing the crude birth rate from about 39 to 25 per 1000 population in 10 to 12 years was adopted. In practice, it has been a moving target and was not achieved even by 1999, the last year for which estimates of birth and death rates are available from the Sample Registration System set up in the 1960s.

Slippages in the achievement of this goal and the resulting frustration led to the outburst of a special drive during the emergency period of 1975–77 to promote sterilisation. The elections following the withdrawal of Emergency led to the fall of the government. The Janata Party government supported a voluntary family welfare programme without any of the alleged excesses of the emergency period. The backlash to the 1975–76 drive continued for several years and was a setback for the programme.

RECOMMENDATIONS OF THE WORKING GROUP ON POPULATION STABILISATION

A Working Group on Population Policy, set up by the Planning Commission, recommended in 1980 an unrealistic goal before the country: a net reproduction rate (NRR) of 1.0 by 1996 as a national average and by 2001 in all the states. On the basis of several assumptions about the method-mix of contraception, the presumed efficacy of different methods, a rise in the age at marriage, and a lowering of the infant mortality rate (IMR) to 60 per 1000 livebirths, a simulation exercise was done. An effective couple protection rate (ECPR) of 60% was expected to lead to a birth rate of 21 and a death rate of 9. These estimates were incorporated in the draft Sixth Five Year Plan as well as the National Health Policy of 1983 and became accepted national goals.

The limitations of the approach adopted by the Working Group are evident in the fact that even in the state of Punjab, where the reported ECPR exceeded 68%, the birth rate in 1996 was 23.7 and the total fertility rate (TFR) in 1997 was 2.7, much above the replacement level of fertility. Of course, Kerala as well as Tamil Nadu reported a below- or near-replacement level of fertility, with a TFR of 1.8 and 2.0, respectively, in 1997. The Eighth plan had recognised that the NRR of 1.0 was likely to be attained only during 2011–16; and the Ninth plan accepted the very real possibility that the replacement level of fertility may be reached only by 2021 in the country as a whole and in some states much later.

In the 1980s, Prime Minister Rajiv Gandhi had initiated an effort to revise the strategy of the family welfare programme, but little came of it. In 1992, the Karunakaran Committee, set up by the National Development Council (NDC) partly in response to the 1991 Census results, recommended the formulation of a National Population Policy. A draft prepared by an expert group under the chairmanship of M.S. Swaminathan in 1994 was circulated widely and its successive variants were considered by the cabinets of three different coalition governments. The drafts underwent several revisions until finally the NPP 2000 was announced.

Regional Variations

In the meanwhile, the state governments have begun to follow the suggestion of the Swaminathan group to formulate state level population policies. Even before the expert group was set up to prepare a draft of the national population policy, the government of Tamil Nadu had formulated a 15-point programme for child welfare, to improve the health and nutrition of women and children in the state. The programme had incorporated in it the goals relating to infant and child mortality and the birth and death rates.

Subsequently, in 1997, the government of Andhra Pradesh prepared a state population policy. At the end of July 1999, the cabinet of Rajasthan state had approved the population policy of Rajasthan. In January 2000, Madhya Pradesh came out with its population policy. More recently, Uttar Pradesh also drafted a population policy. These state-level population policies are expected to help the departments of family welfare in the states to mobilize greater effort towards population goals and related programmes. To place the various population policy statements in perspective, it is essential to review the current population scene. There is considerable confusion and misinformation, and the yardsticks being used to assess the contribution of the family planning programme are rather convoluted. The relevant facts need careful review.

ACHIEVEMENT OF FAMILY WELFARE PROGRAMME

India had a population of 846 million at the time of the Census conducted in February 1991, with a reference date of 1 March. (If account is taken of the net undercount of population, including the greater under-count of young children, the actual population at the time of the Census was 864 million, almost 16 million more than the widely used estimate.) The implicit annual growth rate during the 1980s was 2.1%, only slightly lower than the 2.2% observed during the two decades of 1961–81. This has been misinterpreted as indicating a stagnation in the underlying demographic processes.

Goals of National Population Policy (NPP)

The NPP 2000 has distinguished between immediate, medium-term, and long-term policy objectives. The immediate objective is to address (a) the unmet needs for contraception, (b) health care infrastructure and health personnel, and (c) to provide integrated service delivery for basic reproductive and child health care. The past history suggests, however, that the questions of health infrastructure and health personnel can hardly be addressed in the short run. The resource requirements are so large that the funds will hardly be mobilised immediately or even over a period of five years. The integration of the service delivery is also a longstanding goal that has been difficult to achieve.

The NPP 2000 refers to five schemes that involve incentive payments. For individuals, these include:

(1) The Balika Samridhi Yojana run by the Department of Women and Child Development to promote survival and care of the girl child, with a cash incentive of Rs 500 given at the time of birth of a girl child of birth order 1 or 2.

(2) The Maternal Benefit Scheme run by the Department of Rural Development awards an incentive of Rs 500 for the birth of the first child after 19 years of age and is limited to the first and second births only.

The cash award is now to be linked to 'antenatal check up, institutional delivery by a trained birth attendant, registration of birth, and BCG immunisation.'

(3) A Family Welfare-linked Health Insurance Plan is to be established to offer health insurance (for hospitalisation, not exceeding Rs 5000) to couples (and their children) below the poverty line, if the couple undergoes sterilisation with no more than two living children. The spouse undergoing sterilisation is also to get a personal accident insurance cover.

(4) Couples below the poverty line, who marry after the legal age at marriage, register the marriage, have their first child after the mother reaches the age of 21, accept the small family norm, and adopt a terminal method after the birth of the second child, are to be rewarded.

(5) A fifth scheme provides for group incentives that will reward panchayats and zila (district) parishads for 'exemplary performance in universalizing the small family norm, achieving reductions in infant mortality and birth rates, and promoting literacy with completion of primary schooling.' While it would be a mistake to judge these schemes from the point of view of small sums of money they provide for, the real costs of proving one's eligibility and actually receiving the awards far exceed what is recognised in our metropolitan centres. The proof of age and of the fulfilment of prescribed conditions is difficult to obtain in most areas.

Also, the group incentives can generate misreporting of the level of fertility as well as mortality and it would be a mistake to award them until a system of complete registration of births and deaths, marriages, and pregnancies is actually established. Overall, it is difficult to believe that the incentive schemes will make any material difference to the promotion of fertility decline. It is argued, however, that they have a symbolic role in communicating to the people what is in the social or national interest.

Population Commission

Following the announcement of NPP 2000, a large Population Commission was constituted. The Department of Family Welfare serves as the Secretariat to the Commission, which is expected to 'oversee and review' the implementation of NPP 2000. Similar commissions are envisaged at the state and union territory level. It has often been cynically argued, without convincing reasons, that the Department of Family Welfare/Planning should be abolished and its functions partly transferred to the Directorate

General of Health Services (DGHS) and partly to other departments of the government. However, the DGHS does not have a much better record of performance and the cosmetic change would only make it unwieldy, with no gain in efficiency. The important task is to ensure that the Population Commission is properly briefed to make the best use of the talent and advice it seeks to mobilize. However, there is little doubt that the organised family planning programmes of governments have lowered the costs of obtaining the relevant information and have also provided a modicum of services at an affordable price. Those who denigrate the contribution of the much-maligned family planning programme to the decline in fertility in India are closing their eyes to an important agent of change.

The Technology of Contraception

Several feminist groups are opposed to the idea that Indian women should have access to all the safe and effective methods of contraception available to women in the rest of the world. The 1994 report of the Expert Group had emphasised the need for a careful ethical clearance of all contraceptives, but it also elicited adverse comments. Many scientists of impeccable integrity hold the view that the fears about certain hormonal methods of contraception lack adequate basis. An impartial assessment of all the related issues is necessary. However, it would be a mistake to deny these methods to individual women who are willing to pay for them and find them convenient for their particular situations. All evidence clearly suggests that societies without access to modern methods of contraception can also significantly reduce fertility. However, many of these methods (such as abortion or infanticide) can be harsh and scientific advances must be availed of to facilitate acceleration of the process of transition.

State Level Population Policies

During the past few years, Haryana and Rajasthan have passed laws that prospectively debar persons who do not adopt the two-child norm from contesting elections for panchayats, zila parishads, and nagarpalikas. In Rajasthan, the High Courts have upheld the rationale of the laws. The population policy document of Rajasthan proposes to consider an extension of the law making candidates with two or more children ineligible to contest elections to 'other elected bodies like cooperative institutions.' It may also be made a 'service condition' for state government employees.

The Population Policy of Madhya Pradesh also states that, 'Persons having more than two children after 26 January 2001 would not be eligible for contesting elections for panchayats, local bodies, mandis, or cooperatives in the state. In case they get elected, and in the meantime they have the third child, they would be disqualified for that post.' The policy for Rajasthan proposes 'legal registration of marriage,' compulsory observance of minimum age at marriage for availing of 'government facilities and services', and 'stiffer penal provisions for violation of the legal age at marriage.'

The preceding discussion notes the formulation of state level population policies in Rajasthan, and Madhya Pradesh. In some sense, the pioneer in this respect was Tamil Nadu, even though it did not release a separate document called state population policy. However, all the states have been ambitious in their targets with respect to decline in fertility and mortality.

Andhra Pradesh has traditionally been able to mobilise funds from private and public sector industrial firms for its family welfare camps or programmes.

Experience of Tamil Nadu: The prospects for Madhya Pradesh and Rajasthan states may be illustrated by some aspects of the policy adopted by Tamil Nadu, which had prepared an ambitious early statement of its goals about fertility and mortality. Tamil Nadu has done extremely well in lowering its TFR to the below-replacement level during 1996–97. With an IMR of 53 per 1000 live-births (40 in urban areas and 60 in rural areas), it has already achieved an NRR of 1.0. There is still substantial scope for a further decline in the level of infant and child mortality as well as adult mortality. The life expectancy at birth in Tamil Nadu during 1991 –95 was 63.3 years, 3 years above the national average of 60 years but more than 9 years below the high of 72.9 years achieved by Kerala.

LANDMARKS IN THE EVOLUTION OF INDIA'S POPULATION POLICY

- **1940** The subcommittee on Population, appointed by the National Planning Committee set up by the President of the Indian National Congress (Pandit Jawaharlal Nehru), considered 'family planning and a limitation of children' essential for the interests of social economy, family happiness, and national planning. The committee recommended the establishment of birth control clinics and other necessary measures such as raising the age at marriage and a eugenic sterilisation programme.
- **1946** The Health Survey and Development Committee (Bhore Committee) reported that the control of disease and famine and improvement of health would cause a serious problem of population growth. It considered deliberate limitation of births desirable.

- **1951** The draft outline of the First Five Year Plan recognised 'population policy' as 'essential to planning' and 'family planning' as a 'step towards improvement in health of mothers and children'.
- **1952** The final First Five Year Plan document noted the 'urgency of the problems of family planning and population control' and advocated a reduction in the birth rate to stabilise population at a level consistent with the needs of the economy.
- **1956** The Second Five Year Plan proposed expansion of family planning clinics in both rural and urban areas and recommended a more or less autonomous Central Family Planning Board, with similar state level boards.
- **1959** The Government of Madras (now Tamil Nadu) began to pay small cash grants to poor persons undergoing sterilisation as compensation for lost earnings and transport costs and also to canvassers and tutors in family planning.
- **1961** The Third Five Year Plan envisaged the provision of sterilisation facilities in district hospitals, subdivisional hospitals, and primary health centres as a part of the family planning programme. Maharashtra state organised 'sterilisation camps' in rural areas.
- **1963** The Director of Family Planning proposed a shift from the clinic approach to a community extension approach to be implemented by auxiliary nurse midwives (one per 10,000 population) located in PHCs. Other proposals included: (a) a goal of lowering the birth rate from an estimated 40 to 25 by 1973; and (b) a cafeteria approach to the provision of contraceptive methods, with an emphasis on free choice.
- **1965** The intrauterine device was introduced in the Indian family planning programme.
- **1966** A full-fledged Department of Family Planning was set up in the Ministry of Health. Condoms began to be distributed through the established channels of leading distributors of consumer goods.
- **1972** A liberal law permitting abortions on grounds of health and humanitarian and eugenic considerations came into force.
- **1976** The statement on National Population Policy, made in the Parliament by the Minister for Health and Family Planning, assigned 'top national priority and commitment' to the population problem to bring about a sharp drop in fertility. The Constitution was amended to freeze the representation of different states in the lower house of Parliament according to the size of population in the 1971 Census. The states were permitted to enact legislation providing for compulsory sterilisation.

- **1977** A revised population policy statement was tabled in Parliament by a government formed by the former opposition parties. It emphasised the voluntary nature of the family planning programme. The term 'family welfare' replaced 'family planning'.
- **1982** The draft Sixth Five Year Plan adopted a long term goal of attaining a net reproduction rate of 1.0 on the average by 1996 and in all states by 2001. It adopted the targets for crude birth and death rates, infant mortality rate and life expectancy at birth and the couple protection rate, to be achieved by 2001. (The numbers were based on the illustrative exercises of a Working Group on Population Policy set up by the Planning Commission during 1978.)
- **1983** The National Health Policy incorporated the targets included in the Sixth Five-Year Plan document. While adopting the Health Policy, the Parliament emphasised the need for a separate National Population Policy.
- **1993** A Committee on Population, set up by the National Development Council in 1991, in the wake of the Census results, proposed the formulation of a National Population Policy.
- **1994** The Expert Group, set up by the Ministry of Health and Family Welfare in 1993, to draft the National Population Policy recommended the goal of a replacement level of fertility (a total fertility rate of 2.1) by 2010. Other proposals of the expert group included (i) removal of method-specific targets down to the grassroots level; (ii) an emphasis on improving the quality of services; (iii) a removal of all incentives in cash or kind; (iv) a National Commission on Population and Social Development under the chairmanship of the prime minister. The draft statement was circulated among the members of Parliament and various ministries at the centre and among the states for comments.
- **1997** The cabinet headed by Prime Minister I. K. Gujral approved a draft National Population Policy, to be placed before the Parliament. With the dissolution of the lower house of Parliament, the action was postponed.
- **1999** Another draft of National Population Policy, placed before the cabinet, was remitted to a Group of Ministers (GOM) headed by the Deputy Chairman of the Planning Commission, to examine the scope for the inclusion of incentives and disincentives for its implementation. The GOM consulted various academic experts and women's representatives and finalised a draft, which was discussed by the cabinet on 19 November 1999, and which was revised further for re-submission.
- **2000** National Population Policy was adopted by the cabinet and announced on February 2000.

STRATEGIES TO ACHIEVE POPULATION STABILISATION

India was the first country to evolve a government backed family planning programme in the 1950s when the rest of the world was not aware of the problem. Today, India is still trailing behind in population control. During the notorious Emergency regime between 1975 and 1977, the political leaders, the government officials, and policemen shouted themselves hoarse advocating sterilisations. They devised ambitious programmes and carried them out against popular wishes, and even used such harsh and coercive methods for sterilisation that today one is reluctant to talk of family planning to the populace. The concerned officials in family welfare/planning departments have been scared away from it. In 1977, 'family planning' was rechristened 'family welfare', and tasks beyond its competence embracing all aspects of family welfare, including improvement of women's educational level, were included in it. In its family planning awareness drive, the Government of India adopted the UNEP guideline of delaying the first child and spacing the subsequent birth(s). The methods in family planning are: sterilisation, loop, pill, withdrawal, rhythm, sheath, and diaphragm. The rubber and the pill seems most popular among the high socio-economic groups; so are the withdrawal method among the middle socio-economic groups and sterilisation are preferred by people belonging to the low social strata.

Operations for family planning are not very popular among the socially well-placed, as this group is exposed to other methods of birth control. A good number of women use more than one method, depending on circumstances, availability, and mood of the moment.

Measures Adopted

Officially mobilised in 1951, about 150 family planning clinics were established during the First Five Year Plan period (1951–56). Since then, a network of Community Health Centres (CHCs), Primary Health Centres (PHCs), and Sub-Centres (SCs) have been created for implementing family planning programme through state governments with a 100% assistance. A large number of centres and sub-centres are created in rural areas in each Five Year Plan. In 1998 there were about 1.5 lakh SCs, 25,000 PHCs, and 2500 CHCs in the country. Of the various methods of family planning, the government till recently depended more on the 'camp approach' which relied implicitly on the district authorities applying pressure on their officials to intensify the sterilisation campaign (mostly male sterilisation). The government set targets for different states and districts and adopted persuasive, monetary, as well as coercive measures to achieve targets. The highest rate of target achievement (200%) was in 1976–77, while the achievement rate of sterilisation targets in different years has normally varied between 40 % and 65 %. The highest rate of achievement in 1976–77 has been described as 'Sanjay effect' which was the result of coercion, cruelty, corruption, and inflated achievement figures. The worst victims of cruelty and brutality were the Harijans, peons, clerical staff, school teachers, innocent rural people, hospital patients, jail inmates, and pavement-dwellers. This brutality through family planning (sterilisation) method ultimately led to the fall of the government in 1977.

The Primary Health Centres in villages, engaged in family planning programmes, perform two specific functions: providing services to people and disseminating information about these services in an effective manner in order to motivate people to accept family planning. Nearly half a million medical and paramedical persons are engaged in the programme, besides half a million part-time village health guides.

After the First Five Year Plan, the following Five Year Plans gave increasing priority to the programme but it was only in 1968–69 that the decline in the birth rate became noticeable. The birth rate which stood at 41.7 per thousand in 1961 came down to 28.7 in 1994 and 25.2 in 1995. By the year 2020, as per the World Bank data, the crude birth rate has further reduced to 17.

India has demonstrated its commitment to improving the sexual and reproductive health of its population. Its policy and program environment has shifted from a narrow focus on family planning to a broader orientation that stresses sexual and reproductive health and the exercise of rights.

- The total fertility rate is 2.2 (2015–2016) and has reached replacement level in 18 of its 29 states.
- However, postpartum care eludes many women.
- Contraceptive practice patterns reflect a continued focus on female sterilization, limited use of male methods, limited use of non-terminal methods, and persisting unmet need.
- The overwhelming majority of abortions take place outside of legally sanctioned provider and facility structures.
- Over one-quarter of young women continue to marry in childhood. Comprehensive sexuality education reaches few adolescents, and in general, sexual and reproductive health promoting information needs are poorly met.

POPULATION PROJECTION FOR INDIA (2001–2026)

Population projection is a scientific attempt to peep into the future population scenario, conditioned by making certain assumptions, using data relating to the past available at that point of time. Assumptions used and their probability of adhering in future, forms a critical input in this mathematical effort. Predicting the future course of human fertility and mortality is not easy, especially when looking beyond in time as medical and health intervention strategies, food production and its equitable availability, climatic variability, sociocultural setting, politico economic conditions, and a host of other factors influence population dynamics, making it difficult to predict the growth with certainty. Therefore, caution must be exercised while making or using the population projections in the context of various conditions imposed. The Component Method is the universally accepted method of making population projections because growth of population is determined by fertility, mortality, and migration rates. Twenty-one States have been considered and applied the Component method. They are Andhra Pradesh, Assam, Bihar, Chhattisgarh, Delhi, Gujarat, Haryana, Himachal Pradesh, Jammu & Kashmir, Jharkhand, Karnataka, Kerala, Madhya Pradesh, Maharashtra, Orissa, Punjab, Rajasthan, Tamil Nadu, Uttaranchal, Uttar Pradesh, and West Bengal. The projection of the seven north-eastern states (excluding Assam) has also been carried out as a whole. For the State of Goa and six Union territories, Mathematical Method has been applied. The data used are 2001 Census and Sample Registration System (SRS). SRS provides time series data of fertility and mortality, which has been used for predicting their future levels.

Critical Demographic Issues

The salient features of the population projections at the national level, and some of the underlying assumptions in this regard, are as under:

- The population of India is expected to increase from 1029 million to 1400 million during the period 2001–2026—an increase of 36% in twenty-five years at the rate of 1.2% annually. As a consequence, the density of population will increase from 313 to 426 persons per square kilometer.
- The crude birth rate will decline from 23.2 during 2001–05 to 16.0 during 2021–25 because of falling level of total fertility. In contrast, the crude death rate is expected to fall marginally due to changing age structure of the population with the rising median age as a result of continuing decline in fertility and increase in the expectation of life at birth. It will drop from 7.5 during 2001–05 to 7.2 during 2021–25.

- The infant mortality rate of the country, which is reported to be 63 in 2002, is expected to go down to 40 by the end of the period 2021–25.
- Between 2001 and 2026, because of the declining fertility, the proportion of population aged under 15 years is projected to decline from 35.4 to 23.4%; the proportion of the middle (15–59 years) and the older ages (60 years and above) are set to increase considerably. With the declining fertility, along with the increases in life expectancy, the number of older persons in the population is expected to increase by more than double from 71 million in 2001 to 173 million in 2026—an increase in their share to the total population from 6.9 to 12.4%. The proportion of population in the working age group 15–59 years is expected to rise from 57.7% in 2001 to 64.3% in 2026.
- Another important consequence of the declining fertility will be that, at the national level, the population in the school-going age of 5–14 years is expected to decline from 243 million in 2001 to 222 million in 2026. The share of the population aged 5–14 years to total population of all ages is expected to decrease by 5% from 24% in 2001 to 19% in 2011 and by 3% between 2011 to 2026 (19 to 16%).
- The youth population in the age group 15–24 years is expected to increase from 195 million in 2001 to 224 million in 2026. Its proportion to total population is expected to fall from 19% in 2001 to 16% in 2026.
- The average Indian will be expected to be of 31 years old in 2026 compared to 23 years old in 2001.
- Out of the total population increase of 371 million between 2001 and 2026, the share of the workers in the age group 15–59 years in this total increase is 83%. This has implication in the productivity of labour in future.
- The sex ratio of the total population (females per 1000 males) is expected to decrease (i.e., become less feminine) from 933 in 2001 to 930 during 2026.
- The Total Fertility Rate (TFR) is expected to decline from 2.9 during 2001–2005 to 2.0 during 2021–25. The assumption is that the Total Fertility Rate (TFR) would decline steadily and would touch the floor value of 1.8 in some states. With this, the weighted TFR is projected to reach the replacement level of 2.1 by the period 2021.
- The urban population in the country, which is 28% in 2001, is expected to increase to 38% by 2026. The urban growth would account for over two-thirds (67%) of total population increase by 2026. Out of the total population increase of 371 million during 2001–2026 in the country, the share of increase in urban population is expected to be 249 million.
- The demographic projections suggest that by 2026, the population of India will reach 1,384 million.

4

URBANISATION—PROBLEMS AND REMEDIES

"Urbanisation has lured more people to bustling metropolises, but precious little thought has been given to what happens when these cities fail."—Ben Paynter

INTRODUCTION AND CONCEPT

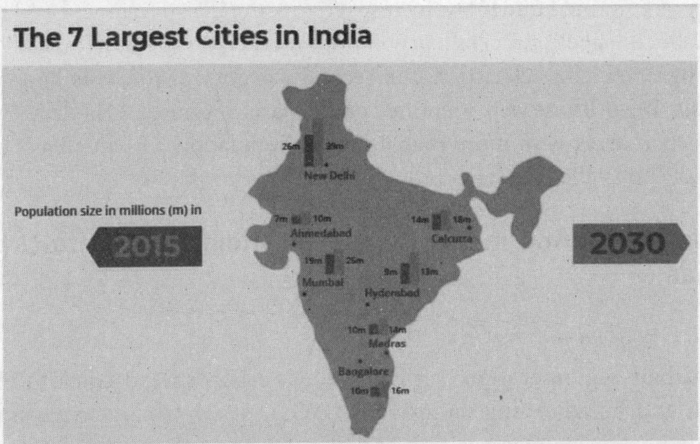

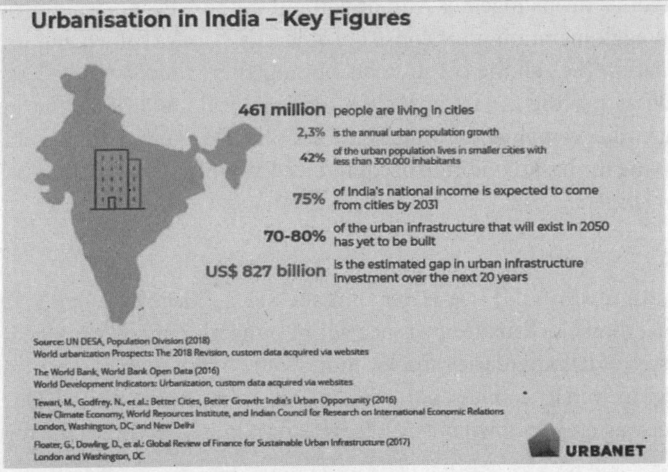

Definitions

India's urban population is estimated to stand at 675 million in 2035, the second highest behind China's one billion, the U.N. has said in a report, noting that after the COVID-19 pandemic, the global urban population is back on track to grow by another 2.2 billion by 2050.

The Census of India, 2011 defines urban settlement as, all the places which have municipality, corporation and cantonment board, or notified town area committee. It includes all the other places which satisfy following criteria:

a. A minimum population of 5000 persons;
b. At least 75% of male main working population engaged in non-agricultural pursuits; and
c. A density of population of at least 400 persons per square kilometre.

The first category of urban units is known as *Statutory town*. These towns are notified under law by respective State/UT government and have local bodies like municipal corporation, municipality, etc, irrespective of demographic characteristics. The second category of towns is known as *Census Town*. These were identified on the basis of Census 2011 data. Cities are urban areas with more than 1,00,000 population. Urban areas below 1,00,000 are called *towns* in India.

Important Terms in the Census of India Related to Urban Areas

Urban Agglomeration (UA)

An urban agglomeration is a continuous urban spread constituting a town and its adjoining outgrowths (OGs), or two or more physically contiguous towns together with or without outgrowths of such towns. An urban agglomeration must consist of at least a statutory town and its total population (i.e., all the constituents put together) should not be less than 20,000 as per the 2011 Census. In varying local conditions, there were similar other combinations which have been treated as urban agglomerations satisfying the basic condition of contiguity. Examples: Greater Mumbai UA, Delhi UA, etc.

Out Growths (OG)

An out growth (OG) is a viable unit such as a village or a hamlet or an enumeration block made up of such village or hamlet and clearly identifiable in terms of its boundaries and location. Some of the examples are railway colony, university campus, port area, military camps, etc., which have come up near a statutory town outside its statutory limits but within the revenue limits of a village or villages contiguous to the town. While determining the outgrowth of a town, it has been ensured that it possesses the urban features in terms of infrastructure and amenities such as pucca roads, electricity, taps, drainage system for disposal of waste water, educational institutions, post offices, medical facilities, banks, etc. and are physically contiguous with the core town of the UA. Each such town together with its outgrowth(s) is treated as an integrated urban area and is designated as an 'urban agglomeration'.

According to 2011 Census, the number of towns are:

Statutory Towns — 4,041
Census Towns — 3,894
Urban Agglomerations — 475
Out Growths — 981

At the central level, nodal agencies which look after programmes and policies for urban development are Ministry of Housing and Urban Poverty Alleviation (MoHUPA) and Ministry of Urban development. Urban development is a state subject. At state level there are respective ministries, but according to the 74th Constitutional Amendment Act, 1992, it is mandatory for every state to form Urban Bocal Bodies (ULBs) and devolve power, conduct regular election, etc. Under the 12th Schedule of the Indian Constitution, 18 such functions have been defined which are to be performed by ULBs and for that, states should support the ULBs through finances and decentralisation of power. But this is not uniform throughout all the states and still more is needed to be done to empower ULBs in India. ULBs look after the service delivery and grievance redressal of citizens. There are eight types of urban local government in India—municipal corporation, municipality, notified area committee, town area committee, cantonment board, township, port trust, and special purpose agencies.

Migration is the key process underlying the growth of urbanisation; and the process of urbanisation is closely related with rural to urban migration of people.

Migration is the key process underlying the growth of urbanisation; and the process of urbanisation is closely related with rural to urban migration of people. In most developing countries of the world, where rate of urban growth is relatively higher, the urban-ward migration is usually high. Rural to urban migration is by far the major component of urbanisation and is the chief mechanism by which urbanisation trends all over the world has been accomplished After independence, urbanisation in India is increasing at a very high pace, but at the same time there are some problems, which are becoming barriers for balanced equitable, and inclusive development.

URBANISATION—INEVITABLE AND DESIRABLE

Background

Urbanisation in the true sense had begun during the British period. In 1687–88, the first municipal corporation in India was set up at Madras (now Chennai). In 1726, Municipal Corporations were set up in Bombay (Mumbai) and Calcutta (Kolkata). In 1882, a resolution was passed and according to which, panchayats were to be formed at village level, district boards, and taluq boards and municipalities also came into existence. At that time Lord Ripon was Viceroy of India, and for this *Lord Ripon is known as father of local self government in India*. Urbanisation since independence has been focused through respective Five year plans. In recent years, there have been various reasons that have led to the growth of urbanisation.

The United Nations-Habitat's World Cities Report 2022 said that rapid urbanisation was only temporarily delayed by the COVID-19 pandemic.

The global urban population is back on track to grow by another 2.2 billion people by 2050, it said.

India's urban population is projected to be 67,54,56,000 in 2035, growing from 48,30,99,000 in 2020 to 54,27,43,000 in 2025 and 60,73,42,000 in 2030, the report said.

By 2035, the percentage of population in India at mid-year residing in urban area will be 43.2%, it said.

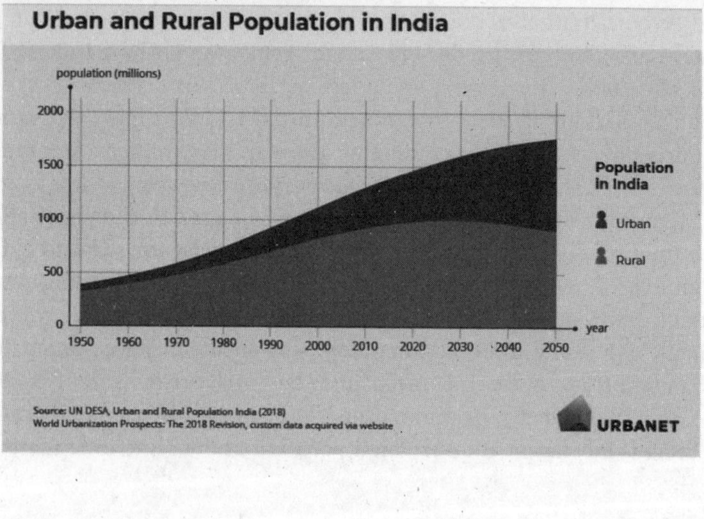

Transportation Problems

Many cities around the world, especially those in developing countries such as China and India, reported unprecedented reductions in the level of airborne pollutants such as PM2.5, PM10, CO_2, NO_2 and SO_2. Declines were significant in cities that imposed lockdowns given the dominance of road transportation and associated emissions in urban areas," (United Nations-Habitat's World Cities Report 2022).

Highlighting the implications of transportation trends during the COVID-19 pandemic, it said that in some countries like India, car dependency increased since the emergence of COVID-19, and people formerly interested in active and public transportation shifted towards private cars.

These trends show that in the absence of safe, affordable and reliable public transportation systems, the future of urban mobility could continue to be dominated by private motorized vehicles.

REASONS FOR URBANISATION

Industrialisation

Industrialisation is a major cause of urbanisation. It has expanded the employment opportunities. Rural people have migrated to cities on account of better employment opportunities.

Social Factors

Many social factors such as attraction of cities, better standard of living, better educational facilities, and need for status also induce people to migrate to cities.

Employment Opportunities

In the rural sector, people have to depend mainly on agriculture for their livelihood. But Indian agriculture is highly dependent on monsoon. So, in drought situations or natural calamities, rural people have to migrate to cities.

Modernisation

Urban areas are characterised by sophisticated technology, better infrastructure, communication, medical facilities, etc. People feel that they can lead a comfortable life in cities and migrate to cities.

Rural Urban Transformation

Not only cities are growing in number, but rural community is adopting urban culture. Rural people are following the material culture of urban people. Urban rural transformation can be observed in areas such as spread of education. The literacy rate has increased among the rural people. They have become more modernised.

Besides these, multiple other changes have occurred due to urbanisation:

i. Change in dress and food habits.
ii. Adoption of modern technology
iii. Empowerment of women.
iv. Modern transport and communication. For example, cell phones have become common even among rural people.
v. Active involvement in politics.
vi. Growth of infrastructure like banks, post office, etc.
vii. Awareness among rural consumers.
viii. Increasing demand for sophisticated products like cosmetics, etc.

Thus, it can be noticed that there are significant changes in the lifestyle of village dwellers. Indian villages have adopted urban culture and urban style of living. However, it is also a lamentable fact that all villages in India have not been able to enjoy the fruits of modernisation.

Effect of Urbanisation

With a high rate of urbanisation, significant changes have taken place. *The effect of urbanisation can be summed up as follows:*

Positive Effect

i. Migration of rural people to urban areas.
ii. Employment opportunities in urban centres.
iii. Transport and communication facilities.
iv. Educational facilities.
v. Increase in the standard of living.

Urbanisation can yield positive effects if it takes place up to a desirable limit. Extensive urbanisation or indiscriminate growth of cities may result in adverse effects.

Negative Effect

i. *Problem of over population*: Concentration of population is a major problem of cities. It has resulted in reduced quality of life, growth of slums, etc.

ii. *Disintegration of joint family*: Joint family can't be maintained in cities on account of high cost of living. People prefer to live in the nuclear type of families.
iii. *Cost of living*: High cost of living is a major problem of cities. In cities like Mumbai, Bengaluru, etc. it is very difficult for lower income groups to maintain a decent standard of living.
iv. *Increase in crime rates*: Urban centres are known for high rate of crimes. Theft, dacoity, murder, cheating, pickpocketing, rape, etc. are common in urban centres.
v. *Impersonal relations*: Urban centres are characterised by highly impersonal relations. The concept of neighbourhood and community life are almost absent in cities. Urban life is highly monotonous. This may have an adverse psychological effect on individuals. People are often self centred and they have no concern for the fellow human beings.
vi. *Problem of pollution*: In industrialised cities, pollution is a major problem. It may be caused by industries or by excessive movement of vehicles.
vii. *Stress*: Urban life is characterised by stress which may even strain family relations.

Thus, urbanisation has its own merits and demerits.

URBANISATION TRENDS AND THEIR IMPLICATIONS

The Background

The degree or level of urbanisation is defined as the relative number of people who live in urban areas. The urban percentage has increased from 11% in 1901 to 31% in 2011, whereas per cent rural has shown the gradual decrease from 89% to around 69% over a century. The urban–rural ratio for India in 2011 turns out to be around 45, meaning that against every 100 ruralites there are 45 urbanites in India in 2011. All these indices pinpoint that India is in the process of urbanisation and it is at the acceleration stage of urbanisation. Urbanisation in India has been relatively slow compared to many developing countries. The percentage of annual exponential growth rate of urban population reveals that in India, it grew at a faster pace from the decade 1921–31 to until 1951. Thereafter, it registered a sharp drop during the decade 1951–61. The decades 1961–71 and 1971–81 showed a significant improvement in the growth which has thereafter steadily dropped to the present level (3.16%). The sharp drop in urban rate during 1951–61 was mainly due to the declassification of a very large number of towns during that period. The decline in rural population growth was within a small range during 1981–91 and 2001–2011. During the process of urbanisation, it is natural that rgtp > rgup > rgrp

where rgtp = rate of growth of total population,

rgup = rate of growth of urban population, and

rgrp = rate of growth of rural population.

The hypothesis that urbanization is necessarily beneficial for economic growth cannot be taken for granted. Our cities have to overcome a number of challenges in order to realize their potential as engines of growth. At present, 34% of India's population lives in urban areas, with a growth rate of 2.4% in the 2010-18 period (World Urbanization Prospects, WUP, 2018). The level of urbanization in India is low as compared to the BRICS economies such as Brazil (86.6%), South Africa (66.4%) and China (59.2%) (WUP 2018).

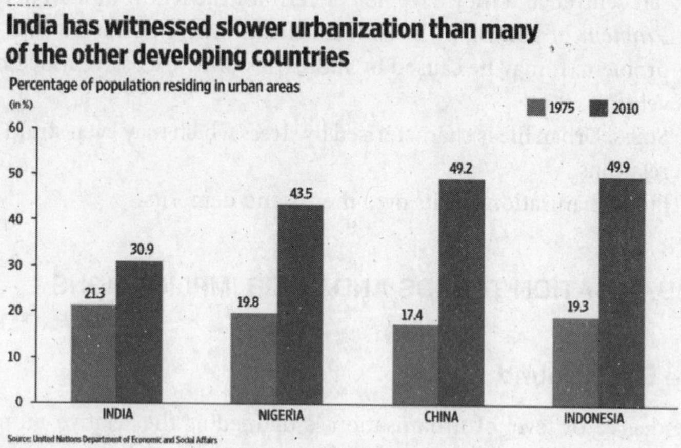

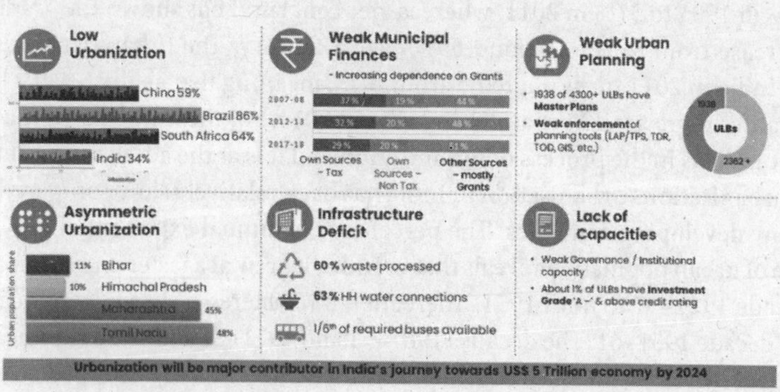

Source: National Institute of Urban Affairs

Low Rural–Urban Migration

The pace of India's rural-urban migration has been low historically because India's rural-urban migration has been driven mostly by male migrants, who go back to their villages instead of settling in cities with their families. The slow pace of rural-urban migration could be because of political incentives. In a country where political success is driven by managing the 3Cs of Indian society—caste, community, and class—any incumbent political leader is disincentivized to see any uncontrolled change in the social configuration of the constituency and, therefore, of the winning coalition.

The McKinsey Report (2010) on India's urbanisation prospects estimates that over the period 2010–2030, urban India will create 70% of all new jobs in India and these urban jobs will be twice as productive as equivalent jobs in the rural sectors.

Concentration of Urban Population in Large Cities

Mumbai and Delhi, India's two biggest cities, account for almost 60% of its billionaires. Those in China are more evenly spread—the top five cities, including Hong Kong, account for just half of China's billionaires.

Back home, not only billionaires but also ordinary urban people seem to be concentrated in a few big cities. Close to 25 million people live in Mumbai and Delhi combined. In other words, 3% of India's entire population occupies only 0.06% of its total area

People have an incentive to migrate from smaller to bigger cities because typically the latter offer higher earnings. However, economic theory suggests that over a period of time as more workers migrate to bigger cities, these will become overcrowded, and see an oversupply of labour, eventually leading to lowering of earnings. Thus, migration should lead to equalisation of earnings, if not between rural and urban areas, then at least between smaller and bigger cities.

However, district-wise data shows otherwise. The chart shows that districts with high urban population density tend to report higher urban incomes. In other words, big cities, like Mumbai and Delhi, still offer higher incomes than other urban areas and that leaves incentive for further migration into such cities.

Emergence and Growth of 'Census' Towns

The places which satisfy the following criteria are called Census towns (CTs):

A. A minimum population of 5000.

B. Atleast 75% of the main male working population is engaged in non-agricultural occupations.

C. A density population of 400 per sq. Km.

URBAN CONDITIONS AND CHALLENGES

Housing Problems

Urban areas today face multifaceted challenges such as population growth, changes in family patterns, growing numbers of urban residents living in slums and informal settlements, constrained urban services, emerging concerns of climate change and upsurge in migration. This has resulted in housing backlog, infrastructure deficit and mushrooming of informal settlements. There were 0.9 million homeless people in urban India [Census 2011], in addition to a slum population of roughly 65 million (or 17% of urban India).

People from India's rural areas, home to 833 million people, are migrating in large numbers to urban centres. As such, housing has gained paramount importance in government policies and private investments. Housing remains the biggest driver of economic growth with strong forward and backward linkages. Increasing the supply and quality of housing has a multiplier effect on the economy by boosting the primary sector (raw materials), manufacturing sector (construction materials) and the service sector (architects and engineers, skilled labours, banking and finance).

Water Problems

By 2050, more than two-thirds of the global population will live in cities. Rapid urbanization creates opportunities for economic developments, but may also increase the use of freshwater resources.

Encroachment is another major threat to urban water bodies. As more people have been migrating to cities, availability of land has been getting scarce. Illegal mining for building material such as sand and quartzite on the catchment and bed of the lake have extremely damaging impact on the water body. For example, the Jaisamand Lake in Jodhpur, once the only source of drinking water for the city, has been suffering from illegal mining in the catchment area for the last 20 years

Using water bodies to attract tourists has become a threat to several urban lakes in India. Tso Morari and Pongsho lakes in Ladakh have become polluted because of unplanned and unregulated tourism.

The biggest challenge is the government apathy towards water bodies. This can be understood from the fact that the it does not even have any data on the total number of urban water bodies in the country. *A 2010-11 Comptroller and Auditor General of India report on the plight of 22 lakes in 14 states said*:

The Union Ministry of Environment & Climate Change (MoEF&CC) had not identified wetlands associated with each river / lake and no identifications of risks to these wetlands due to pollution of river water / lake water had been carried out by the Central Pollution Control Board (CPCB). Further, CPCB had not identified major aquatic species, birds, plants and animals that faced threat due to pollution of rivers and lakes.

Sanitation Problems

Around 40 per cent of the urban population is serviced with sewerage systems, while the remaining 60 per cent is dependent on sub-optimally regulated on-site sanitation systems, according to the Advisory on On-Site and Off-Site Sewage Management Practices. This was issued by the Central Public Health and Environmental Engineering Organisation under the Union Ministry of Housing and Urban Affairs.

This necessitates the need of regulation, guidelines and a management strategy for wastewater and septage, including technology for treatment and disposal options for septage and ways to maximise resource recovery.

The National Policy on Faecal Sludge and Septage Management (FSSM) issued in 2017 aims to facilitate the nationwide implementation of FSSM services in all urban local bodies (ULB).

It sets the context, priorities and direction for safe and sustainable sanitation in every household in India. Since then, there is a great momentum to scale FSSM, with many states also issuing policies in this regard.

The advisory is in line with the efforts made by Delhi-based think-tank Centre for Science and Environment (CSE), whose report, Excreta Matters 2012, detailed how the unaffordable conventional paradigm of water-sewage management needs to be changed. The institute has pushed the agenda of decentralised wastewater management as an alternative to the current conventional wastewater approach.

Industrial Pollution

The increase in the number of industries has led to the growth of urban population and economy. Different industries produce different pollutants and release them into the environment. If we look at the pollution level in cities with the population size of million plus, a city like Surat releases maximum sulphur dioxide in the form of ash, smoke, automobiles exhaust, and household burning of coal and wood. Other cities like Kolkata, Mumbai,

Delhi, Faridabad also send maximum polluting elements to the atmosphere. The increase in sulphur dioxide level in the atmosphere results in diseases like asthma, chronic bronchitis, respiratory problems, and lung cancer among city dwellers. Six cities—Mumbai, Delhi, Hyderabad, Surat, Kochi, and Vishakhaptnam have nitrous oxide levels beyond the permissible limit and causes discoloration of skin. Patna and Surat have almost four times higher than maximum permissible limit of SPM (Suspended Mass Particles) followed by other cities like Delhi, Kolkata, Indore, Kanpur, Lucknow, and Jaipur. SPM consists of benzene soluble organic matter which is highly toxic and carcinogenic. Industrial workers are exposed to poisonous gases, chemicals, and dust that produce serious headache, chest pain, eye, nose, and skin irritation. Similarly, an effective way of collection and treatment of industrial waste water is a severe problem in most of the developing countries like India. Effluent and waste water treatment is expensive and hence it is not followed in many industries. Most of the treated waste water should be recycled to meet its own requirement. Reuse of waste water for the purpose of agriculture and other uses has been well recognised in some of the developed countries.

Transportation Problems

Assuming a decadal increase of around 32%, India's urban population is expected to increase from 377 million in 2011 to 500 million in 2021. In terms of percentage of total population, the urban population has gone up from 17% in 1951 to 31.8% in 2011 and is expected to increase up to around 35% by the year 2021. This growth has envisaged the demand for transport from one place to the other. Many of the Indian cities are less accessible to the surrounding rural areas due to inadequate roads and transportation facilities. Within and between cities, mobility of individuals have increased tremendously and the people are experiencing severe problems such as delays, traffic congestion, air pollution, noise pollution, and energy waste, etc. Improper transport policy adversely affects traffic congestion and also causes significant disruption of business and commercial activities. The policy should aim at reducing the social costs of accidents and pollution. As per the report 'Basic Road Statistics in India-2018-19', India has a network of over 63, 31,757 kilometres of roads on 31.03.2019, which is the second largest in the world. There has been a consistent increase in the construction of roads under various categories during the period 1950-51 to 2018-19. The total road constructed has increased to 63, 31,757 km in 2019 from 62,15,797 km in 2018 and has registered a growth of 1.9 percent. Despite this, urban India suffers from transport issues. The main reason for all these is the prevailing imbalance in modal split besides inadequate transport infrastructure and its sub-optimal use. Public transport systems in cities have not been able to keep pace with the rapid and substantial increases in

Cities cannot afford to cater only to the private vehicles and there has to be a general recognition that a policy should be designed in such a way that reduces the need to travel by personalised modes and boosts public transport, particularly bus transport system.

demand over the past few years. As a result, people have turned towards personalised modes such as mopeds, scooters, motorcycles, and cars and intermediate public transport modes such as auto-rickshaws, tempos, and taxis. Cities cannot afford to cater only to the private vehicles and there has to be a general recognition that a policy should be designed in such a way that reduces the need to travel by personalised modes and boosts public transport, particularly bus transport system. Measures need to be taken to enhance the quality as well as quantity of public transport services and to impose constraints on the use of private vehicles.

Global Warming and Air Quality

The protective atmospheric ozone layer is becoming thin resulting in the rise of global temperatures and greenhouse effect. The UNO is keen on environmental protection. The increase in the urban sprawl increases the number of buildings, extensive road networks, and other paved surfaces. Urban areas generally have higher solar radiation; heat is stored during daytime and is released by night. Built up areas in the urban belt tend to have relatively higher temperatures compared to those of non-urban areas. This thermal difference combined with heat generated by the urban houses, burning of fossil fuel in automobiles, and industrial pollution contributes to the development of heat in urban areas. To protect the ozone layer from the environmental pollution, the Government has to think on proper zoning policies and use of building materials and paved surfaces that minimizes the absorption of heat. The Government should insist on the use of light colour to the buildings and roofing materials in commercial and residential properties, restrict use of reflective glasses on private and commercial properties, encourage tree planting in residential areas to provide shade, and keep the city cool and educate the people about effect of urban heat. The technology through Geographical Information System (GIS) links urban population with environmental problems and it displays the data in a coloured map form. GIS provides useful colour pictures which can be used to educate the people regarding environmental problems. The health status of a citizen can be known by integrating geographic information on polluting factories, major roadways, and air and water quality monitoring. These maps should be made available to the public so that they can help the Government to initiate steps for pollution control measures.

INITIATIVES FOR URBAN DEVELOPMENT IN INDIA

Impact of Pradhan Mantri Awas Yojana (Urban) – Housing for All Scheme

To tackle the urban housing backlog, Pradhan Mantri Awas Yojana (Urban) was launched in 2015 to provide housing for all by 2022 and focuses on in-situ rehabilitation of slum dwellers (ISSR), subsidy for beneficiary led construction/ enhancement of houses (BLC), providing institutional credit through credit-linked subsidy (CLSS) and affordable housing via a partnership model between the public and private sectors (AHP). A Technology Sub-mission had been introduced to bring in a basket of new technologies that can invigorate the construction market. The scheme has been progressive and largely holistic for ownership based housing in the country. The mission verticals, originally designed for the Economically Weaker Section (EWS) and Lower Income Group (LIG) segment, have been protracted to include the Middle Income Group (MIG) as well, thus magnifying the total net of beneficiaries.

As per the report 'Assessing Employment Generation under PMAY-Urban (February, 2019)' by National Institute of Public Finance and Policy, PMAY (U) has been able to generate 12 million jobs through forward and backward linkages in 21 sectors. The construction of sanctioned houses has consumption for more than 17 million metric tons of cement and 13 million tons of steel.

The Advisory on On-Site and Off-Site Sewage Management Practices highlights the following:

- Guides states / Union territories and other stakeholders on safe and holistic management of sewage and faecal matter.
- It discusses on-site sewage treatment methods along with FSSM, apart from off-site sewage treatment methods as affordable and rapid approach to cover remaining population with safe sanitation.
- Showcases integrated planning of sanitation in a city by using city sanitation planning (CSP) and shit-flow diagrams (SFDs).

- Identifies interventions for optimal performance of on-site systems and subsequent progressive coverage of on-site systems with off-site systems as and when necessity arises.
- It emphasises FSSM as an important element of operation and maintenance of on-site sewage management system and is essential for its optimum performance, but in no way an alternative for conventional sewerage systems.
- Space and freedom to plan sanitation facilities in a city according to availability of resources over time.

Jal Jeevan Mission

Jal Jeevan Mission, is envisioned to provide safe and adequate drinking water through individual household tap connections by 2024 to all households in rural India. The programme will also implement source sustainability measures as mandatory elements, such as recharge and reuse through grey water management, water conservation, rain water harvesting. The Jal Jeevan Mission will be based on a community approach to water and will include extensive Information, Education and communication as a key component of the mission. The Jal Jeevan Mission will be based on a community approach to water and will include extensive Information, Education and communication as a key component of the mission. JJM looks to create a jan andolan for water, thereby making it everyone's priority..

Atal Mission for Rejuvenation and Urban Transformation

Atal Mission for Rejuvenation and Urban Transformation (AMRUT), first focused national water Mission was launched in June 2015 to facilitate ease of living to citizens in 500 cities by providing tap connections and sewer connections.

The purpose of Atal Mission for Rejuvenation and Urban Transformation (AMRUT) is to

- Ensure that every household has access to a tap with the assured supply of water and a sewerage connection.
- Increase the amenity value of cities by developing greenery and well maintained open spaces (e.g. parks) and
- Reduce pollution by switching to public transport or constructing facilities for non-motorized transport (e.g. walking and cycling). All these outcomes are valued by citizens, particularly women, and indicators and standards have been prescribed by the Ministry of Housing and Urban Affairs (MoHUA) in the form of Service Level Benchmarks (SLBs).

Deendayal Antyodaya Yojana (National Urban Livelihoods Mission)

The Ministry of Housing and Urban Poverty Alleviation had been implementing a Centrally Sponsored Scheme Swarna Jayanti Shahari Rozgar Yojana (SJSRY) since 1997 which has been restructured as Deendayal Antyodaya Yojana - National Urban Livelihoods Mission since September, 2013. The NULM has been under implementation w.e.f. September 24, 2013 in all district headquarters (irrespective of population) and all the cities with population of 1 lakh or more.

NULM adopts the following strategy:

- Building capacity of the urban poor, their institutions and the machinery involved in the implementation of livelihoods development and poverty alleviation programmes through handholding support
- Enhancing and expanding existing livelihoods options of the urban poor
- Building skills to enable access to growing market-based job opportunities offered by emerging urban economies
- Training for and support to the establishment of micro-enterprises by the urban poor – self and group
- Ensure availability and access for the urban homeless population to permanent 24- hour shelters including the basic infrastructural facilities like water supply, sanitation, safety and security
- Cater to the needs of especially vulnerable segments of the urban homeless like the dependent children, aged, disabled, mentally ill, and recovering patients etc., by creating special sections within homeless shelters and provisioning special service linkages for them
- To establish strong rights-based linkages with other programmes which cover the right of the urban homeless to food, healthcare, education, etc. and ensure access for homeless populations to various entitlements, including to social security pensions, PDS, ICDS, feeding programmes, drinking water, sanitation, identity, financial inclusion, school admission etc., and to affordable housing
- To address livelihood concerns of the urban street vendors by facilitating access to suitable spaces, institutional credit, social security and skills to the urban street vendors for accessing emerging market opportunities.

Note: The Self Employment Programme of urban poor is a component of the National Urban Livelihoods Mission (NULM). It provides financial assistance to individuals/groups of urban poor for setting up gainful self-employment ventures/ micro-enterprises, suited to their skills, training, aptitude and local conditions.

Members of Parliament Local Area Development Scheme

The Members of Parliament Local Area Development Scheme (MPLADS) is an ongoing Central Sector Scheme which was launched in 1993-94. The Scheme enables the Members of Parliament to recommend works for creation of durable community assets based on locally felt needs to be taken up in their constituencies in the area of national priorities namely drinking water, education, public health, sanitation, roads etc.

The Ministry of Statistics and Programme Implementation has been responsible for the policy formulation, release of funds and prescribing monitoring mechanism for implementation of the Scheme.

Features

- The MPLADS is a Plan Scheme fully funded by Government of India. The annual MPLADS fund entitlement per MP constituency is Rs. 5 crore.
- MPs are to recommend every year, works costing at least 15 per cent of the MPLADS entitlement for the year for areas inhabited by Scheduled Caste population and 7.5 per cent for areas inhabited by S.T. population.
- In order to encourage trusts and societies for the betterment of tribal people, a ceiling of Rs. 75 lakh is stipulated for building assets by trusts and societies subject to conditions prescribed in the scheme guidelines.
- Lok Sabha Members can recommend works within their Constituencies and Elected Members of Rajya Sabha can recommend works within the State of Election (with select exceptions). Nominated Members of both the Rajya Sabha and Lok Sabha can recommend works anywhere in the country.
- All works to meet locally felt infrastructure and development needs, with an emphasis on creation of durable assets in the constituency are permissible under MPLADS as prescribed in the scheme guidelines. Expenditure on specified items of non durable nature are also permitted as listed in the guidelines.

Implementation

- A Member of Parliament shall give his/ her choice of Nodal District in a prescribed format to the Ministry of Statistics and Programme Implementation with copy to the State Government and to the District Magistrate of the chosen District.
- The annual entitlement of Rs 5 crore shall be released, in two equal instalments of Rs 2.5 crore each, by Government of India directly to the

District Authority of the Nodal District of the Member of Parliament concerned.

- Each MP shall recommend eligible work on the MP's letter head duly signed by the MP to the district authority.
- The District Authority shall identify the Implementing Agency capable of executing the eligible work qualitatively, timely and satisfactorily. It shall be responsible for timely and effective implementation of such works. All recommended eligible works should be sanctioned within 75 days from the date of receipt of the recommendation, after completing all formalities. The District Authority shall, however, inform MPs regarding rejection, if any, within 45 days from the date of receipt of recommendations, with reasons thereof.
- MPLAD Scheme can be converged in individual/stand-alone projects of other Central and State Government schemes provided such works of Central/State Governments Schemes are eligible under MPLADS. Funds from local bodies can similarly also be pooled with MPLADS works. Wherever such pooling is done, funds from other scheme sources should be used first and the MPLADS funds should be released later, so that MPLADS fund results in completion of the project.
- As soon as a work under the Scheme is completed, it should be put to public use. For greater public awareness, for all works executed under MPLADS a plaque (stone/metal) carrying the inscription 'Member of Parliament Local Area Development Scheme Work' indicating the cost involved, the commencement, completion and inauguration date and the name of the MP sponsoring the project should be permanently erected.
- One MP - One Idea : In order to foster a grass-root bottoms-up approach to innovation and development and to arrive at solutions for local problems, which are sustainable and scalable, there is a need for seeking out and campaigning for ideas that have the potential to solve challenges. Accordingly, based on the innovative ideas received from the local people regarding developmental projects, a 'One MP – One Idea' Competition may be held in each Lok Sabha constituency annually to select the three best innovations for cash awards and certificate of appreciation for next five best innovations

National Transit-Oriented Development Policy

The Ministry of Housing and Urban Affairs (MoHUA) estimates that INR 39,20,000 crore (USD 600 billion) needs to be invested, between 2011-31, of which about 55% is to be allocated to urban roads and mass transit systems – a move that clearly highlights the importance of transport in urban development.

The National Transit Oriented Development (NTOD) policy has various elements that can contribute to creating a green mobility framework for Indian cities. The NTOD stresses on sustainable aspects of mobility, such as encouraging high-density, mixed-use spaces and compact developments with mandatory inclusive housing. It focuses on aspects of transport like traffic calming and universal accessibility with the creation of vibrant public spaces, and encourages the monetisation of these developments through various mechanisms like Value Capture Financing, thus ensuring NMT strategies will have enough funds to be adopted.

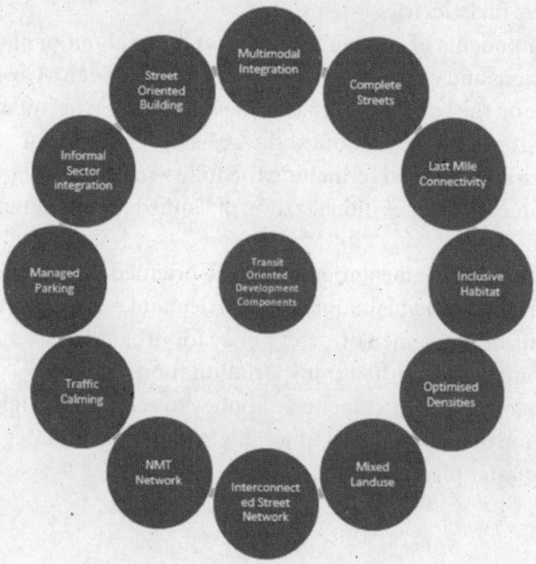

Source: *National Transit Oriented Development Policy*

National Electric Mobility Mission Plan

The 2020 National Electric Mobility Mission Plan (NEMMP) was first proposed by the Department of Heavy Industries, Ministry of Heavy Industries and Public Enterprises in 2012. Its goal was to encourage the faster adoption of electric and hybrid vehicles in the country through government-industry collaborations, to allow India to emerge as a leader in EV manufacturing by 2020.

Green Urban Mobility Initiative

To boost green and sustainable alternatives under the Smart Cities Mission, the Indian government launched the Green Urban Mobility Initiative (GUMI) in 2017. The thrust of the initiative is on two components:

- **Sustainable urban mobility:** This provides impetus to solutions like public transport and NMT, and increases the adoption of technological solutions for transport integration, using BRTS, walking and cycling tracks.
- **Sustainable vehicles and fuels:** This advances the adoption of EVs, and clean and renewable alternatives to fossil fuels for public transport projects. It aims to create over 1000 kilometres of BRT networks and redevelop 550 buses, 20,000 paratransit services and 6,000 buses on alternative fuel/electric systems.
- Both components of the initiative aim to bring about public transport interventions and will involve local government through a Green Mobility challenge on the lines of the Smart Cities Challenge. The initiative targets different zones in India amongst the 103 smart cities so far.

The GUMI was expanded to include the following components:

- Establishment and operationalization of Unified Metropolitan Transport Authorities
- Adoption and implementation of transit-oriented development
- Adoption and implementation of travel demand management measures
- Adoption and implementation of policy for urban street vendors
- Establishment of an urban transportation fund
- Adoption of an anti-encroachment policy to reclaim the right of way
- Preparation of comprehensive mobility plans and their integration with the city master plan

5

TACKLING POVERTY IN INDIA

"There are people in the world so hungry, that God cannot appear to them except in the form of bread."

—Mahatma Gandhi

INTRODUCTION

According to the new global poverty line of $2.15 per day adopted recently by the World Bank in September 2022, 10 per cent of Indians were poor in 2019, down from 22.5 per cent in 2011. Rural India had more poor than the urban: 11.9 per cent in rural areas and 6.4 per cent in urban areas. As per the estimate of the World Bank, poverty in India had declined over the last decade but not as much as previously thought

As compared to 2011, the extreme poverty is 12.3 percentage points lower in 2019, with greater poverty reductions in rural areas. At the same time, the level of poverty was considerably higher than earlier projected by other agencies, based on consumption figures in India's national accounts. However, Consumption inequality in India has moderated since 2011.

India has not declared its poverty figures since 2011, measured on the basis of consumption expenditure surveys by the National Sample Survey organisation (NSSO). A consumption expenditure survey by NSSO in 2017-18 was to be released but the government stopped its publication. This one showed that poverty had increased in India.

Multidimensional Poverty Index (MPI)

The MPI provides a comprehensive picture of acute multidimensional poverty to inform the work of countries and communities building a more just future for the global poor. It was developed by OPHI with the United Nations Development Programme (UNDP) in 2010. It is a part of UNDP's Human Development Report (HDR) and is released annually. India ranked 62 in the Global MPI 2020 which ranked 107 countries.

MPI Dimensions and Indicators

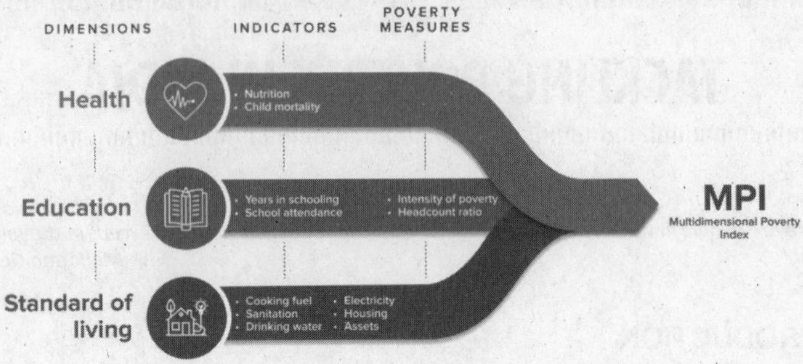

Source: UNDP

Key Findings with respect to India

In India five out of six multidimensionally poor people are from lower tribes or castes.

- 9.4% of the Scheduled Tribe group lives in multidimensional poverty
- 33.3% of the Scheduled Caste group lives in multidimensional poverty.
- 27.2% of the Other Backward Class group lives in multidimensional poverty.

National Multidimensional Poverty Index

According to Global MPI 2021, India's rank is 66 out of 109 countries. The National MPI Project is aimed at deconstructing the Global MPI and creating a globally aligned and yet customised India MPI for drawing up comprehensive Reform Action Plans with the larger goal of improving India's position in the Global MPI rankings.

MEASUREMENT OF POVERTY

The Planning Commission (now NITI Aayog) is the nodal agency in the Government of India for estimation of poverty. It estimates the incidence of poverty at the national and state level separately in rural and urban areas. The incidence of poverty is measured by the poverty ratio, which is the ratio of number of poor to the total population expressed as percentage. It is also known as head-count ratio. The poverty ratio is measured from an exogenously determined poverty line quantified in terms of per capita consumption expenditure over a month and the class distribution of persons obtained from the large sample survey of consumer expenditure data of the National Sample Survey Office (NSSO).

After the Working Group of the Planning Commission delineated the methodology of poverty estimation in 1962, it has been intensely debated by the academicians, experts, policy planners, etc. over the years. In response, the Planning Commission has constituted Task Force/Expert Group from time to time to review the methodology. These include the Task Force under the chairmanship of Dr. Y. K. Alagh in 1977; the Expert Groups under the chairmanship of Prof. D.T. Lakdawala in 1989, and Prof. S.D. Tendulkar in 2005. This chapter takes a look at the evolution of the methodology of measurement of poverty as recommended by the Working Group 1962, Task Force (Alagh), Expert Group (Lakdawala), and Expert Group (Tendulkar).

The Planning Commission constituted a Working Group in 1962 to find out a desirable minimum level of living for the population. The Working Group recommended that the national minimum consumption expenditure for a household of five persons (four adult consumption units) should be not less than Rs. 100 per month or Rs. 20 per capita per month in terms of 1960–61 prices. For urban areas, this figure was Rs. 125 per month or Rs. 25 per capita per month to cover the higher prices there. The poverty line excluded expenditure on health and education, both of which, it was assumed, were to be provided by the state. The Working Group (1962) appeared to have taken into account the recommendation of balanced diet made by the Nutrition Advisory Group of the Indian Council of Medical Research (ICMR) in 1958. This poverty line was widely used in the 1960s and 1970s to estimate the poverty ratio at national and state level.

The Planning Commission in July 1977 constituted the Task Force on "Projections of Minimum Needs and Effective Consumption Demand" under the Chairmanship of Dr. Y. K. Alagh. The Task Force submitted its report in January 1979 and the Planning Commission accepted its recommendations in the same month. *The Task Force provided a quantitative measure of poverty by estimating:*

(a) The average calorie requirements separately for the all-India rural and urban areas as a population-weighted average of the age-gender-activity specific calorie allowances recommended by the Nutrition Expert Group (1968) by reference to the 1971 population Census, and
(b) The poverty line corresponding to the calorie requirement.

The estimated calorie norm was 2400 kcal per capita per day in rural areas and 2100 kcal per capita per day in urban areas.

The Task Force used the percentage distribution of persons in different expenditure classes in the National Sample Survey (NSS) data on household consumer expenditure to estimate the percentage of persons living below the poverty line. The NSS distribution of private consumption was adjusted pro rata to correspond to the consumption estimates of National Accounts Statistics (NAS) made by the Central Statistical Office (CSO). Using the poverty line and the adjusted distribution of persons by expenditure classes for the reference year the percentage of persons below the poverty line was estimated. Applying the projected population of the year, the number of persons in poverty was estimated from the percentage of persons. The poverty line was defined at national level (separately for rural and urban areas).

The Planning Commission methodology for estimating poverty at national and state level was regarded by some as inappropriate in giving a representative picture of the incidence of poverty in the country. *The main points of the criticism were:*

(a) the adjustment procedure;
(b) the choice of deflators to represent price changes in the poverty line;
(c) application of the same poverty line in all the states, which imply the absence of price differentials across the states;
(d) use of a fixed consumption basket over time; and
(e) the uniform consumption basket for all the states.

The Planning Commission, in September 1989, constituted the Expert Group on Estimation of Proportion and Number of Poor to "look into the methodology for estimation of poverty and to redefine the poverty line, if necessary". The Expert Group submitted its Report in July 1993. The Government accepted the Expert Group methodology in March 1997 as the basis for computing the official estimates of poverty in India.

The Expert Group (Lakdawala) did not redefine the poverty line. It retained the one defined by the Task Force (Alagh) which was at national level in rural and urban areas. It disaggregated these national poverty lines into state-specific poverty lines in order to reflect the inter-state price differentials.

The Expert Group (Lakdawala) could estimate the poverty lines in rural and urban areas of eighteen states. These eighteen states are: Andhra Pradesh, Assam, Bihar, Gujarat, Haryana, Himachal Pradesh, Jammu and Kashmir, Karnataka, Kerala, Madhya Pradesh, Maharashtra, Orissa, Punjab, Rajasthan, Tamil Nadu, Uttar Pradesh, West Bengal, and Delhi. In the remaining states/UTs, the poverty lines could not be computed similarly because of non-availability of state-specific prices data. In these states, the poverty ratios were equated with one of these eighteen states based on the criteria of physical contiguity of areas and similarity of economic profile.

Two factors largely distinguish the Expert Group (Lakdawala) methodology of poverty estimation from those of the Task Force (Alagh). First, the Expert Group (Lakdawala) method uses state-specific poverty lines as against national poverty line for estimation of poverty in the state; it thereby captures the cost of living in the states more accurately (as compared to the Task Force method). Second, the Expert Group (Lakdawala) uses the state-wise consumption distribution of the NSS without any adjustment to the NAS consumption. This is a major departure from the Task Force method, which did this adjustment on a pro rata basis.

In March 1997, the Government adopted the Expert Group (Lakdawala) methodology for poverty estimation as the basis for computing the official estimates of poverty and using this methodology the Planning Commission estimated the poverty ratios in rural and urban areas of different states/UTs for the year 1973–74 (NSS 28th Round consumer expenditure data, which was used to estimate the poverty line by the Task Force), and for the years 1977–78, 1983, 1987–88, and 1993–94 for which the large sample survey consumer expenditure data were then available from the 32nd, 38th, 43rd, and 50th Rounds of the NSS. Subsequently, using the same methodology, the Planning Commission estimated the poverty ratios at the national and states level for the years 1999–2000 and 2004–05, using the NSS large sample survey consumer expenditure data of 55th and 61st Rounds respectively.

The Expert Group under the chairmanship of Suresh D. Tendulkar was constituted by the Planning Commission in December, 2005. It was mandated to: (a) examine the issues relating to the comparability of the NSS 50th (1993–94), NSS 55th (1999–2000), and NSS 61st (2004–05) . The Expert Group (Tendulkar) submitted its recommendations to the Planning Commission in November 2009.

The Expert Group (Tendulkar) outlined the methodology for updation of the state specific rural and urban poverty lines of 2004–05 for future years.

The Planning Commission released estimates of poverty for 1993–94 and 2004–05 derived from the Expert Group (Tendulkar) method In January 2011. Subsequently, based on the same methodology, the poverty ratio for 2009–10 and 2011–12 were derived by the Planning Commission in March 2012 and July 2013 respectively.

Number and Percentage of Population below poverty line by states. 2009-12 (Tendulkar Methodology)

		Poverty Estimates (combined)			
		lakhs		Number below poverty line (Lakhs)	
S.No.	State	2009-10	2011-12	2009-10	2011-12
1.	Andhra Pradesh	21.1	9.2	176.6	78.8
2.	Arunachal Pradesh	25.9	34.7	3.5	4.9
3.	Assam	37.9	32	116.4	101.3
4.	Bihar	53.5	33.7	543.5	358.2
5.	Chhattisgarh	48.7	39.9	121.9	104.1
6.	Goa	14.2	9.9	23.3	17.0
7.	Gujarat	8.7	5.1	1.3	0.8
8.	Haryana	23	16.6	136.2	102.2
9.	Himachal Pradesh	20.1	11.2	50.0	28.8
10.	Jammu & Kashmir	9.5	8.1	6.4	5.6
11.	Jharkhand	9.4	10.3	11.5	13.3
12.	Karnataka	39.1	37	126.2	124.3
13.	Kerala	23.6	20.9	142.3	129.8
14.	Madhya Pradesh	12	7.1	39.6	23.9
15.	Maharashtra	36.7	31.6	261.8	234.1
16.	Manipur	24.5	17.4	270.8	197.9
17.	Meghalaya	47.1	36.9	12.5	10.2
18.	Mizoram	17.1	11.9	4.9	3.6
19.	Nagaland	21.1	20.4	2.3	2.3
20.	Orissa	20.9	18.9	4.1	3.8
21.	Punjab	37	32.6	153.2	138.5
22.	Rajasthan	1.2	8.3	0.1	23.2
23.	Sikkim	15.9	14.7	43.5	102.9
24.	Tamil Nadu	24.8	8.2	167.0	0.5
25.	Tripura	13.1	11.3	0.8	82.6
26.	Uttar Pradesh	17.1	14	121.8	5.2

27.	Uttarkhand	17.4	29.4	6.3	598.2
28.	West Bengal	37.7	11.3	737.9	11.6
29.	A & N Islands	18	20	17.9	185.0
30.	Chandigarh	26.7	9.7	240.3	1.2
31.	Dadra & Nagar Haveli	0.4	1	0.0	0.0
32.	Daman & Diu	9.2	21.8	1.0	2.3
33.	Delhi	39.1	39.3	1.3	1.4
34.	Lakshadweep	33.3	9.9	0.8	0.3
35.	Puducherry	6.8	2.8	0.0	0.0
36.	India	29.8	21.9	3,546.8	2,697.8

ADDITIONAL CONCEPTS OF POVERTY

Relative and Absolute Poverty

Absolute poverty refers to a set standard which is the same in all countries and which does not change over time. Relative poverty refers to a standard which is defined in terms of the society in which an individual lives and which therefore differs between countries and over time. Absolute poverty and relative poverty are both valid concepts. The concept of absolute poverty is that there are minimum standards below which no one anywhere in the world should ever fall. The concept of relative poverty is that, in a rich country such as the UK, there are higher minimum standards below which no one should fall, and that these standards should rise if and as the country becomes richer. It is absolute poverty which is (by far) the more serious issue. This is the case in much of the third world, where the focus is therefore on fixed income thresholds (typically $1 or $2 a day, on the grounds that this is the minimum needed for mere survival). There is no obvious way of defining an absolute poverty threshold except the $1 or $2 a day threshold defined on the grounds that this is the minimum needed for mere survival.

The Human Development Index (HDI) and the Human Poverty Index (HPI)

The HDI was created to emphasize that people and their capabilities should be the ultimate criteria for assessing the development of a country, not economic growth alone. The HDI can also be used to question national policy choices, asking how two countries with the same level of Gross National Income (GNI) per capita can end up with different human development outcomes. These contrasts can stimulate debate about government policy priorities. The Human Development Index (HDI) is a summary measure of average achievement in key dimensions of human development: a long and healthy life, being knowledgeable, and having a decent standard of living. The HDI is the geometric mean of normalized indices for each of the three dimensions. The health dimension is assessed by life expectancy at birth, and the education dimension is measured by mean of years of schooling for adults aged 25 years and more and expected years of schooling for children of school entering age. The standard of living dimension is measured by gross national income per capita. The HDI uses the logarithm of income to reflect the diminishing importance of income with increasing GNI. The scores for the three HDI dimension indices are then aggregated into a composite index using geometric mean.

Poverty and Development

Indian economy since her independence has gradually been moving towards the achievements of faster rate of growth of GDP after surpassing the long term (1950–75) persistence of high growth rate. It has been found that Indian economy continued to achieve high growth between 1975 and 1990, but eventually confronted the crisis of 1991 caused by high fiscal deficit vis-à-vis the current account deficit. The fallout of the crisis was the switching of the economy from plan to market.

Simultaneously, it has also been found that in course of structural transformation of the Indian economy, the service sector has been enjoying a comparative advantage in playing a leading role towards the achievements of remarkable growth rate such that the service sector driven growth has been christened as 'service sector revolution' in our economy.

Nevertheless, during the post-reform period and especially during the first five years of new millennium, the growth rate of GDP has reached such a conspicuous level (i.e., 8%–9% per annum) that India has been recognized as one of the fastest growing economies in the world. During the period of half a century, the economy has also experienced remarkable structural transformation in respect of her composition of GDP. Simultaneously, it has also been found that in course of structural transformation of the Indian economy, the service sector has been enjoying a comparative advantage in playing a leading role towards the achievements of remarkable growth rate such that the service sector driven growth has been christened as 'service sector revolution' in our economy.

The reform process has given a tremendous boost to the growth performance of all the states such that the states have been able to reap the benefits of the market in varying degrees. No definite conclusion on the performance of decadal as well as pre- and post-reform agricultural growth can be drawn. In fact, the states with high degree of application of new seed fertilizer technology during sixties have achieved higher growth rates in agriculture, but the states with delayed application of new technology have achieved higher growth rates during 1970s and 1980s. However, there has been sluggishness in the growth rates of agriculture in almost in all the states during the 1990s coupled with a bit improvement in the first decades of the new millennium. So, one can plausibly conclude that liberalisation of agricultural sector after the formation of WTO has not produced favourable impact on the growth of agriculture across the states of India. On the other hand, as far as the industrial sector is concerned, all the states have achieved growth of Net State Domestic Product (NSDP) originating from industry in varying degrees with some states like Andhra Pradesh, Himachal Pradesh, Gujarat, Karnataka, etc. achieving high growth rates and some achieving moderate growth rates, and very few states like West Bengal and Orissa, achieving lower growth rates. We also find that the first decades of reform has registered sluggishness in the growth rates of industrial production across all the states excepting Assam, Gujarat, and to some extent West Bengal. The estimates of industrial growth rates during pre- and post-reform period also reveal that some states have performed better during the post-reform period and some have performed better during the entire pre-reform period. It seems to be the outcome of the variability in the access to market economy on the part of the states. On the other hand, as far as the cross-state growth of service sector in concerned, almost all the states have experienced tremendous increase in the growth of service sector in varying degrees. The post-reform period has witnessed a tremendous breakthrough in the growth rates of the service sector in almost all the states as compared to their growth performance of service sector during the pre-reform period. We can conclude that the reform process in India has not only helped bring about the service sector revolution that we have experienced, but also reducing inter-state disparity in the growth rates of service sector tremendously. So one can expect that the higher growth rates of the service sector and the declining trend in inter-state disparity would have produced a favourable impact on the incidence of poverty at the cross state level.

Poverty and Shared Prosperity Report 2022 by World Bank

The World Bank's Poverty and Shared Prosperity series provide the latest estimates and trends in global poverty and shared prosperity. The 2022 edition provides the first comprehensive look at the landscape of poverty in the aftermath of an extraordinary series of shocks to the global economy. Global progress in reducing extreme poverty has virtually come to a halt.

After COVID-19 dealt the biggest setback to global poverty in decades, rising food and energy prices—fueled by climate shocks and conflict among the world's biggest food producers—have hindered a swift recovery.

Major Highlights of the Report

Poverty: The world is unlikely to meet the goal of ending extreme poverty by 2030. 70 million people were plunged into poverty in 2020, the largest one-year increase since global poverty monitoring began in 1990. An estimated 719 million people subsisted on less than $2.15 a day by the end of 2020.

Covid pandemic and the war in Ukraine: The global poverty reduction has been slowing down since 2015 but the Covid pandemic and the war in Ukraine have completely reversed the outcomes.

Inequalities: They too have risen. The poorest people bore the steepest costs of the pandemic: income losses averaged 4 per cent for the poorest 40 per cent, double the losses of the wealthiest 20 percent of the income distribution. Global inequality rose for the first time in decades.

Global median income: It declined by 4 per cent in 2020, the first decline since measurements of median income began in 1990. The median divides the income distribution into two equal parts: one-half of the cases falling below the median income and one-half above the median.

India's poverty levels: Poverty has gone up in India too. Previous estimates suggested a poverty headcount rate at the US$1.90 poverty line of 10.4 percent in 2017. The latest estimate based on Sinha Roy and van der Weide (2022) shows that poverty at the US$1.90 poverty line was 13.6 percent in 2017.

Major Challenges to India as Cited by the Report

The report uses data from the Centre for Monitoring Indian Economy (CMIE), because there are no official estimates of poverty available since 2011. The most recent survey data released by the National Sample Survey Office of India used to measure poverty is the 2011/12 National Sample Survey (NSS). The government decided not to release the 2017/18 NSS round because of concerns about data quality. Lack of data could not have left India out of the poverty estimates simply because India is one of the countries with the biggest poor population. Because of India's size, the lack of recent survey data for the country significantly affects the measurement of global poverty, as was evident in Poverty and Shared Prosperity 2020.

INDIA—POVERTY ESTIMATES

Earlier, India used to define the poverty line based on a method defined by a Task Force in 1979. It was based on expenditure for buying food worth 2,400 calories in rural areas, and 2,100 calories in urban areas. In 2011, the Suresh Tendulkar Committee defined the poverty line on the basis of monthly spending on food, education, health, electricity, and transport. According to this estimate, a person who spends Rs. 27.2 in rural areas and Rs. 33.3 in urban areas a day are defined as living below the poverty line. For a family of five that spends less than Rs. 4,080 and Rs. 5,000 in rural and urban areas respectively is considered below the poverty line. This has been criticized for fixing the poverty line too low. According to a committee headed by former Reserve Bank Governor C. Rangarajan, there were 363 million people, or 29.5% of India's 1.2 billion people, who lived in poverty in 2011–12. The Rangarajan panel considered people living on less than Rs. 32 a day in rural areas and Rs. 47 a day in urban areas as poor.

RANGARAJAN REPORT ON POVERTY

Poverty lines estimated using the methodology provided by the Expert Group (Tendulkar) did not reflect the changing times and aspirations of the people of India. There was a need to re-examine the poverty line and its composition.

The methodology developed and adopted by the Expert Group (Rangarajan) and the results based on these are outlined here:

i. The poverty line should be based on certain normative levels of adequate nourishment, clothing, house rent, conveyance, and education, and a behaviourally determined level of other non-food expenses.
ii. The Expert Group (Rangarajan) computed the average requirements of calories, proteins, and fats based on ICMR norms differentiated by age, gender, and activity for all-India rural and urban regions to derive the normative levels of nourishment. Accordingly, the energy requirement works out to 2,155 kcal per person per day in rural areas and 2,090 kcal per person per day in urban areas.
iii. The protein and fat requirements have been estimated on the same lines as for energy. These requirements are 48 gms and 28 gms per capita per

day, respectively, in rural areas; and 50 gms and 26 gms per capita per day in urban areas.

iv. A food basket that simultaneously meets all the normative requirements of the three nutrients defines the food component of the poverty line basket proposed by the Expert Group (Rangarajan).

v. The new poverty line thus works out to monthly per capita consumption expenditure of Rs. 972 in rural areas and Rs. 1,407 in urban areas in 2011–12. For a family of five, this translates into a monthly consumption expenditure of Rs. 4,860 in rural areas and Rs. 7,035 in urban areas.

vi. The Expert Group (Rangarajan) therefore estimates that the 30.9% of the rural population and 26.4% of the urban population was below the poverty line in 2011–12. The all-India ratio was 29.5%. In rural India, 260.5 million individuals were below poverty and in urban India, 102.5 million were under poverty. Totally, 363 million were below poverty in 2011–12.

vii. The poverty ratio has declined from 39.6% in 2009–10 to 30.9% in 2011–12 in rural India and from 35.1% to 26.4% in urban India. The decline was thus a uniform 8.7 percentage points over the two years. The all-India poverty ratio fell from 38.2% to 29.5%. Totally, 91.6 million individuals were lifted out of poverty during this period.

INDIA'S POVERTY CHALLENGE

Poverty is considered to be a vicious circle—Low level of saving reduces the scope for investment; low level of investment yields low income, and thus, the circle of poverty goes on indefinitely. *The factors of India's challenge against poverty can be grouped under four categories:*

1. Climatic Factors

Climatic conditions constitute an important cause of poverty. The hot climate of India reduces the capacity of people especially the ruralites to work for which production severely suffers. Frequent floods, famines, earthquakes, and cyclones cause heavy damage to agriculture. Moreover, absence of timely rain, excessive, or deficient rain affect the country's agricultural production severely.

2. Demographic Factors

The following demographic factors are accountable for poverty in India.

(i) Rapid growth of population

Rapid growth of population aggravates the poverty of the people. The growth of population exceeds the rate of growth in national income. Population growth not only creates difficulties in the removal of poverty, but also lowers the per capita income which tends to increase poverty. The burden of this reduction in per capita income is borne heavily by the poor people. Population growth at a faster rate increases labour supply which tends to lower the wage rate.

(ii) Size of family

Size of the family has significant bearing on rural poverty. The larger the size of family, the lower is the per capita income, and the lower is the standard of living. The persistence of the joint family system has contributed to the health and earning capacity of the ruralites.

3. Personal Causes

Lack of motivation

Lack of motivation is an important cause of rural poverty. Some ruralites do not have a motive to work hard or even to earn something. This accounts for the poverty of the ruralites.

4. Economic Causes

(i) Low agricultural productivity

Poverty and real income are very much interrelated. Increase in real income leads to reduction of the magnitude of poverty. So far as agricultural sector is concerned, the farmers even today are following the traditional method of cultivation. Hence, there is low agricultural productivity resulting in rural poverty.

(ii) Unequal distribution of land and other assets

Land and other forms of assets constitute sources of income for the ruralites. But, unfortunately, there has been unequal distribution of land and other assets in our economy. The size-wise distribution of operational holdings indicates a very high degree of concentration in the hands of a few farmers leading to poverty of many in the rural sector.

(iii) Decline of village industries

At present, consequent upon industrialisation, new factories and industries are being set up in rural areas. Village industries fail to compete with them in terms of quality and price. As a result they are closed down. The workers are thrown out of employment and lead a life of poverty.

(iv) Immobility of labour

Immobility of labour also accounts for rural poverty. Even if higher wages are offered, labourers are not willing to leave their homes. The joint family system makes people lethargic and stay-at-home. Poverty is considered as God-given, something preordained. All these factors lead to abysmal poverty in rural India.

(v) Lack of employment opportunities

Unemployment is the reflection of poverty. Because of lack of employment opportunities, people remain either unemployed or underemployed. Most of these unemployed and underemployed workers are the small and marginal farmers and the landless agricultural labourers.

5. Social Causes

(i) Education

Education is an agent of social change and egalitarianism. Poverty is also said to be closely related to the levels of schooling and these two have a circular relationship. The earning power is endowed in the individual by investment in education and training. But this investment in people takes away money and lack of human investment contributes to the low earning capacity of individuals. In this way people are poor because they have little investment in themselves and poor people do not have the funds for human capital investment.

(ii) Caste system

Caste system in India has also been responsible for rural poverty. The subordination of the low caste people by the high caste people caused the poverty of the former. Due to rigid caste system, the low caste people could not participate in the game of economic progress. A shudra was not allowed to become a trader and a vaisya could earn his bread only by trade. Birth would decide their occupation and their economic fate. K. V. Verghese rightly observes, "Caste system acted as a spring board for class exploitation with the result that the counterpart of the poverty of the many is the opulence of the few. The second is the cause of the first."

(iii) Joint family system

The joint family system provides social security to its members. Some people take undue advantage of it. They live upon the income of others. Their normal routine of life consists in eating, sleeping, and begetting children. In this way poverty gets aggravated through joint family system.

(iv) Social customs

The ruralites spend a large percentage of annual earnings on social ceremonies like marriage, death, feast, etc. As a result, they remain in debt and poverty.

(v) Growing indebtedness

In the rural sector, most of the ruralites depend on borrowings from the moneylenders and landlords to meet even their consumption expenses. Moneylenders, however, exploit the poor by charging exorbitant rates of interest and by acquiring the mortgaged land in the event of non-payment of loans. Indebted poor farmers cannot make themselves free from the clutches of moneylenders. Their poverty is further accentuated because of indebtedness. Such indebted families continue to remain under the poverty line for generations because of this debt-trap.

WELFARE SCHEMES BY CENTRE

The poverty welfare scheme has seen an evolution since the time India got independence till the present time. Over this period the general nature of these schemes has transformed from 'the top down' approach to the 'targeted approach' to the more recent 'multidimensional approach'. These approaches varied as the State's perception and understanding with respect to poverty changed over time.

Top-down Approach

This approach was adopted in the initial years after India got independence. The idea was to focus on the agricultural productivity (1st Five Year Plan) and industrial growth (2nd FYP) with the assumption that overall growth in these macro sectors will eventually bring the people out of poverty.

Land consolidation, land ceiling measures and import substitution measures are some examples of such schemes. These policies did not perform as per the expectation as these were not based on ground realities like caste-class nexus, capabilities deficit, poverty of culture; and also because of the inherent loopholes in the policy design, administrative apathy and caste-politics nexus.

Targeted Approach

The unsatisfactory results of Top-down' schemes convinced the government to come up with a more 'targeted approach'. The idea was to provide the welfare measure to those who needed them the most. Many targeted poverty alleviation schemes were rolled out during the period of 3rd FYP.

1. The beginning was made with the rural manpower programme in 1960-1961, followed by the Crash Scheme for Rural Employment (CSRE) in 1971-72.
2. Drought Prone Area Programme (DPAP) in 1972 aimed to minimize the adverse effect of drought on production of crops and livestock and productivity of land water.

- Marginal Farmers and Agricultural Labour Scheme (MFALS) in 1973- 74, aimed at technical and financial assistance to marginal and small farmers and agriculture labour in maximum productive use of their small holding and skill by undertaking animal husbandry, horticulture, etc.
- Small Farmers Development Agency (SFDA) in 1974-75, was created with the main objective to investigate and identify the problems of small farmers and ensure technical and financial assistance to small farmers.
- The Desert Development Programme (DDP) was created in 1977-78 and the Food for Work Programme (FWP) was introduced in 1977-78, for providing food grains to labour for the works of development.
- Training of Rural Youth for Self Deployment (TRYSEM) in 1979 was also introduced for education and vocational training for youth.

Multidimensional Approach

Multidimensional approach is based on a whole new way of looking at the issue of poverty. The cause and consequences of poverty were linked to multiple socio-economic factors, and, therefore, the newer poverty alleviation schemes are more broad in terms of their vision and objectives. Poverty is connected to the wider issue of human development. It is also inspired by the notion of 'Amartya Sen' on poverty who connects it with poverty and empowerment. Some of the major schemes in this category are:

(i) MGNREGA

The Mahatma Gandhi National Rural Employment Guarantee Act (MGNREGA) is Indian legislation enacted on August 25, 2005. It provides a legal guarantee for one hundred days of employment in every financial year to adult members of any rural household willing to do public work-related unskilled manual work at the statutory minimum wage. The Ministry of Rural Development (MRD), Govt of India is monitoring the entire implementation of this scheme in association with state governments
This act was introduced with an aim of improving the purchasing power of the rural people, primarily semi or unskilled work to people living below

the poverty line in rural India. It attempts to bridge the gap between the rich and poor in the country. Roughly one-third of the stipulated work force must be women.

Adult members of rural households submit their name, age and address with a photo to the Gram Panchayat. The Gram Panchayat registers households after making enquiry and issues a job card. The Panchayat/Programme officer will accept the valid application and issue a dated receipt of application, a letter providing work will be sent to the applicant and also displayed at the Panchayat office. The employment will be provided within a radius of 5 km: if it is above 5 km extra wage will be paid

(ii) Pradhan Mantri Jan Dhan Yojana

The National Mission of Financial Inclusion named as the Pradhan Mantri Jan Dhan Yojana seeks to integrate the poorest of the poor with bank accounts. All the households across the country - both rural and urban are to be covered under the scheme. Bank accounts will be opened for 15 crore poor persons. All bank accounts opened under the scheme are to have an overdraft facility of Rs 5, 000 for Aadhar-linked accounts after satisfactory operation in the account for 6 months. A minimum monthly remuneration of Rs 5, 000 to business correspondents who will provide the last link between the account holders and the bank.

The scheme will also enable to better target the beneficiaries through Direct Benefit Transfers. Combined with Aadhar, Jan Dhan Account can eliminate the inclusion exclusion errors of targeting.

(iii) Pradhan Mantri Awas Yojana

The Pradhan Mantri Awas Yojana (Urban) Programme launched by the Ministry of Housing and Urban Poverty Alleviation (MoHUPA), in Mission mode envisions provision of Housing for All by 2022, when the Nation completes 75 years of its Independence. The Mission seeks to address the housing requirement of urban poor including slum dwellers through following programme verticals:

- Slum rehabilitation of Slum Dwellers with participation of private developers using land as a resource
- Promotion of Affordable Housing for weaker section through credit linked subsidy
- Affordable Housing in Partnership with Public & Private sectors
- Subsidy for beneficiary-led individual house construction /enhancement

(iv) National Social Assistance Programme

NSAP was launched on 15th August, 1995. The National Social Assistance Programme (NSAP) represents a significant step towards the fulfillment of the Directive Principles in Article 41 and 42 of the Constitution recognizing the concurrent responsibility of the Central and the State Governments in the matter. It is a social security and welfare programme to provide support to aged persons, widows, disabled persons and bereaved families on death of primary breadwinner, belonging to below the Poverty line households. Presently NSAP comprises of five schemes, namely –

- Indira Gandhi National Old Age Pension Scheme (IGNOAPS),
- Indira Gandhi National Widow Pension Scheme (IGNWPS),
- Indira Gandhi National Disability Pension Scheme (IGNDPS),
- National Family Benefit Scheme NFBS) and
- Annapurna.

(v) Pradhan Mantri Matru Vandana Yojana

PMMVY is a Maternity Benefit Programme that is implemented in all the districts of the country in accordance with the provision of the National Food Security Act, 2013. The scheme was launched with the objective to provide partial compensation for the wage loss in terms of cash incentives so that the woman can take adequate rest before and after delivery of the first living child. The cash incentive provided would lead to improved health seeking behaviour amongst the Pregnant Women and Lactating Mothers (PW& LM).

WELFARE SCHEMES BY STATES

Kudumbashree Scheme (Kerala)

It is a Self-Help Group (SHG) in Kerala that is empowering the poor women by enhancing their livelihood opportunities, microcredit availability, and entrepreneurship.

Janmabhoomi (Andhra Pradesh)

The scheme was launched by the Andhra Pradesh Government to bring people-centered development aimed at the comprehensive rebuilding of villages and towns with people's participation in the decision-making process.

Gokul Yojana (Gujarat)

It provides the basic infrastructure to all villages within a time frame of five years, such as all-weather approach roads, drinking water, and construction of village ponds with bathing ghats, construction of primary school rooms, community halls, community work sheds, and village afforestation.

Namakku Naame Thittam (Tamil Nadu): This scheme involves village level development such as the construction of buildings, creation and improvement of minor irrigation works, and construction of bridges, culverts, and roads.

FINANCIAL INCLUSION

There are a number of schemes by the government for financial inclusion. They are:

SCHEME	DATE OF LAUNCH	PROVISIONS
Atal Pension Yojana	May 9, 2015	Social sector scheme pertaining to pension sector
Bachat Lamp Yojana	2009	Reduce the cost of compact fluorescent lamps
Central Government Health Scheme	1954	Comprehensive medical care facilities to Central Government employees and their family members
Deendayal Disabled Rehabilitation Scheme	2003	Create an enabling environment to ensure equal opportunities, equity, social justice, and empowerment of persons with disabilities
Deen Dayal Upadhyaya Gram Jyoti Yojana	2015	It is a Government of India program aimed at providing 24x7 uninterrupted power supply to all homes in Rural India
Digital India Programme	July 1, 2015	Aims to ensure that government services are available to citizens electronically and people get benefitted from the latest information and communication technology
Gramin Bhandaran Yojana	March 31, 2007	Creation of scientific storage capacity with allied facilities in rural areas to meet the requirements of farmers for storing farm produce, processed farm produce, and agricultural inputs. Improve their marketability through promotion of grading, standardisation, and quality control of agricultural produce.
Indira Awaas Yojana	1985	Provides financial assistance to rural poor for constructing their houses themselves.
Indira Gandhi Matritva Sahyog Yojana	2010	A cash incentive of Rs. 4000 to women (19 years and above) for the first two live births

SCHEME	DATE OF LAUNCH	PROVISIONS
Integrated Child Development Services	October 2, 1975	Tackle malnutrition and health problems in children below 6 years of age and their mothers
Integrated Rural Development Program	1978	Self-employment program to raise the income-generation capacity of target groups among the poor. The scheme has been merged with another scheme named Swarnajayanti Gram Swarozgar Yojana (SGSY) since 01/04/ 1999.
Janani Suraksha Yojana	2005	One-time cash incentive to pregnant women for institutional/home births through skilled assistance
Jawaharlal Nehru National Urban Renewal Mission (JnNURM)	December 3, 2005	A programme meant to improve the quality of life and infrastructure in the cities. To be replaced by Atal Mission for Rejuvenation and Urban Transformation.
Kasturba Gandhi Balika Vidyalaya	July 2004	Educational facilities (residential schools) for girls belonging to SC, ST,OBC, minority communities, and families below the poverty line (BPL) in Educationally Backward Blocks
INSPIRE Programme		Scholarships for top Science students, Fellowships for pursuing PhD, Research Grants to researchers
Kishore Vaigyanik Protsahan Yojana	1999	Scholarship program to encourage students to take up research careers in the areas of basic sciences, engineering, and medicine
Livestock Insurance Scheme (India)		Insurance to cattle and attaining qualitative improvement in livestock and their products
Mahatma Gandhi National Rural Employment Guarantee Act	February 6, 2006	Legal guarantee for one hundred days of employment in every financial year to adult members of any rural household willing to do public work-related unskilled manual work at the statutory minimum wage of Rs. 120 per day in 2009 prices.
Members of Parliament Local Area Development Scheme	December 23, 1993	Each MP has the choice to suggest to the District Collector for works to the tune of Rs. 5 crores per annum to be taken up in his/her constituency. The Rajya Sabha Member of Parliament can recommend works in one or more districts in the State from where he/she has been elected.

SCHEME	DATE OF LAUNCH	PROVISIONS
Midday Meal Scheme	August 15, 1995	Lunch (free of cost) to school-children on all working days
Namami Gange Programme	March 1995	Integrates the efforts to clean and protect the River Ganga in a comprehensive manner
National Literacy Mission Programme	May 5, 1988	Make 80 million adults in the age group of 15–35 literate
National Pension Scheme	January 1, 2004	Contribution based pension system
National Scheme on Welfare of Fishermen		Financial assistance to fishers for construction of house, community hall for recreation, and common working place and installation of tubewells for drinking water
National Service Scheme	1969	Personality development through social (or community) service
National Social Assistance Scheme	August 15, 1995	Public assistance to its citizens in case of unemployment, old age, sickness and disablement and in other cases of undeserved want
Pooled Finance Development Fund Scheme		
Pradhan Mantri Adarsh Gram Yojana	July 23, 2010	Integrated development of Schedule Caste majority villages in four states
Pradhan Mantri Suraksha Bima Yojana	May 9, 2015	Accidental Insurance with a premium of Rs. 12 per year.
Pradhan Mantri Jeevan Jyoti Bima Yojana	May 9, 2015	Life insurance of Rs . 2 lakh with a premium of Rs. 330 per year.
Pradhan Mantri Jan Dhan Yojana	August 28, 2014	National Mission for Financial Inclusion to ensure access to financial services, namely banking savings and deposit accounts, remittance, credit, insurance, and pension in an affordable manner
Pradhan Mantri Gram Sadak Yojana	December 25, 2000	Good all-weather road connectivity to unconnected villages
Rajiv Awas Yojana	2013	It envisages a "Slum Free India" with inclusive and equitable cities in which every citizen has access to basic civic infrastructure and social amenities and decent shelter

SCHEME	DATE OF LAUNCH	PROVISIONS
Rajiv Gandhi Grameen idyutikaran Yojana	April 2005	Programme for creation of Rural Electricity Infrastructure and Household Electrification for providing access to electricity to rural households
Rashtriya Krishi Vikas Yojana	August 1, 2007	Achieve 4% annual growth in agriculture through development of agriculture and its allied sectors during the XI Plan period
Rashtriya Swasthya Bima Yojana	April 1, 2008	Health insurance to poor (BPL), domestic workers, MGNERGA workers, rikshawpullers, building and other construction workers, and many other categories as may be identified by the respective states
RNTCP	1997	Tuberculosis control initiative
Saksham or Rajiv Gandhi Scheme for Empowerment of Adolescent Boys	2014	Aims at all-round development of adolescent boys and make them self-reliant, gender-sensitive and aware citizens when they grow up. It cover all adolescent boys (both school going and out of school) in the age group of 11 to 18 years subdivided into two categories, viz. 11-14 & 14–18 years. In 2014–15, an allocation of Rs . 25 crore was made for the scheme.
Sabla or Rajiv Gandhi Scheme for Empowerment of Adolescent Girls	2011	Empowering adolescent girls (Age of 11–18 years) with focus on out-of-school girls' by improvement in their nutritional and health status and upgrading various skills like home skills, life skills, and vocational skills. Merged Nutrition Programme for Adolescent Girls (NPAG) and Kishori Shakti Yojana (KSY).
Sampoorna Grameen Rozgar Yojana	September 25, 2001	Providing additional wage employment and food security, alongside creation of durable community assets in rural areas
Swabhiman	February 15, 2011	To make banking facility available to all citizens and to get 5 crore accounts opened by March 2012. Replaced by Pradhan Mantri Jan Dhan Yojana.
Swarnajayanti Gram Swarozgar Yojana	April 1, 1999	Bring the assisted poor families above the poverty line by organising them into Self Help Groups (SHGs) through the process of social mobilisation, their training and capacity building, and provision of income generating assets through a mix of bank credit and government subsidy.

SCHEME	DATE OF LAUNCH	PROVISIONS
Swavalamban	September 26, 2010	Pension scheme to the workers in unorganized sector. Any citizen who is not part of any statutory pension scheme of the Government and contributes between Rs. 1000 and Rs. 12000/- per annum, could join the scheme. The Central Government shall contribute Rs. 1000 per annum to such subscribers.
Udisha		Training Program for ICDS workers
Voluntary Disclosure of Income Scheme	June 18, 1997	Opportunity to the income tax/wealth tax defaulters to disclose their undisclosed income at the prevailing tax rates
National Rural Livelihood Mission (NRLM)	June 2011	This scheme will organize rural poor into Self Help Group (SHG) groups and make them capable for self-employment. The idea is to develop better livelihood options for the poor
HRIDAY—Heritage City Development and Augmentation Yojana	Jan 2015	The scheme seeks to preserve and rejuvenate the rich cultural heritage of the country
Sukanya Samridhi Yojana (Girl Child Prosperity Scheme)	22 Jan 2015	The scheme primarily ensures equitable share to a girl child in resources and savings of a family in which she is generally discriminated as against a male child
Smart Cities Mission	June 25, 2015	To enable better living and drive economic growth stressing on the need for people centric urban planning and development
Atal Mission for Rejuvenation and Urban Transformation (AMRUT)	June 25, 2015	To enable better living and drive economic growth stressing on the need for people centric urban planning and development
Pradhan Mantri Awas Yojana (PMAY)	June 25, 2015	To enable better living and drive economic growth stressing on the need for people centric urban planning and development.
National Child Labour Projects (NCLP)	Launched in 9 districts in 1987 and has been expanded in January 2005 to 250 districts in 21 different states of the country	The objective of this project is to eliminate child labour in hazardous industries by 2010. Under this scheme, the target group is all children below 14 years of age who are working in occupations and processes listed in the Schedule to the Child Labour (Prohibition & Regulation) Act, 1986 or occupations and processes that are harmful to the health of the child.

SCHEME	DATE OF LAUNCH	PROVISIONS
Antyodaya Anna Yojna	25 December, 2000	Under the scheme 1 crore of the poorest among the (Below Poverty Line) BPL families covered under the targeted public distribution system are identified. Issue of Ration Cards Following the recognition of Antyodaya families, unique quota cards to be recognized an "Antyodaya Ration Card" must be given to the Antyodaya families by the chosen power. The scheme has been further expanded twice by additional 50 lakh BPL families each in June 2003 and in August 2004 , thus covering 2 crore families under the AAY scheme
Pradhan Mantri Kaushal Vikas Yojana	July 15, 2015	Seeks to provide the institutional capacity to train a minimum 40 crore skilled people by 2022
National Food Security Mission	2007 for 5 years	It launched in 2007 for 5 years to increase production and productivity of wheat, rice, and pulses on a sustainable basis so as to ensure food security of the country. The aim is to bridge the yield gap in respect of these crops through dissemination of improved technologies and farm management practices.
Pradhan Mantri Ujjwala Yojana	1 May, 2016	Launched to provide free LPG connections to women from below poverty line families.

EMPOWERING WOMEN

Beti Bachao, Beti Padhao Campaign

This program seeks to promote gender sensitisation, awareness against female foeticide, and education for girls.

Highlights

- Launched from Panipat in Haryana on January 22, 2015.
- PM Modi invited suggestions for the program from citizens on the MyGovportal.
- In addition, a special deposit scheme for the girl child called the Sukanya Samriddhi account has been launched, where parents or legal guardians of a girl child under 10 years can open an account with a minimum deposit of Rs . 1,000 in any post office or authorized branches of commercial bank. Interest received is 9.2% and is tax free.

Nai Roshni

For women empowerment, the Ministry started "Nai Roshni", a Leadership Development Programme for Minority Women in 2012–13. The objective of the scheme is to empower and instill confidence among minority women, including their neighbours from other communities living in the same village/locality, by providing knowledge, tools, and techniques for interacting with Government systems, banks, and other institutions at all levels.

The effort would embolden minority women to move out of the confines of their home and community and assume leadership roles and assert their rights, collectively or individually, in accessing services, facilities, skills, and opportunities, besides claiming their due share of development benefits of the Government for improving their lives and living conditions.

"Nai Roshni" programme is run with the help of NGOs, civil societies, and government institutions all over the country. It includes various training modules like leadership of women, educational programmes, health and hygiene, Swachch Bharat, financial literacy, life skills, legal rights of women, digital literacy, and advocacy for social and behavioural change.

SOCIAL INFRASTRUCTURE, EMPLOYMENT AND HUMAN DEVELOPMENT

PISA Ranking

PISA (Program for International Student Assessment) is a competency-based test designed to assess the ability of the 15-year-old candidates that measures their reading, mathematics, and science literacy every three years to apply their knowledge to real-life situations.

It is an international survey coordinated by the Organization for Economic Cooperation and Development (OECD) and was first conducted in 2000. India has participated in the PISA test only once before, in 2009. Since then, it stopped participating till only recently when it decided to join back. The field trial was scheduled to happen in 2021 but was postponed till 2022 due to the pandemic.

The 2009 round of PISA, where students from Himachal Pradesh and Tamil Nadu sat for the test, India ranked 72nd out of 73 countries, outranking only Kyrgyzstan.

Learnings from participation in PISA will help to introduce competency-based examination reforms in the school system and help move away from rote learning. The CBSE and NCERT will be part of the process and activities leading to the actual test. It would lead to recognition and acceptability of Indian students and prepare them for the global economy in the 21st century.

ASER 2021—Annual Status of Education Report

THE SIXTEENTH ANNUAL STATUS OF EDUCATION REPORT (RURAL) 2021 RELEASED

The sixteenth Annual Status of Education Report (Rural) 2021 released

Every year from 2005 to 2014, and then every alternate year till 2018, ASER has reported on the schooling status of children in the 5-16 age group across rural India.

Due to the COVID-19 pandemic in 2020, ASER developed an entirely new design, consisting of a phone-based survey that explored children's access to learning opportunities. This was the format employed for ASER 2021 as well.

The survey was conducted September-October 2021, in 25 states and 3 Union Territories. It reached a total of 76,706 households and 75,234 children in the age group of 5-16 years, as well as teachers or head teachers from 7,299 government schools offering primary grades.

A summary of the report's findings is provided below:

School Enrollment Patterns A shift from private to government schools with enrollment in private schools decreasing from 32.5% in 2018 to 24.4% in 2021 among children aged 6-14. The proportion of children not currently enrolled in school increased from 1.4% to 4.6% in 2020 and remained static in 2021. Among children in the age group of 15-16, an increase in government school enrollment from 57.4% in 2018 to 67.4%.
Tuition Big increase in children taking tuition from 30% in 2018 to almost 40% in 2021, across gender, grades and school types. The proportion of children with parents in the 'low' education category who are taking tuition increased by 12.6 percentage points, as opposed to a 7.2 percentage point increase among children with parents in the 'high' education category. Tuition is up across the country in all states except Kerala.

Access to Smartphones

Smartphone ownership has almost doubled from 36.5% in 2018 to 67.6% in 2021. More children in private schools have a smartphone at home (79%) than government school going children (63.7%).

Although over two thirds of all enrolled children have a smartphone at home (67.6%), over a quarter of these have no access to it (26.1%).

Learning Support at Home

Learning support at home has decreased over the last year from three quarters of all enrolled children in 2020 to two thirds in 2021, with the sharpest drops visible among children in higher grades.

Among both government and private school going children, those whose schools have reopened get less support from home.

Access to Learning Materials

Almost all enrolled children have textbooks for their current grade (91.9%).

Among enrolled children whose schools had not reopened, 39.8% children received some kind of learning materials or activities (other than textbooks) from their teachers during the reference week.

In the reference week, 46.4% children in reopened schools received learning materials/activities as compared to 39.8% children whose schools had not reopened.

EMPLOYMENT ISSUES

Skilling the Youth

The Ministry of Skill Development and Entrepreneurship is responsible for coordination of all skill development efforts across the country, removal of disconnect between demand and supply of skilled manpower, building the vocational and technical training framework, skill upgradation, building of new skills, and innovative thinking not only for existing jobs but also jobs that are to be created. The Ministry aims to skill on a large scale with speed and high standards in order to achieve its vision of a 'Skilled India'. It is aided in these initiatives by its functional arms

- National Skill Development Agency (NSDA),
- National Skill Development Corporation (NSDC),
- National Skill Development Fund (NSDF), and
- 33 Sector Skill Councils (SSCs) as well as 187 training partners registered with NSDC.

The Ministry also intends to work with the existing network of skill development centres, universities, and other alliances in the field. Further, collaborations with relevant Central Ministries, State governments, international organisations, industry, and NGOs have been initiated for multilevel engagement and more impactful implementation of skill development efforts.

Nai Manzil

On New Year's eve , the Indian government and the World Bank signed a 50 million dollar project which has the potential of transforming the lives of thousands of disadvantaged young people from minority communities through a series of educational and training programmes.

'Nai Manzil' (New Goal), is an ambitious educational and skills development programme funded by the World Bank. It has been designed to help minority youth (17–35 age group) from poorer backgrounds. It is particularly aimed at school dropouts and those who lack the necessary skills to find jobs even after completing their education.

Key Features

Under a two-pronged approach, help will be afforded to those who sign up for the programme by providing them an opportunity to complete their education through open schooling, followed by hands-on vocational training that will equip them for the job market. The programme is aimed at reaching out to Muslim students who have studied in madrassas and need help with formal schooling—and vocational skills. The government reckons that there are more than three lakh madrassas across the country; each of these on an average teach at least 100 students.

MGNREGA and the Intensive and Participatory Planning Exercise (IPPE)

MGNREGA is job guarantee scheme of India. The MGNREGA (Mahatma Gandhi National Rural Employment Guarantee Act) is designed to provide job guarantee for at least 100 days in rural parts of the country. Through this scheme, all the adult members (at least 18 years of age) of the any family in rural part of the country are given non-skilled work.

The MGNREGA Act was presented with an aim of helping the buying power of the rural individuals; mainly partial or unskilled perform to individuals living in rural parts of the country, whether or not they are below the hardship line. About one-third of the predetermined workforce is women. In the year of 2011, the program was commonly criticized as no more effective than other hardship decrease programs in the country of India.

TOWARDS A HEALTHY INDIA

Ayushman Bharat programme

Ayushman Bharat is a National Health Protection Scheme, which will cover over 10 crore poor and vulnerable families (approximately 50 crore beneficiaries) providing coverage upto 5 lakh rupees per family per year for secondary and tertiary care hospitalization. Ayushman Bharat - National Health Protection Mission will subsume the on-going centrally sponsored schemes - Rashtriya Swasthya Bima Yojana (RSBY) and the Senior Citizen Health Insurance Scheme (SCHIS).

The initiatives are as follows

(i) Health and Wellness Centre

The National Health Policy, 2017 has envisioned Health and Wellness Centres as the foundation of India's health system. Under this 1.5 lakh centres will bring health care system closer to the homes of people. These centres will provide comprehensive health care, including for non-communicable diseases and maternal and child health services. These centres will also provide free essential drugs and diagnostic services. The Budget has allocated Rs.1200 crore for this flagship programme. Contribution of private sector through CSR and philanthropic institutions in adopting these centres is also envisaged.

(ii) National Health Protection Scheme

The second flagship programme under Ayushman Bharat is National Health Protection Scheme, which will cover over 10 crore poor and vulnerable families (approximately 50 crore beneficiaries) providing coverage upto 5 lakh rupees per family per year for secondary and tertiary care hospitalization. This will be the world's largest government funded health care programme. Adequate funds will be provided for smooth implementation of this programme.

The expenditure incurred in premium payment will be shared between Central and State Governments in specified ratio as per Ministry of Finance guidelines in vogue. The total expenditure will depend on actual market determined premium paid in States/ UTs where Ayushman Bharat - National Health Protection Mission will be implemented through insurance companies. In States/ UTs where the scheme will be implemented in Trust/ Society mode, the central share of funds will be provided based on actual expenditure or premium ceiling (whichever is lower) in the pre-determined ratio.

Mission Indradhanush

Full immunisation against preventable childhood diseases is the right of every child. With a view to provide this right to every child, the Government of India launched the Universal Immunisation Program (UIP) in 1985, one of the largest health programs of its kind in the world. Despite being operational for over 30 years, UIP has been able to fully immunize only 65% children in the first year of their life and the increase in coverage has stagnated in the past 5 years to an average of 1% every year. To strengthen and invigorate the program and achieve full immunisation coverage for all children at a rapid pace, the Government of India launched *Mission Indradhanush* in December 2014. *Mission Indradhanush* will ensure that all children under the age of two years and pregnant women are fully immunized with all available vaccines.

National Ayush Mission (NAM)

Department of AYUSH (Ayurveda, Yoga and Naturopathy, Unani, Siddha and Homeopathy), Ministry of Health and Family Welfare, Government of India has launched National AYUSH Mission (NAM) during the 12th Plan for implementing through states/UTs. The basic objective of NAM is to promote AYUSH medical systems through cost effective AYUSH services, strengthening of educational systems, facilitate the enforcement of quality control of Ayurveda, Siddha, and Unani & Homoeopathy (ASU &H) drugs, and sustainable availability of ASU & H raw materials. It envisages flexibility of implementation of the programmes which will lead to substantial participation of the State Governments/UT. The NAM contemplates establishment of a National Mission as well as corresponding Missions in the state level. NAM is likely to improve significantly the Department's outreach in terms of planning, supervision, and monitoring of the schemes.

The vision of this scheme is:

a. To provide cost effective and equitable AYUSH healthcare throughout the country by improving access to the services.

b. To revitalize and strengthen the AYUSH systems making them as prominent medical streams in addressing the health care of the society.

c. To improve educational institutions capable of imparting quality AYUSH education.

d. To promote the adoption of quality standards of AYUSH drugs and making available the sustained supply of AYUSH raw materials.

The objectives are:

a. To provide cost effective AYUSH Services, with a universal access through upgrading AYUSH Hospitals and Dispensaries, co-location of AYUSH facilities at Primary Health Centres (PHCs), Community Health Centres (CHCs), and District Hospitals (DHs).
b. To strengthen institutional capacity at the state level through upgrading AYUSH educational institutions, state government ASU&H pharmacies, drug testing laboratories, and ASU & H enforcement mechanisms.
c. Support cultivation of medicinal plants by adopting Good Agricultural Practices (GAPs) so as to provide sustained supply of quality raw materials and support certification mechanism for quality standards, good agricultural/collection/storage practices, and
d. Support setting up of clusters through convergence of cultivation, warehousing, value addition, and marketing and development of infrastructure for entrepreneurs.

Components of the Mission

a. AYUSH Services
b. AYUSH Educational Institutions
c. Quality Control of ASU &H Drugs
d. Medicinal Plants

HUMAN DEVELOPMENT: INTERNATIONAL COMPARISON

The Human Development Report 2021–22, brought out by the United Nations Development Programme, shows that India's global rankings have gone down from 130 in 2020 to 132 in 2021. This is not surprising as the growth in India's Human Development Index (HDI) values have decelerated faster than the global values during the pandemic. India's HDI values, which were stagnant in 2019, fell marginally in 2020—the first year of the pandemic—and the fall accelerated almost threefold to -1.4% in 2021. However, at the global level, the fall in HDI indicators was stemmed in 2021 at 0.4%, which is marginally lower than in 2020. This sharp deterioration in India's HDI values by implication tends to have declining impact on that of both South Asia and medium HDI countries, which include India. The regional numbers show that the highest decline in HDI values in 2021 was in South Asia (0.9%) primarily on account of India's poor performance.

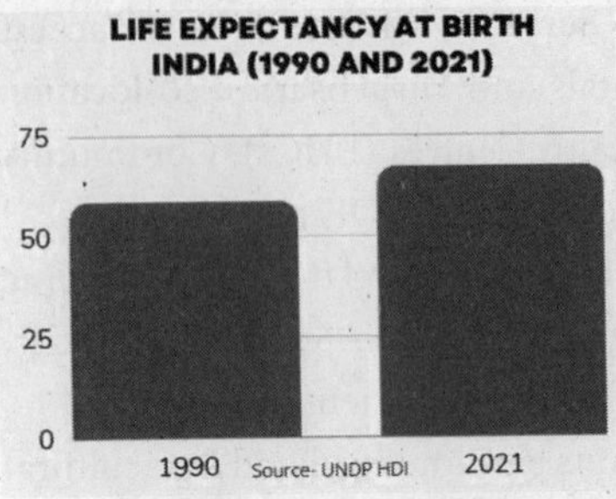

Life expectancy at birth, India (1990 and 2021)

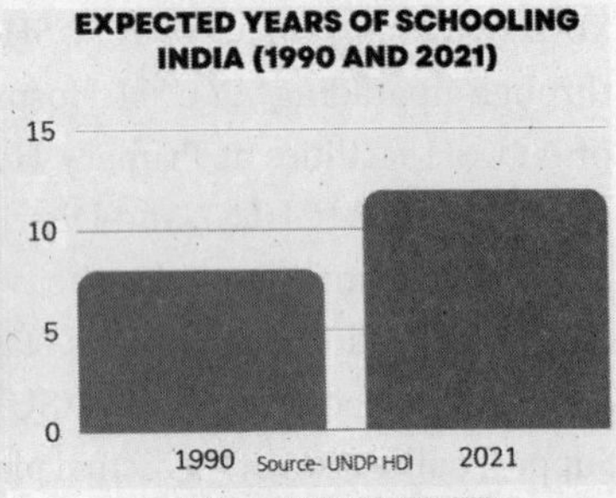

Expected years of schooling, India (1990 and 2021)

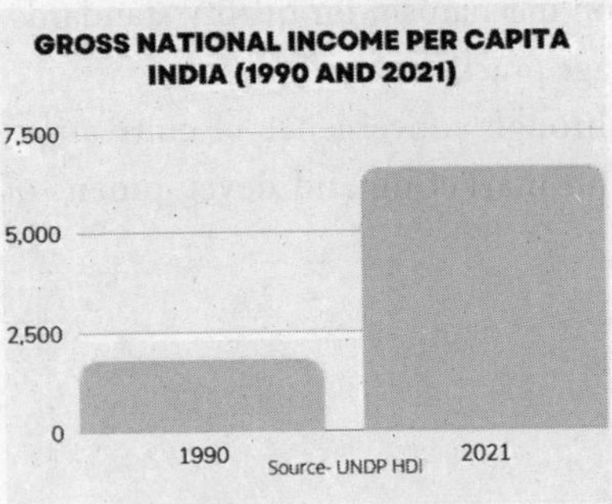

Gross national income per capita, India (1990 and 2021)

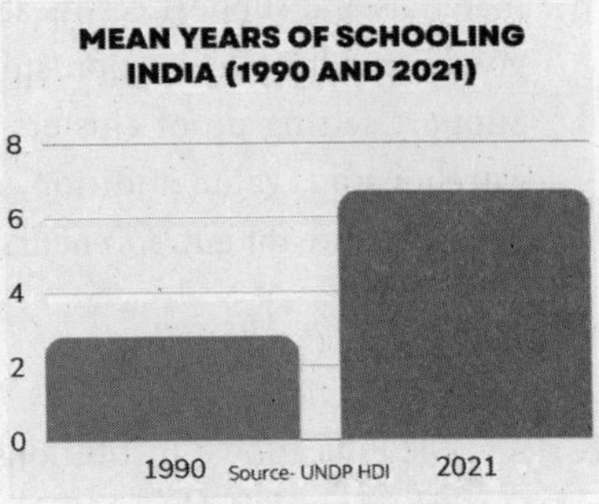

Mean years of schooling, India (1990 and 2021)

The current HDI value of the country is 0.633, which is significantly below the global average of 0.732. As if that is not bad enough, India is ranked behind the world average on all the four parameters: Bangladesh, Bhutan, China, and Sri Lanka have performed better. Strikingly, India's dismal performance pulled down that of South Asia, which registered the steepest decline in HDI values in 2021. Admittedly, India's showing is consistent with the global trend: 90 per cent of the countries surveyed have recorded a fall on the index. In fact, this is the first time since 1990 — when the HDI was constituted — that the global HDI value has decreased for two years in a row owing to factors such as the Covid-19 pandemic and the Ukraine war. This dip leads to two concerns: first, the momentum gained in realising sustainable development goals has suffered reversals; second, the report mentions that economies are facing a "new uncertainty complex" as a result of intersecting factors like widening inequalities and a polarising political ethic. The Inequality-adjusted Human Development Index (IHDI) indicates a percentage loss in HDI due to inequality. For India, the IHDI value for 2019 is 0.537 (16.8% overall loss).

Gender Inequality Index (GII)

GII is a composite metric of gender inequality using three dimensions: reproductive health, empowerment and the labour market. A low GII value indicates low inequality between women and men, and vice-versa. India has been ranked 122 on the Gender Inequality Index.

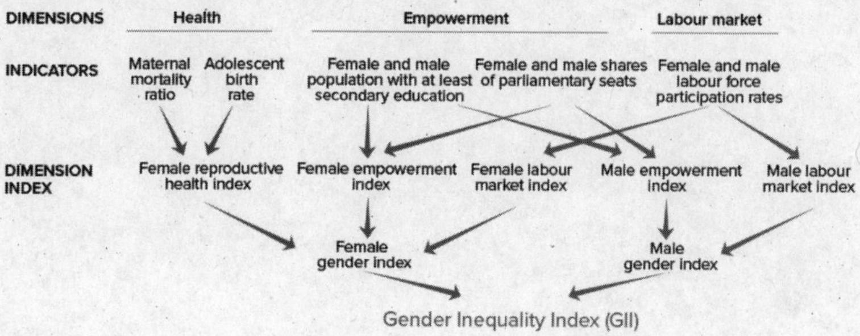

Source: UNDP

Gender Development Index (GDI)

GDI measures gender inequalities in achievement in three basic dimensions of human development. GDI measures gender inequalities in achievement in three basic dimensions of human development: health, measured by female and male life expectancy at birth; education, measured by female and male expected years of schooling for children and female and male mean years of schooling for adults ages 25 years and older; and command over economic resources, measured by female and male estimated earned income. For India, the GDI value for 2021 is 0.490. The key HDI metric where women seem to lag behind men the most is the income per capita.

6

ROLE OF WOMEN AND WOMEN EMPOWERMENT IN INDIAN SOCIETY

We need women at all levels, including the top, to make sure women's voices are heard and heeded, not overlooked and ignored. *—Sheryl Sandberg, CEO, Facebook*

INTRODUCTION

The role of women in India has undergone a significant change in the last few decades. Equipped with economic empowerment, women in many areas have assumed a comparable position with men. Yet, several evils still persist that undermines the efforts to constitute a gender equitable society.

The status of women in India has been subject to many changes over the past few millennia. From equal status with men in ancient times through the low points of the medieval period, to the promotion of equal rights by many reformers, the history of women in India has been eventful. In modern India, women have adorned high offices in India including that of the President, Prime Minister, Speaker of the Lok Sabha, Leader of Opposition, etc. yet, in the present times the gender inequality prevails.

STATUS OF WOMEN DOWN THE AGES

Women in Ancient India

In the ancient Indus valley civilisation of India, evidences show the worship of the mother goddess. Hence, the veneration for the mother is evident during that period. During the Rig Vedic period, it is believed that the position of wife was honoured and women's position was acknowledged, especially in the performance of religious ceremonies. Education of young girls was considered as an important qualification for marriage. There are references in Vedic literature that in the Kshatriya society, brides had exclusive right of selecting their own consorts, which was known as 'Swayamvara'. In Rig Vedic society, dowry system was unknown. However, the concept of marriage as a *dan* or gift was prevalent. Monogamy was the general practice though Bigamy was also in practice, but it was limited to the aristocratic classes. The wife was respected in her new house. The wife participated in the sacrificial offerings of her husband. However, being a patriarchal system, the women were expected to bear sons since the son performed the last rites and continued the lineage. Remarriage of widows was permitted under certain conditions. Female morality maintained a high standard although the same degree of fidelity was not expected from the husband. In this age there was no practice of divorce. The Rig Veda states that the widow had the right to marry again with her husband's brother. Rig Veda recognised the right of inheritance of unmarried daughters on the property of her father but married daughters were exempted.

Gradually, religious ceremonies were increasingly conducted by the priests resulting in weakening of the women's eminent position in the household. Later, in the Age of the Upanishads, the 'anuloma' system of marriage, i.e., between the male of a higher caste and female of a lower caste prevailed

In case a grown up girl was not married at a proper time by her father, she could choose her husband after three years of waiting. The most pleasing feature of this period is the presence of women teachers, many of whom possessed high spiritual knowledge. As in all patriarchal societies during that age, the birth of a daughter was unwelcome.

during this period. In the Age of Sutras and Epics, the 'Grihya-sutras' give detailed rules regarding the proper seasons for marriage and qualifications of bride and bridegroom. The bride was supposed to be at a mature age, over 15 or 16. The elaborate rites indicate that marriage was a holy bond and not a contract. The women held an honoured position in the household. She was allowed to sing, dance, and enjoy life. *Sati* was not generally prevalent. Widow Remarriage was allowed under certain circumstances. On the whole, the Dharma-sutras take a more lenient attitude than the Smritis of a later age. The 'Apastamba' imposes several penalties on a husband who unjustly forsakes his wife. On the other hand, a wife who forsakes her husband has to only perform penance. In case a grown up girl was not married at a proper time by her father, she could choose her husband after three years of waiting. The most pleasing feature of this period is the presence of women teachers, many of whom possessed high spiritual knowledge. As in all patriarchal societies during that age, the birth of a daughter was unwelcome. The son lived with his parents, earned money for the family, protected the family from enemies, and perpetuated the name of the family. The *Ramayana* along with the *Mahabharata* and the *Puranas* constitute the epic literature in India. The position of women gradually deteriorated not only in the society but also in the family. The discontinuance of Upanayana, the neglect of education, and lowering of the marriage age had a negative consequence upon the position and status of woman. During this period, a woman was considered to be a commodity which could be kept on bet and could be sold or purchased. But we also get quite contrary views from *Ramayana* and *Mahabharata*. Sita is regarded as one of the five ideal and revered women in India, the other four being Ahalya, Draupati, Tara, and Mandodari. There are references in *Mahabharata* which reflects that women used to guide men on religious and social questions. It was expected of a good woman to cooperate with her husband in religious pursuits. Marriage was a religious sacrament. A woman was considered unfit for independence at any time as she required protection throughout her life. In the Age 600 BC to 320 AD, marriage between the same caste was preferred although inter caste marriages were prevalent. Of the eight forms of marriage prescribed by the Dharma-sutras, the Arsha

---

Chandragupta Maurya, the founder of the Maurya dynasty, was reputedly assisted by Kautilya, a Brahman prime minister, who composed the Arthasastra, a handbook of statecraft. The elaborate documents states that women had property rights to the stridhan, which was the gift made to a woman at the time of her marriage by her parents and afterwards augmented by her husband. Marriage was both a secular and sacred institution.

---

form of marriage was most popular. The bridegroom was selected by the girl's father. According to Nearchus, the Indians "marry without giving or taking dowries but the girls, as soon as they are marriageable, are brought forward by their fathers and exposed in public, to be selected by a person who excels in some form of physical exercise". This indicates a modified form of Svayamvara.

Lowering of the marriage age affected their education and culture adversely. Emphasis was now laid on the physical chastity of women which discouraged widow remarriage, divorce, and encouragement of *Sati*. There is also evidence that women were active in such public economic activities as wage-labour, as well as serving as temple dancers, courtesans, and court attendants. During the earlier part of this period, there were highly educated women holding an honorable position in the society and household. Women also received training in arts, music, painting, and for some, military training also. Buddhist and Jain nuns renounced the world for the sake of spiritual salvation. Jain texts refer to Jayanti who carried on discussions with Mahavira himself and later on became a nun. In spite of the progress,

Historical References to Women in Early Medieval Period

Like the earlier period, women were generally considered mentally inferior. Their duty was to obey their husband blindly. Women continued to be denied the right to study the Vedas. Furthermore, the marriageable age for girls was lowered, thereby destroying their opportunities for higher education. However, from some of the dramatic works of the period, we find the court ladies and even the queen's maids-in-waiting were capable of composing excellent Sanskrit and Prakrit verses. Various stories point to the skill of princesses in the fine arts, especially in painting and music. Daughters of high officials, courtesans, and concubines were also supposed to be highly skilled in the various arts, including poetry. As for marriage, the Smriti writers say that girls were to be given away by their parents, between the ages of six and eight or between their eighth year and attending puberty. Medhatithi made inter-caste marriages exceptional. Marriage with the daughter of a maternal uncle is condemned. Marriage by mutual love is condemned by Medhatithi and he said that one should marry a girl who is much younger than himself, she must get married between the age of eight and achieving puberty. If a girl's guardian cannot find her a match before she becomes of marriageable age, then she can choose her partner after staying in her father's house for three years after attaining puberty. Sometimes, girls with the approval of their parents opted for a Svayamvara ceremony. Remarriage was allowed under certain condition when the husband had deserted or died or adopted the life of a recluse, or was impotent or had become an outcaste. In general, women were distrusted. However, within the home they were honoured. If a husband abandoned even a guilty wife, she was to be given maintenance. With the growth of property rights in land, the property rights of women also increased. In order to preserve the property of a family, women were given the right to inherit the property of their male relations. With some reservation, a widow was entitled to the entire estate of her husband if he died sonless. Daughters also had the right to succeed to the properties of a widow. Thus, the growth of feudal society strengthened the concept of private property. The practice of *Sati* was made obligatory by some writers, but condemned by others. According to an Arab writer, Sulaiman, wives of a king sometimes burnt themselves on the funeral pyre of their husbands, but it was for them to exercise their option in the matter. Purdah was not prevalent during this period. The general level of their culture is high. Several Queens of the Kara dynasty ruled in Ores. Sugandha and Didda of Kashmir administered extensive kingdoms. There were learned women as well as administrators. Sarasvati, wife of Mandanamisra, who acted as an arbitrator in her husband's disputations with Sankaracharya, was a learned scholar herself.

there were growing regression. Upanayana ceremony was reduced to only a formality. Manu laid down that marriage was equal to Upanayana while Yajnavalkya took the step of prohibiting Upanayana ceremony for girls. The wife who used to perform Vedic sacrifices was denied the right to do so. *Sati* existed but was confined to the warrior class only. Women courtesans were not looked down by religious leaders or kings. A famous courtesan Amrapali who lived during the reign of Bimbisara (300 to 273 BC) was a beauty whom Buddha visited. Chandragupta Maurya, the founder of the Maurya dynasty, was reputedly assisted by Kautilya, a Brahman prime minister, who composed the *Arthasastra*, a handbook of statecraft. The elaborate documents states that women had property rights to the *stridhan*, which was the gift made to a woman at the time of her marriage by her parents and afterwards augmented by her husband. Marriage was both a secular and sacred institution. Widows could remarry, although, when they did so, they lost rights to any property inherited from their deceased husbands. In 320 to 750 AD, the Gupta Empire is seen as the classical age of Indian culture because of its high literary and artistic accomplishments. Some information on roles for elite women comes from the *Kama Sutra*, a manual about the many ways to acquire pleasure, a legitimate goal for Hindu men in the householder, or the second stage, of their lives. Women were expected to be educated, to give and to receive sexual pleasure, and to be faithful wives. Courtesans were trained in poetry and music as well as the skills of sexual pleasure and were esteemed members of society. An important example is of a noble-hearted courtesan Vasantesena, the heroine of the "The Little Clay Cart," a popular play in Sanskrit ascribed to Sudraka (ca. A.D. 400). The other major dramatic female heroine of classical Indian literature is Shakuntala, a docile young woman who yearned for her distant lover in Kalidasa's "Shakuntala and the Ring of Remembrance." There was a growing tendency to lower the marriageable age of girls with girls being married before or after puberty. Marriage within the same caste was preferred but prohibited within certain degrees of relationship. Girls of high families had adequate opportunities for acquiring proficiency in higher learning. In Vatsyayana's *Kamasutra*, instances of princesses are mentioned whose intellect was sharpened by knowledge of the Sastras. The literary evidence of the Gupta age proves that girls of high families as also those living in hermitages read works on ancient history and legend. Girls living in royal courts were trained in singing and dancing too. Vatsyanana draws a picture of a good wife which may be taken as a reflection of the real life during that period. *Sati* was extolled by some but strongly disapproved by others.

The only direction in which the position of women improved was in the sphere of proprietary rights. As society began to discourage widow remarriages, there began to arise a class of childless widows who needed money to maintain themselves. Due to a lowering of the age of marriage, girls were not educated as before. This reduced the position and status of women. Brides being too young had no say in choosing their partners. Love marriages were a thing of the past. During this period, marriage became an irrevocable union, but it was one sided in favour of the husband. Since women were not as educated as before, they did not know what their rights were. Among the most striking changes may be the increased recognition in Katyayana of the women's right to property and a remarkable rule in Atri that allowed women molested by robbers to regain her social status.

Women in Medieval India

Medieval Indian history spreads over 500 years. It is predominantly the history of Muslim rulers. Muslims appeared in India as a warrior class. Their rule in India is divided into two Eras; The Era of Delhi Sultanate and the Mughal Era. The only woman who had ever occupied the throne of Delhi was Razia Sultan. Gulbadan Begum was a woman of exceptional poetic talent who wrote *Humayun-namah*. Nur Jahan and Jahan Ara took an active part in the state affairs. Nurjahan was the greatest Muslim queen of India. She was the very embodiment of beauty and military valour. Mumtaj Mahal a princess of a rare beauty combined with superb intellectual talents and aesthetic tastes. India has also produced heroic women such as Chandbibi, who appeared on the ramparts of the fort of Ahmednagar dressed in male attire; Tara Bai, the Maharata heroine who was the life and soul of Maharata resistance during the last determined onslaught of Aurangazeb; Mangammal, whose benign rule is still a green memory in the South, and Ahalya Bai Holkar, to whose administrative genius Sir John Malcolm has paid a magnificent tribute. The Moghul princesses of course played a notable part in the court life of Agra and Delhi. Jehanara, the partisan of Dara Shikoh, Roshanara, the partisan of Aurangazeb, Zebunnissa, the daughter of Aurangazeb, whose poems (under the pen name of Makhfi) have come down to us, and others represented the culture of the court. Jija Bai, the mother of

Shivaji, was a devoted mother, who was strong-willed and autocratic at home, but subordinated herself to the interests of her son. During the medieval period the social life of women underwent great changes. Dependence of women on their husbands or other male relatives was a prominent feature of this period. Devoid of avenues of any education, having lost the access to Stridhana or dowry, they virtually became the exploited class with disastrous results for themselves and the nation. Indian women were politically, socially, and economically inactive except for those engaged in farming and weaving. Political subordination includes the exclusion of women from all important decision-making processes.

With the advent of Muslims in India, the social movement of Indian women was restricted. They were prohibited to attend public functions and were not free to participate as men's equals in religious functions. Another social evil that existed in society during this period was child marriage. These child brides were denied all intellectual, physical, and spiritual development. Similarly, most of the women were made to believe that their ideal place

With the advent of Muslims in India, the social movement of Indian women was restricted. They were prohibited to attend public functions and were not free to participate as men's equals in religious functions. Another social evil that existed in society during this period was child marriage. These child brides were denied all intellectual, physical, and spiritual development.

was the home. Thus, they were persuaded by circumstances to accept their inferiority and secondary position. Men being providers, women became dependent on them economically for their subsistence except for the labour classes, where both men and women participated in subsistence farming and other occupations. Many social evils like female infanticide, *Sati*, child marriages, Purdah system, or zenana (the seclusion of women), developed during the middle ages due to the political instability of Northern India, especially due to various invasions. Polygamy came into practice. Muslim rulers in India had large harems. Thus, women came to be regarded as instruments of sensual satisfaction. Even among the Hindus there was no limit set to the number of wives a man could take, and a Muslim man could have as many as four wives. Islam also made the husband the head of the family and insisted that a wife should obey all his commands and should serve him with utmost loyalty. Another social evil that existed in medieval India was female infanticide. This particular system was prevalent among Rajputs and other high castes. Even among the Muslims this custom existed. This social evil originated from the belief that only the birth of a son could make salvation possible for parents as only a son had the privilege of performing Samskaras. The son began to be considered as the maintainer of the race. Purdah gained popularity with the advent of the Muslims. The Purdah system existed among Kshatriyas in the period of Dharma Sastras. Dowry system was a common phenomenon. It actually meant "Stridhana" which included gifts, ornaments, property, and cash presented to her by her father or her relatives. But in the medieval period the term acquired special significance. It meant money or "Dakshina" which was actually presented to the bridegroom along with the bride. In Vedic times it ensured some sort of security for her. During the Middle Ages, the term "Stridhana" acquired huge dimensions. The Hindus and Muslims favoured this custom of dowry. This in a way contributed to female infanticide, as it became a heavy burden on the poor. The birth of girls came to be seen as a misfortune by the majority of the population.

The condition of the Hindu widows became more miserable during the medieval period. Rigidity of caste system denied them the right to freedom and social mobility. A widow was secluded from society and was devoid of any worldly pleasure. The condition of the Muslim widow was slightly better owing to the fact that she could marry after a certain lapse of time following her husband's death. Jauhar refers to the practice of voluntary immolation by wives and daughters of defeated warriors, in order to avoid capture and consequent molestation by the enemy. The practice was followed by the wives of defeated Rajput rulers, who are known to place a high premium on honour. The feudal society of the time encouraged "*Sati*" which meant self-immolation of the widow. The Devadasi system was prevalent among the Hindus. Under the Devadasi system women were the brides of gods. But they were supposed to entertain kings, priests, and even members of the upper classes.

Bhakti movements which flourished during the medieval age gave rise to a new class of man and women who cared little for gender bias. This liberal stream to some extent widened the horizon of women. Female poet-saints also played a significant role in the Bhakti movement. Nonetheless, many of these women had to struggle for acceptance within the largely male dominated movement. Injustices and the patriarchal order itself were not a major focus of these poet-saints. Akkamahadevi, also known as Akka or Mahadevi was a bhakta from the southern region of Karnataka and a devotee of Shiva in the 12th century CE. Mirabai, or Mira is said to have been born into a ruling Rajput family. Mirabai's poetry tells of her vision of Lord Krishna when she was a child.

Women in Modern India

Modern India refers to the period from 1700 A.D. to 1947 A.D. In the background of the intellectual upheaval of the 18th and 19th century, there was a worldwide demand for establishing of independent and egalitarian nationalist societies which invariably emphasised the equality of women with men. Women in modern India have largely been influenced by the programs of reform and upliftment largely influenced by the western democratic and liberal ideology. Before the advent of the British in India, the life of women was rather oppressive, and they were subject to a constant process of subjugation and social oppression. During the British rule, a number of changes were made in the economic and social structures of Indian society, and some substantial progress was achieved in elimination of inequalities between men and women, in education, employment, social rights, etc. After the Bhakti Movement, the Christian Missionaries took interest in the education of the girls. The Hunter Commission too emphasised on the

Before the advent of the British in India, the life of women was rather oppressive, and they were subject to a constant process of subjugation and social oppression. During the British rule, a number of changes were made in the economic and social structures of Indian society, and some substantial progress was achieved in elimination of inequalities between men and women, in education, employment, social rights, etc.

need for female education in 1882. The Calcutta, Bombay, and Madras (now Kolkata, Mumbai, and Chennai) institutions did not permit the admission of girls till 1875. It was only after 1882 that girls were allowed to go for higher education. Since then, there has been a continuous progress in the area of education among females. Though the number of girls studying at various levels was low, yet there has been a marked increase in the number of female students at every level from 1941 onwards. During the 19th century, women in India suffered from disabilities like child-marriage, practice of polygamy, sale of girls for marriage purposes, severe restrictions on widows, non-access to education, and restricting oneself to domestic and child-bearing functions. The Indian National Conference started in 1885 by Justice Ranade contained these disabilities. Raja Ram Mohun Roy, who played an important role in getting the *Sati* system abolished raised voices against the child-marriage and fought for the right of inheritance for women. Ishwar Chandra Vidyasagar launched a movement for the right of widows to remarry and also pleaded for educating women. Maharaja S. Rao, ruler of Baroda State worked for prevention of child-marriages, Polygamy, and getting the rights of education to women, and the right of remarriage to widows. Swami Vivekananda, Annie Besant, Mahatma Gandhi, and Swami Dayanand Saraswati also took interest in the social and political rights of women. Some women organisations like the Banga Mahila Samaj, and the Ladies Theosophical Society functioned at local levels to promote modern ideas for women. These organisations took up issues like women's education, abolition of social evils like Purdah and Child marriage, Hindu law reform, moral and material progress of women, equality of rights and opportunities, etc. It can be said that, the Indian women's movement worked for two goals:

(i) Uplift of women.

(ii) Equal rights for both men and women.

During the 19th and 20th centuries, some laws were enacted with the sincere efforts of Indian social reformers, humanists, and some British administrators to improve the condition of women in Indian society. The first effort in this direction was the enactment of law against the practice of *Sati*. From about 1812, the Bengali reformer Raja Rammohan Roy started his own campaign against the practice. On 4 December 1829, the practice was formally banned in the Bengal Presidency lands, by the then-governor general, William Bentick. **Female Infanticide** was another inhuman practice afflicting the 19th century Indian society. It was particularly in vogue in Rajputana, Punjab, and the North Western Provinces. Some laws were enacted against this practice in 1795, 1802, and 1804, and then in 1870. Gradually, this evil practice came to be done away through education and public opinion. Social reformers made sincere efforts to popularize **Widow Remarriage** by writing in newspapers and contemporary journals. Prominent among these reformers were Raja Rammohan Roy and Iswar Chandra Vidyasagar. They carried out large scale campaigns in this regard mainly through books, pamphlets, and petitions with scores of signatures. Finally, the Widow Remarriage Act came into force in 1856. The practice of **Child Marriage** was another social stigma for the women. In November 1870, the Indian Reforms Association was started with the efforts of Keshav Chandra Sen. In 1846, the minimum marriageable age for a girl was only 10 years. In 1891, through the enactment of the Age of Consent Act, this was raised to 12 years. In 1930, through the Sharda Act, the minimum age was raised to 14 years. After independence, the limit was raised to 18 years in 1978. Voices were raised against the practice of **Purdah** during the 19th and 20th century. In Southern India and among the peasantry, Purdah was not prevalent. Through the large scale participation of women in the national freedom movement, the system disappeared without any specific legislative measure taken against it.

ROLE OF WOMEN'S ORGANISATIONS IN INDIAN NATIONAL MOVEMENT

Women's Organisations

The WIA (Women's Indian Association), founded by Margaret Cousins in Madras, worked extensively for the social and educational emancipation of women. Associated with the Theosophical Society, it encouraged non-sectarian religious activity and did creditable work in promoting literacy, setting up shelters for widows, and providing relief for disaster victims. Women in Bombay, Madras, and Calcutta (now Mumbai, Chennai, and Kolkata) through networks developed during World War I work, linked their associations together and created the NCWI in 1925. The most important of the women's organisations of the time—the All India Women's Conference (AIWC)—first met in Poona in 1927. Though its initial efforts were directed towards improving female education, its scope later expanded to include a host of women's issues such as women's franchise, inheritance rights, to name a few. Post-independence, the Constitution of India drafted in 1950

Women joined the Chipko movement in 1974 and with their united strength prevented the contractor from cutting trees. It was the women of Chipko who brought to public attention the importance of trees and the need to protect the environment.

granted equal rights to men and women. A slew of rights such as the right to vote, right to education, and right to entry into public service and political offices brought in complacency among women's groups. Though scores of women took part in the sharecroppers' movement in Telangana in Andhra Pradesh in 1948–50 and in anti-alcohol movements in Uttarakhand in the 1960s, this period saw limited activity in the area of women's rights. There was an anti-alcohol agitation as men used to get drunk and beat their wives. Women went round villages breaking pots in liquor dens.

The Chipko movement got its name from the Hindi word 'chipko' which means to cling. This clinging to trees was a particular action people used to save trees from being felled, which were crucial to their lives. The movement began in 1973 in the small hilly town of Gopeshwar in Chamoli district when representatives from a sports factory came to cut trees. Women joined the chipko movement in 1974 and with their united strength prevented the contractor from cutting trees. It was the women of Chipko who brought to public attention the importance of trees and the need to protect the environment. The publication of Towards Equality, the Report of the Committee on the Status of Women in 1974 and the United Nation's declaration of 1975 as the International Year of Women beginning with the First World Conference on Women in Mexico, generated a new interest in and debate on women's issues. The 1970s and 1980s witnessed the growth of numerous women's groups that took up issues such as dowry deaths, bride burning, rape, *Sati*, and focused on violence against women. Some of the earliest autonomous women's groups were the Progressive Organisation of Women (POW, Hyderabad), the Forum Against Rape (now redefined as Forum Against Oppression of Women), Stree Sangharsh, and Samata (Delhi). Among the first campaigns that women's groups took up was the struggle against rape in 1980. The amended law was enacted in 1983 after long discussions with women's groups. The POW in Hyderabad organised new and fresh protests against dowry. In the late 1970s, Delhi became the focus of the movement against dowry and the violence inflicted on women in the marital home. Groups which took up the campaign included 'Stree Sangharsh' and 'Mahila Dakshita Samiti'. Later, a joint front called the 'Dahej Virodhi Chetna Mandal' (organisation for creating consciousness against dowry) was formed under whose umbrella a large number of organisations worked. The anti-dowry campaign attempted to bring social pressure to bear on offenders so that they would be isolated in the community in which they lived. Experience in the campaign revealed the need for counselling, legal aid, and advice to women. Women's organisations also succeeded in getting the dowry law changed. *Sati* was declared a punishable offence in 1829. Yet in 1987, Roop Kanwar, a young widow, was forcibly put on the funeral pyre of her husband and burnt to death in a village in Rajasthan. Women's groups rose in protest and declared this to be a coldblooded murder. They demanded a new *Sati* Prevention Bill. There were several campaigns in the eighties relating to women's rights. Among them was a campaign, in 1985, in support of the Supreme Court judgment in the divorce case where Shah Bano, a Muslim woman, had petitioned the Court for maintenance from her husband under Section 125 of the Criminal Procedure Act and the Court granted her demand. The orthodox Muslims, however, protested against interference with their personal law. In 1986, the government introduced the Muslim Women's (Protection of Rights in Divorce) Bill denying Muslim women redress under Section 125. Women's associations protested against this outside the Parliament. Over the years it has become clear that changing laws alone means little unless there is a will to implement them and unless there is education and literacy which makes women aware of their rights and allows them to exercise them effectively. Women's studies spread to India slowly at first and then more rapidly following the UN Mid Decade

Conference in Copenhagen in 1980. The Indian Association of Women's Studies established in 1981 is an institution of women academics and activists involved in research and teaching. In the last three decades, a large number of books and journals by and on women have appeared. There are publishing houses that bring out books exclusively on feminist subjects. Efforts are being made to prepare reading and teaching material with a feminist perspective. A number of universities and colleges have women's study centers. All the major political parties, the Congress, BJP, CPI, and CPI (M) have their women's wings. The new women's groups declare themselves to be feminist. They are dispersed with no central organisation but they have built informal networks among themselves. Their political commitment is more leftist than liberal. The Indian women's movement is often accused of being urban based and middle class in character. While the urban feminists

The last few years have seen the broadening and expansion of the movement to take in a whole range of issues. Women's organisations not only lead campaigns and march on the streets, they, including the older ones such as AIWC, YWCA, and others, run shelters for battered wives and women who are victims of violence, and provide counselling and legal aid.

are more visible and articulate, rural women have also mobilised themselves. While street level protests and demonstrations give the women's movement visibility, this is clearly not enough. What is needed is attention to basic survival needs such as food, safe drinking water, sanitation, and housing. Women need education, healthcare, skill development and employment; and safety in the home and at work.

The last few years have seen the broadening and expansion of the movement to take in a whole range of issues. Women's organisations not only lead campaigns and march on the streets, they, including the older ones such as AIWC, YWCA, and others, run shelters for battered wives and women who are victims of violence, and provide counselling and legal aid. They conduct training workshops on various issues. They also help in forming Self-Help Groups to make women economically self-reliant. The success of the women's movement has not been in the number of women appointed to office or in the number of laws passed but in the fact that it has brought about a new consciousness on the entire question of women in Indian society. History shows that though the struggle for women's rights is long and hard, it is a struggle that must be waged and won. The women's movement thus has a long way to go in its struggle for bringing about new values, a new morality, and a new egalitarian relationship.

ROLE OF GANDHI AND NEHRU IN WOMEN EMPOWERMENT

As part of the larger independence movement, Mahatma Gandhi called for an end to the British monopoly and tax on salt in January 1930. On the famous Dandi march through the villages of Gujarat, thousands of people were walking with Gandhi and among them were many women. On the last day of the march, Sarojini Naidu, Gandhi's close friend and a nationalist leader in her own right, insisted on joining him. Sarojini Naidu was among the most visible leaders (male or female) of pre-independent India. As president of the Indian National Congress and the first woman governor of free India, she was a fervent advocate for India, avidly mobilizing support for the Indian independence movement. She was also the first woman to be arrested in the salt march. Her presence signaled thousands of other women to join the protest. Some of the women who joined the salt march

In fact, it is generally understood that the salt protest was made so successful precisely because of the many women who not only made salt, but who also sat openly in markets selling and buying it. This time marked a new level of participation by Indian women in the nationalist movement.

were wealthy elite women from cities, but the majority were ordinary village women. After the march to Dandi, thousands of women were breaking the salt law and leading protests all over the country. In fact, it is generally understood that the salt protest was made so successful precisely because of the many women who not only made salt, but who also sat openly in markets selling and buying it. This time marked a new level of participation by Indian women in the nationalist movement. The event is generally remembered as the first time masses of Indian women participated in the struggle for independence and marked the involvement of women from all walks of life, extending the movement out of its upper class enclave. At first, Gandhi's choice of salt as a symbol of protest had amused and bewildered many people. Making salt, in defiance of British laws, became a way for Indian women to declare independence in a very personal way and in their own daily life. Emphasizing their feminine qualities and their role as mothers, specifically as mothers of the nation, empowered women to find places in the public arena of protest.

Mahatma Gandhi worked not only for the political emancipation of the nation but also for the liberation of all the suppressed and oppressed sections of society. One of his noteworthy achievements has been the awakening of the women of India. He advocated social emancipation before political emancipation. Women, urban and rural, educated and uneducated, Indian and foreign, were attracted to his ideas and deeds. While some like Sarojini Naidu, Lakshmi Menon, Sushila Nayyar, and Rajkumari Amrit Kaur rose to prominence, there were thousands of unsung and unnoticed followers who learnt the meaning of liberation from him and contributed with all their energy to the struggle for independence. *Gandhiji was against:*

1. The pernicious system of child marriage. He considered such marriage as initio null and void and as such, no marriage at all.
2. All social and religious barriers to widow remarriage.
3. The Purdah system.
4. The dowry system.
5. Heavy expenditure in connection with marriages.

Mahatma Gandhi worked not only for the political emancipation of the nation but also for the liberation of all the suppressed and oppressed sections of society. One of his noteworthy achievements has been the awakening of the women of India. He advocated social emancipation before political emancipation.

Gandhiji's View on Participation of Women in Politics

Mahatma Gandhi is known to be one of the few people who encouraged women's active participation in the freedom struggle, marking him as a rare promoter of women's liberation. Women's entry into national politics through non-violent methods brought miraculous results. On the one hand, women became aware of their inner strength, and on the other, the process brought human and moral elements into politics. Gandhiji had tremendous faith in women's inherent capacity for non-violence. And his experience of participation by women in politics from his days in South Africa till the end of his life bears testimony to the fact that they never failed his expectations. With Gandhiji's inspiration, they took the struggle right into their homes and raised it to a moral level. Women organised public meetings, sold Khadi and prescribed literature, started picketing shops of liquor and foreign goods, prepared contraband salt, and came forward to face all sorts of atrocities, including inhuman treatment by police officers and imprisonment. They came forward to give all that they had—their wealth and strength, their jewellery and belongings, their skills and labour—all with sacrifices for this unusual and unprecedented struggle. Gandhiji's call to women to involve themselves in the freedom struggle had far-reaching results in changing their outlook. Many women in their individual lives shed their age-old prejudices against the caste system. They had no hesitation in leaving the boundaries of their protected homes and going to the jail. Women's participation in the freedom struggle feminised nationalism and the nationalist struggle helped them to liberate from age-old traditions. Though Gandhiji never challenged the traditional setup, he inspired women to carve out their own destinies within it, and thereby changing its very essence. Women learnt from Gandhiji that one can be strong, even if seemingly weak, to protest against injustice. His advice to women was to teach people in villages simple lessons of hygiene and sanitation. They realised that they do not have to accept the norms of male-dominated politics. They evolved their own perspectives and formulated their own methods. In a way they presented a critique of the colonial unethical state.

Role of Jawaharlal Nehru in Emancipation of Women

Jawaharlal Nehru had famously said, "You can tell the condition of a Nation by looking at the status of its Women". The basic instruments that Nehru adopted for his 'assault on the barriers of ages' to clear "the way for the majority of Indian women to have full social, as well as political equality" were the Constitution, special legislation for the protection of women, and expanding educational opportunities. Apart from the Preamble, the section on 'Fundamental Rights' guarantees, to men and women equally, various freedoms, equality before law, and opportunity for employment or office under the State, and forbids discrimination on the grounds only of religion, race, caste, sex, descent, place of birth, or residence. Article 15(3) empowers the State to make special provisions for women and children even in violation of fundamental rights of non-discrimination. Like the women's movement, Nehru had placed maximum faith in the spread of education to bring about women's equality. The first official step in this direction was the appointment of a National Committee on Women's Education (1958–59) and the consequent setting up of a National Council for Women's Education under the aegis of the Ministry of Education. Another instrument on which Nehru placed equal faith was political equality.

WOMEN'S ORGANISATIONS AND ISSUES

Women's organisations emerged in India as a result of the spread of education and the establishment of the notion of the new woman. There was an improved level of communication among women which made them aware of the different problems that they faced and their rights and accountabilities in society. This awareness led to the upsurge of women's organisations that fought for and signified women's causes.

Pre-Independence

An exclusive feature of the Indian women's crusade is the fact that early efforts at women's liberation were set in motion by men. Social reformers such as Raja Ram Mohan Roy, Maharishi Karve, and Swami Dayanand Saraswati challenged the conventional subservience of women, stimulated widow remarriage, and supported female education and impartiality in matters of religion, among other issues. Mahila mandals organised by Hindu reformist organisations such as the Arya Samaj and Brahmo Samaj encouraged women to go out of the boundaries of their homes and interact with other members of the society. Pandita Ramabai, who was considered as one of the innovators of the feminist movement, with the help of Justice Ranade established the Arya Mahila Samaj in 1882. She envisioned creating

An exclusive feature of the Indian women's crusade is the fact that early efforts at women's liberation were set in motion by men. Social reformers such as Raja Ram Mohan Roy, Maharishi Karve, and Swami Dayanand Saraswati challenged the conventional subservience of women, stimulated widow remarriage, and supported female education and impartiality in matters of religion, among other issues.

a support network for newly educated women through weekly lectures and lessons at homes, where women could learn and gain confidence through interactions. Women's auxiliaries of general reform associations also served as a ground for women to deliberate social issues, express opinions, and share experiences. The Bharata Mahila Parishad of the National Social Conference was the most protruding among such opportunities. Though the National Social Conference was formed at the third meeting of the Indian National Congress in 1887, the Mahila Parishad was launched only in 1905. These initiatives greatly influenced the social status of women. Early attempts at encouraging women to converse outside their families and local committees thus, stemmed from the broader social reform movement and efforts to upgrade the conditions of women. But a major inadequacy of the movement at this juncture was that it was essentially exclusive in character. The reforms were planned for restricted upper caste women and did not take up the cause of the huge masses of poor and working class women. Also, male-guided organisations still perceived the household as the woman's first priority and did not make efforts to employ education as an instrument to improve their contribution in society.

In the beginning of nineteenth century, there was concerted effort towards education of women. Schools and educational institutions promoting female public education mushroomed across the country. The pre-Independence period saw women's issues related to the nationalist agenda at various junctures. In this period, major enhancement of women was in terms of political participation of women, calling for a redefinition of conventional gender roles. Women began openly demonstrating their opposition to foreign control by supporting civil disobedience actions and other forms of protest against the British. Opportunities to organize and participate in agitations gave women the much-needed confidence and a chance to develop their leadership skills. Cutting across communal and religious barriers, women associated themselves with larger problems of society and opposed sectarian issues such as communal electorates. Political awareness among women grew, owing to a general understanding that women's issues could not be separated from the political environment of the country. *During this period, the initial women's organisations formed within the historical background of the social reform movement and the nationalist movement were as follows.*

1. The Women's India Association (WIA)
2. National Council of Women in India (NCWI)
3. The All India Women's Conference (AIWC) in 1917, 1925, and 1927 correspondingly

The Post-Independence Period and Women's Rights

The Constitution of India in 1950 permitted equal rights to men and women. Rights such as the right to vote, right to education, and right to entry into public service and political offices brought in satisfaction among women's groups. In this period, there was limited activity in the area of women's rights. Many women's organisations such as National Federation of Indian Women (1954) and the Samajwadi Mahila Sabha (1559) were formed to work for supporting the cause of Indian women. Since the country was facing a social, political crisis after the British rule, many demands of the women activists were not supported by the Government. But during this period from 1945, the Indian women got an opportunity to participate in confrontational politics. In post-independent India, the women's crusade was divided, as the common opponent, foreign rule, was no longer there. Some of the women leaders formally joined the Indian National Congress and took powerful position as Ministers, Governors, and Ambassadors. Free India's Constitution gave universal adult franchise and by the mid-fifties India had fairly liberal laws concerning women. Most of the demands of the women's movement had been met and there seemed few issues left. Women's organisations now observed that there was an issue of implementation and consequently there was a pause in the women's movement. Women displeased with the status quo joined struggles for the rural poor and industrial working class such as the Tebhaga movement in Bengal, the Telangana movement in Andhra Pradesh, or the Naxalite movement. Shahada, which acquired its name from the area in which it occurred, in Dhulia district in Maharashtra, was a tribal landless labourers' movement against landlords. Women actively participated and led demonstrations, developed, and yelled militant slogans and mobilised the masses.

As women's belligerency developed, gender based issues were raised. In the meantime in Ahmedabad, the first attempt at a women's trade union was made with the establishment of the Self Employed Women's Association (SEWA) at the initiative of Ela Bhat in 1972. Major objective was to improve the condition of poor women who worked in the unorganised sector by providing training, technical aids, and collective bargaining. Based on Gandhian ideals, SEWA has been a remarkable success. The Nav Nirman movement, initially a student's movement in Gujarat against rising prices,

The 1970s and 1980s observed the development of numerous women's groups that took up issues such as dowry deaths, bride burning, rape, and Sati, and focused on violence against women.

black marketing, and dishonesty launched in 1974 was soon joined by huge number of middle class women. The 1970s and 1980s observed the development of numerous women's groups that took up issues such as dowry deaths, bride burning, rape, and *Sati*, and focused on violence against women. They stressed the sexual coercion of women in a way previous reform or feminist groups had never done. They questioned the patriarchal assumptions underlying women's role in the family and society based on the biological sex differences implying a "natural" separation of human activities by gender differentials, the public political sphere being the male domain, and the private familial sphere as that of the female which eventually translates into a supremacy of male over female. Some of the earliest autonomous women's groups such as POW and Samata have been covered earlier in this chapter.

In 1975, the Lal Nishar Party structured a joint women's conference which was well attended by women in Pune in Maharashtra. Similarly, the communist party in India in 1975 organised a National Seminar which was attended by women in Maharashtra. The famous women's organisations which were established during this time are the Stree Mukhti Sangkatana, the Stree Sangharsh, and Mahila Dakshata in Delhi, Vimochana in Chennai, Baijja in Maharashtra, and Pennurumai in Chennai. The *Feminist Network* in English and *Manushi* in Hindi were some of the first women's newsletters and magazines to appear. The issues that they raise are rape, wife-battering, divorce, maintenance, and child custody along with legislative reforms. This progressive outlook is indeed a by-product of the changing economic, social, and political climate in the country. Therefore, the women's movement in India after Independence struggle not only struggled for liberation but also averred the need for creating a non-class socialist society where women can be completely free from apprehension and violence. The reverberations of changes, recurrent and sporadic at the beginning, began to be heard rather loudly from the middle of the 20th century. Some women organisations such as the Banga Mahila Samaj, and the Ladies Theosophical Society functioned at local levels to promote contemporary ideas for women. These organisations deal with issues like women's education, abolition of social evils like Purdah and Child marriage, Hindu law reform, moral and material progress of women, and equality of rights and opportunities.

Currently there are many women organisations in India:

i. All India Federation of Women Lawyers
ii. All India Women's Conference
iii. Appan Samachar
iv. Association of Theologically Trained Women of India
v. Bharatiya Grameen Mahila Sangh
vi. Bharatiya Mahila Bank
vii. Confederation of Women Entrepreneurs
viii. Durga Vahini
ix. Friends of Women's World Banking
x. Krantikari Adivasi Mahila Sangathan

The National Alliance of Women (NAWO) is a national web of women. Its affiliation or membership is open to all liberal minded women's groups and institutions, non-governmental organisations, women workers, women's unions, individuals, and others who share the principles, objectives and values of NAWO, as defined in the NAWO vision. *Major objectives of this organisation are:*

1. Strengthening and building new initiatives, networks, forums etc., for protecting women's rights.
2. Monitoring the Government of India's commitments, implementing the Platform for Action with special focus on the eight point agenda discussed at the Conference of Commitment, CEDAW, the Human Rights, and other United Nations Convention.

3. Advocacy, lobbying, and campaigning on women related issues.
4. Information dissemination and documentation.
5. Solidarity and linkages with other regional and global forums.

Another women organisation in India is *Swadhina* (Self-esteemed Women) which was formed in 1986. It is principally a civil society organisation focused on Empowerment of Women and Child Development based on Sustainable Development and Right Livelihood. At Swadhina, it is believed that positive social change has a direct effect on the lives of women and that change is possible only through an equal and spontaneous participation of women. Organisation members are active in five states across the country in remote tribal districts of Singbhums in Jharkhand, Purulia and West Midnapur in West Bengal, Kanya Kumari in Tamil Nadu, Mayurbhanj in Orissa, and East Champaran in Bihar. Major projects of this organisation include women's empowerment and child development.

It promotes women's empowerment through:

- Promoting grass-root level women's organisation
- Fostering functional literacy, education, and social awareness generation
- Augmenting participation of women in local governance
- Encouraging women's income generation and economic capacity building
- Strengthening women's participation in agriculture and food security support
- Upholding non-violence and social empowerment
- Improving family health and nutrition

It promotes child development through:

- Supporting child education
- Promoting sports and games
- Advancing environment and ecological awareness

All India Democratic Women's Association (AIDWA) is also a dominant woman organisation which is an independent left oriented women's organisation committed to achieving democracy, equality, and women's emancipation. AIDWA members are from all strata in society, regardless of class, caste, and community. It has an organisational presence in 22 states in India. AIDWA was created in 1981 as a national level mass organisation of women. AIDWA believes the liberation of women in India requires fundamental systemic change. It upholds secular values and challenges and resists cultural practices demeaning to women.

To summarise, women from earlier times have played a significant role in shaping of civilisation. Historical data indicated that though the struggle for women's rights is long and hard, but currently, status of women is enhanced and society has recognised their importance.

Indian Women NGOs

All India Coordinating Forum of the Adivasi/Indigenous Peoples (AICAIP) at Delhi was established as a forum for Adivasi/indigenous people's movements all over India. Its objective is to strengthen the process of building solidarity and alliances amongst struggle oriented indigenous people's organisations. AICAIP aims to identify shared issues and problems, to generate debate on these issues, and to provide support to help deal with them. One of the five working groups AICAIP has established is focused on Adivasi Women Issues. *A list of other Indian Women NGOs is provided here:*

- Joint Women's Programme - NGOs Delhi
- National Council of Women in India, Pune
- Centre for Women's Development Studies, Delhi

A research centre comprised of a group of professionals working for the realisation of women's equality and development in all spheres of life. The centre maintains a specialised library with a collection on women and development in India, open to students, research scholars, gender consultants, policy makers, journalists, etc.

- Committee on the Portrayal of Women in the Media, Delhi
- Institute of Social Studies Trust: Delhi.
- The YWCA of India – NGOs, Delhi

An umbrella organisation affiliated to the World YWCA with 65 local associations in India. The organisation works for women's empowerment through a variety of programmes, the most important of which are leadership training for women, advocacy work on all women's issues, and community development work. The YWCA also runs 40 women's residences across the country providing housing for working women as well as emergency shelter for women. The YWCA of India is also a part of a network of 7 women's organisations based in Delhi and works together with them on common issues.

- National Commission of Women, Delhi.
- Diverse Women for Diversity, Delhi.
- Kali For Women, Delhi, Feminist Publisher.
- Women's Foundation, Delhi.
- Saheli, a women's organisation, Delhi.
- Sakhi, Lesbian Organisation, Delhi.
- Center for Women's Studies and Development, Chandigarh.
- Centre for Women's Studies and Development, Faculty of Social Sciences,Varansai, Aroda .
- Women and Media Group, Mumbai.
- The Women's Centre of India, Mumbai.

- Women's Studies Unit, Mumbai
  The Women's Studies Unit attempts to sensitise students and policymakers about women and development issues by teaching social work students and government employees, by producing teaching materials, consulting various groups about women and development, and by conducting research.
- Maitreyi, Mumbai
  The major objective of Maitreyi is to develop a feminist perspective in understanding women's issues and the women's movement, and to sensitize everyone about women's issues.
- Shreemati Nathibai Damodar Thackersey (SNDT)
  Women's University Library, Mumbai. SNDT Women's University was established in 1916 as the first women's university in India.
- Akshara, Mumbai
  A Women's Resource Centre, Akshara began informally in 1987 as result of the women's movement and its campaigns in Mumbai.
- Center for Health Education, Training and Nutrition Awareness (CHETNA), Ahmedabad
  Chetna's mission is to contribute towards the empowerment of disadvantaged women and children to enable them to gain control over their own, their families', and their communities' health.
- Centre for Social Justice:
- Feminist Support Group, Ahmedabad
- Single Women's Organisation:
- Networking Organisation, Ahmedabad
- Women's Studies Research Centre
- Forum Against Oppression of Women (FAOW), Mumbai
  FAOW was formed in 1979 as a platform to respond to an extremely unjust judgement on a rape case. Soon from a Forum Against Rape as it was earlier called, it changed its name to the present one to encompass varied forms of women's oppression. FAOW is part of what in India is recognised as the Autonomous Women's groups which has played a crucial role in this third phase of the women's movement [late 70's onwards].
- Research Center for Women's Studies, Mumbai.
- Women's Studies Unit, Tata Institute of Social Sciences, Mumbai.
- Majlis, Mumbai
  Majlis is a legal and cultural resource centre working in the area of women and minority rights. Majlis is also involved in research and documentation on issues concerning women.

- India Women Scientist's Association (IWSA), Mumbai:
- It promotes women's participation in Science. Membership is open to all science graduates.
- Centre for Documentation and Research on Women (Aalochana). Pune, Maharastra.
- Anveshi Research Center for Women's Studies, Osmania University Campus, Hyderabad.
- Streelekha, Bengaluru.
- Bangalore Joint Women's Programme.
- Center for Informal Education and Development Studies, Bengaluru.
- St. Ignatius Social Centre, Karnataka.
- Working Women's Forum, Chennai.
- Madras Women's Indian Association, Chennai.
- Mother Teresa Women's University, Chennai.

STATUS OF WOMEN IN THE INDIAN CONSTITUTION

The principle of gender equality is enshrined in the Indian Constitution in its Preamble, Fundamental Rights, Fundamental Duties, and Directive Principles. The Constitution not only grants equality to women, but also empowers the State to adopt measures of positive discrimination in favour of women. Within the framework of a democratic polity, our laws, development policies, plans, and programmes have aimed at women's advancement in different spheres. India has also ratified various international conventions and human rights instruments committing to secure equal rights of women. Key among them is the ratification of the Convention on Elimination of All Forms of Discrimination against Women (CEDAW) in 1993.

Constitutional Provisions

The Constitution of India not only grants equality to women but also empowers the State to adopt measures of positive discrimination in favour of women for neutralizing the cumulative socio-economic, education, and political disadvantages faced by them. Fundamental Rights, among others, ensure equality before the law and equal protection of law; prohibits discrimination against any citizen on grounds of religion, race, caste, sex or place of birth, and guarantees equality of opportunity to all citizens in matters relating to employment. Articles 14, 15, 15(3), 16, 39(a), 39(b), 39(c), and 42 of the Constitution are of specific importance in this regard. *The Constitutional Privileges are:*

(i) Equality before law for women (Article 14)

(ii) The State not to discriminate against any citizen on grounds only of religion, race, caste, sex, place of birth or any of them (Article 15 (i))

(iii) The State to make any special provision in favour of women and children (Article 15 (3))

(iv) Equality of opportunity for all citizens in matters relating to employment or appointment to any office under the State (Article 16)

(v) The State to direct its policy towards securing for men and women equally the right to an adequate means of livelihood (Article 39(a)); and equal pay for equal work for both men and women (Article 39(d))

(vi) To promote justice, on a basis of equal opportunity and to provide free legal aid by suitable legislation or scheme or in any other way to ensure that opportunities for securing justice are not denied to any citizen by reason of economic or other disabilities (Article 39 A)

(vii) The State to make provision for securing just and humane conditions of work and for maternity relief (Article 42)

(viii) The State to promote with special care the educational and economic interests of the weaker sections of the people and to protect them from social injustice and all forms of exploitation (Article 46)

(ix) The State to raise the level of nutrition and the standard of living of its people (Article 47)

(x) To promote harmony and the spirit of common brotherhood amongst all the people of India and to renounce practices derogatory to the dignity of women (Article 51(A) (e))

(xi) Not less than one-third (including the number of seats reserved for women belonging to the Scheduled Castes and the Scheduled Tribes) of the total number of seats to be filled by direct election in every Panchayat to be reserved for women and such seats to be allotted by rotation to different constituencies in a Panchayat (Article 243 D (3))

(xii) Not less than one-third of the total number of offices of Chairpersons in the Panchayats at each level to be reserved for women (Article 243 D (4))

(xiii) Not less than one-third (including the number of seats reserved for women belonging to the Scheduled Castes and the Scheduled Tribes) of the total number of seats to be filled by direct election in every Municipality to be reserved for women and such seats to be allotted by rotation to different constituencies in a Municipality (Article 243 T (3))

(xiv) Reservation of offices of Chairpersons in Municipalities for the Scheduled Castes, the Scheduled Tribes, and women in such manner as the legislature of a State may by law provide (Article 243 T (4))

Legal Provisions

To uphold the Constitutional mandate, the State has enacted various legislative measures intended to ensure equal rights, to counter social discrimination and various forms of violence and atrocities, and to provide support services especially to working women. Although women may be victims of any of the crimes such as 'Murder', 'Robbery', 'Cheating', etc., the crimes, which are directed specifically against women, are characterised as 'Crime against Women'. These are broadly classified under two categories:

(1) The Crimes Identified Under the Indian Penal Code (IPC)

(i) Rape (Sec. 376 IPC)
(ii) Kidnapping and Abduction for different purposes (Sec. 363–373)
(iii) Homicide for Dowry, Dowry Deaths or their attempts (Sec. 302/304-B IPC)
(iv) Torture, both mental and physical (Sec. 498-A IPC)
(v) Molestation (Sec. 354 IPC)
(vi) Sexual Harassment (Sec. 509 IPC)
(vii) Importation of girls (up to 21 years of age)

(2) The Crimes Identified under the Special Laws (SLL)

Although all laws are not gender specific, the provisions of law affecting women significantly have been reviewed periodically and amendments carried out to keep pace with the emerging requirements. Some Acts which have special provisions to safeguard women and their interests are:

(i) The Employees State Insurance Act, 1948
(ii) The Plantation Labour Act, 1951
(iii) The Family Courts Act, 1954
(iv) The Special Marriage Act, 1954
(v) The Hindu Marriage Act, 1955
(vi) The Hindu Succession Act, 1956 with amendment in 2005
(vii) Immoral Traffic (Prevention) Act, 1956
(viii) The Maternity Benefit Act, 1961 (Amended in 1995)
(ix) Dowry Prohibition Act, 1961
(x) The Medical Termination of Pregnancy Act, 1971
(xi) The Contract Labour (Regulation and Abolition) Act, 1976
(xii) The Equal Remuneration Act, 1976
(xiii) The Prohibition of Child Marriage Act, 2006
(xiv) The Criminal Law (Amendment) Act, 1983
(xv) The Factories (Amendment) Act, 1986

(xvi) Indecent Representation of Women (Prohibition) Act, 1986
(xvii) Commission of *Sati* (Prevention) Act, 1987
(xviii) The Protection of Women from Domestic Violence Act, 2005

Special Initiatives For Women

(i) **National Commission for Women:** In January 1992, the Government set up this statutory body with a specific mandate to study and monitor all matters relating to the constitutional and legal safeguards provided for women, review the existing legislation to suggest amendments wherever necessary, etc.

(ii) **Reservation for Women in Local Self-Government:** The 73rd Constitutional Amendment Acts passed in 1992 by Parliament ensure one-third of the total seats for women in all elected offices in local bodies whether in rural areas or urban areas.

(iii) **Sexual Harassment of women at the workplace (Prevention, Prohibition and Redressal) Act, 2013:** In the year 1997 the Supreme Court through *Vishakha vs State of Rajasthan* gave Vishakha Guidelines to be followed at the workplace to ensure the safety of women. These guidelines were removed from the effect with the passing of Sexual Harassment of women at the workplace (Prevention, Prohibition, and Redressal) Act, 2013. It provided the definition of sexual harassment for the first time together with a list of actions that will constitute an act of such harassment and prohibited such acts especially by those in the workplace who exercise the power of authority over women which is common in organizational structure so as to save them from sexual exploitation whether it is a public or private organization

(iv) **Maternity Benefit (Amendment) Act 2017:** This Act amends the Maternity Benefit Act of 1961 providing 26 weeks of Maternity Benefit to the first two children and 12 weeks for mothers adopting a child below the age of three months. The act is applicable to all those women employed in factories, mines, and shops or commercial establishments employing 10 or more employees. The Act has introduced an enabling provision relating to "work from home" that can be exercised after the expiry of the 26 weeks leave period. It has mandated a crèche facility for every establishment employing 50 or more employees.

CRIMES AGAINST WOMEN AND THE LAW

Crimes against women rose 15 per cent in India in 2021 and Delhi is the most unsafe metropolitan city according to the latest National Crime

Records Bureau (NCRB) report 2021 which covers crimes against women, kidnappings, suicides, and traffic accidents in India

The year 2021 also witnessed a spike in the rate of crimes against women (number of incidents per one lakh population) from 56.5 per cent in 2020 to 64.5 per cent, as per Indian Express.

Amongst the majority of the crimes against women, 31.8 per cent were cases registered under 'cruelty by husband or his relatives', 20.8 per cent cases were 'assault on women with intent to outrage her modesty', kidnapping and abduction accounted for 17.6 per cent cases and 7.4 per cent were rapes.

With 56,083 cases, Uttar Pradesh topped the list of crimes against women, followed by Rajasthan (40,738) and Maharashtra (39,526).

According to the NCRB data, Nagaland reported the lowest number of crimes against women with 5.5 per cent rate in 2021. The northeastern state also had the lowest number of actual cases (54) last year. As many as 31,677 rape cases were registered in 2021 as compared to 28,046 cases in 2020 in the country. Rajasthan reported highest number of rapes in 2021

Delhi accounted for the highest rate of crimes against women in 2021 among the Union territories, showed NCRB data. The number of cases surged over the past three years from 13,395 in 2019 to 14,277 in 2021. Crimes against women in the National Capital accounted for 32.20 per cent of total crimes in the 19 metropolitan cities, followed by Mumbai (12.76 per cent) and Bengaluru (7.2 per cent). Two minor girls were raped every day last year in Delhi.

The National Capital logged 13,892 cases of crimes against women in 2021, a 40 per cent jump from 2020 when the official figure was 9,782. Of a total of 8,664 instances in various categories of crimes against women in 19 cities across the country with a population exceeding two million, Delhi recorded 4674 cases of cruelty by husbands, abduction and kidnapping of women stood at 3,948 cases.

EMPOWERMENT

Empowerment is the process by which the disempowered or powerless people can change their circumstances and begin to have control over their lives. It results in a change in the balance of power, in the living conditions, and in the relationships. Women empowerment may mean equal status to women, opportunity, and freedom to develop themselves. The concept of empowerment flows from the power. Empowerment of women would mean equipping women to be economically independent, self-reliant, and having positive esteem to enable them to face any difficult situation. The empowered women should be able to participate in the process of decision-making.

Why Women Need to be Empowered

Today we have noticed different Acts and Schemes of the central government as well as state government to empower the women of India. But in India women are discriminated and marginalised at every level of the society whether it is social participation, political participation, economic participation, access to education, and also reproductive healthcare. Women are found to be economically very poor all over the India. The National Statistical Office (NSO) conducted a nationwide study on 'Household Social Consumption: Education in India as part of the 75th round of National Sample Survey (NSS) - from July 2017 to June 2018. As per the report, India's country-wide female literacy rate is 70.3%, while the male literacy rate is estimated at 84.7%. Thus, increasing education among women is of very important in empowering them. It has also noticed that some of the women are too weak to work. They consume less food but work more. Another problem is that of workplace harassment of women. There are so many cases of rape, kidnapping of girls, dowry harassment, and so on. For these reasons, they require empowerment of all kinds in order to protect themselves and to secure their purity and dignity. To sum up, women empowerment cannot be possible unless women come with help to self-empower themselves. There is a need to formulate reducing feminised poverty, promoting education of women, and prevention and elimination of violence against women.

Political Empowerment

In India, the Ministry of Human Resource Development (MHRD-1985) and the National Commission for Women (NCW) have been working to safeguard the rights and legal entitlement of women. The 73rd and 74th Amendments (1993) to the Constitution of India have provided some special powers to women for reservation of seats (33%). In India 'The New Panchayati Raj' is the part of the effort to empower women at least at the village level. The government of India has ratified various international conventions and human rights instruments committing to secure equal rights to women. These are CEDAW (1993), the Mexico Plan of Action (1975), the Nairobi Forward Looking Strategies (1985), the Beijing Declaration, as well as the platform for Action (1995), and other such instruments. The year of 2001 was observed as the year of women's empowerment. During the year, a landmark document has been adopted, 'the National Policy for the empowerment of women.' For the beneficiaries of women, the government has adopted different schemes and programmes like Stand Up India scheme, Jan Dhan Yojana, Pradhan Mantri Matru Vandana Yojana, POSHAN Abhiyan, 'National Repository of Information for Women' (NARI)portal etc. The most positive development during the last few years has been the growing involvement of women in the Panchayati Raj institutions. There are many elected women representatives at the village council level. At the central and state levels too women are progressively making a difference. Today, we have seen women chief ministers, women president, different political parties leaders, well established businesswomen, etc. The most notable amongst these are Mrs. Pratibha Devisingh Patil, Sheila Dixit, Mayawati, Sonia Gandhi, Brinda Karat, Najma Heptulla, Indira Nooyi (Pepsico), Sushma Swaraj, 'Narmada Bachao' leader Medha Patkar, etc.

Social Empowerment

Women's empowerment in India is heavily dependent on many different variables that include geographical location (urban/rural), educational status, social status (caste and class), and age. Policies on women's empowerment exist at the national, state, and local (Panchayat) levels in many sectors, including health, education, economic opportunities, gender-based violence, and political participation. However, there are significant gaps between policy advancements and actual practice at the community level. One key factor for the gap in implementation of laws and policies to address discrimination, economic disadvantages, and violence against women at the community level is the largely patriarchal structure that governs the community and households in much of India. As such, women and girls have restricted mobility, access to education, access to health facilities, and lower decision-making power, and experience higher rates of violence. Political participation is also hindered at the Panchayat (local governing bodies) level and at the state and national levels, despite existing reservations for women. The impact of the patriarchal structure can be seen in rural and urban India, although women's empowerment in rural India is much less visible than in urban areas. This is of particular concern, since much of India is rural despite the high rate of urbanisation and expansion of cities. Rural women, as opposed to women in urban settings, face inequality at much higher rates, and in all spheres of life. Urban women and, in particular, urban educated women enjoy relatively higher access to economic opportunities, health and education, and experience less domestic violence. Women (both urban and rural) who have some level of education have higher decision-making power in the household and the community. Furthermore, the level of women's education also has a direct implication on maternal mortality rates, and nutrition and health indicators among children. Among rural women, there are further divisions that hinder women's empowerment. The most notable ones are education levels and caste and class divisions. Women from lower castes (the scheduled castes, other backward castes, and tribal communities) are particularly vulnerable to maternal mortality and infant mortality. They are often unable to access health and educational services, lack decision-making power, and face higher levels of violence. Among women of lower caste and class, some level of education has shown to have a positive impact on women's empowerment indicators.

Social divisions among urban women also have a similar impact on empowerment indicators. Upper class and educated women have better access to health, education, and economic opportunities, whereas lower class, less educated women in urban settings enjoy these rights significantly less. Women and children in slums are among the most vulnerable to violence and abuse, and are deprived of their basic human rights. As a result of a vibrant women's movement in the last 50 years, policies to advance human rights for women in India are substantial and forward-thinking, such as the Domestic Violence Act (2005), and the 73rd and 74th Amendments to the

---

Women (both urban and rural) who have some level of education have higher decision-making power in the household and the community.

Constitution that provide reservations for women to enter politics at the Panchayat level. There are multiple national and state level governmental and non-governmental mechanisms such as the Women's Commission to advance these policies, and the implementation of these policies is decentralised to state and district-level authorities and organisations that include local non-governmental organisations. Financial corruption hinders the government's ability to invest in social capital, including initiatives to advance women's empowerment. Since the 1990's, India has put in place processes and legislative acts such as the Right to Information Act (2005) for information disclosure to increase transparency and hold government officials accountable. Mistrust of political institutions and leaders remains high in the society with corruption and graft allegations often covering media headlines. In addition to corruption and inadequate resources for implementation of initiatives at the community level, women's empowerment in India is negatively impacted by the pervasive discrimination of women in the family and the community.

Discrimination against women in most parts of India (particularly the north) emerges from the social and religious construct of women's role and their status. As such, in many parts of India, women are considered to be less than men, occupying a lower status in the family and community, which consequentially restricts equal opportunity in women and girls' access to education, economic possibilities, and mobility. Discrimination also limits women's choices and freedom. These choices are further dependent on structural factors like caste and class. Empowerment for women in India requires a cross-cutting approach and one which addresses the diversity of social structures that govern women's lives. Access to education is part of a larger structural concern, including the practice of son preference, which creates inherent discriminatory practices. Education initiatives therefore cannot rely solely on building educational infrastructure, but also need to address some of the root causes of discrimination against women and girls which affect the decisions made by parents. Women's security, decision-making power, and mobility are three indicators for women's empowerment. In India, and more so for rural and less educated women, these three indicators are significantly low. Data from survey on women's decision-making power shows that only about one-third of the women interviewed took decisions on their own regarding household issues and

---

Discrimination against women in most parts of India (particularly the north) emerges from the social and religious construct of women's role and their status.

---

their health. The survey also found that older married women had more decision-making power than the younger married women. Younger women and girls experience an additional layer of discrimination as a result of their age.

Data on women's mobility in India indicates the lack of choices women have, and that urban and educated women have more mobility choices than rural women. Mobility restrictions for women are dependent upon how the family and community view women's rights. They also, however, are intrinsically dependent on the prevailing levels of violence against women in the household and the community. Abuse and violence towards women is predominantly perpetrated within the household, and marital violence is among the most accepted by both men and women. The gap in policy and practice in women's empowerment is most visible when it comes to the level and kinds of violence women face in India. Despite the policies, laws, and initiatives by civil society institutions, violence against women in India is widespread and the consequences for perpetrators rarely match the crime. Enforcement of laws and sentencing of perpetrators are long and arduous processes, and the gaps in these processes are further widened by corruption.

Additionally, social stigma and the fear of abandonment by the family play a big role in women and girls' ability or inability to access laws and policies to address sexual and physical violence.

In general, women in India are restricted in matters of decision- making, freedom of mobility, and access to money, though wide variations exist depending on the socio-demographic context (IIPS and ORC Macro, 2000). Certain periods in a woman's life like early childhood, adolescence, and old age may be especially vulnerable to discrimination and neglect.

About 25 per cent of women aged 18-29 and 15 per cent of men aged 21-29 got married before reaching the minimum legal age of marriage, according to the latest National Family Health Survey (NFHS) conducted between 2019-21. In India, the legal age of marriage for women is 18 and 21 for men. However, the government is planning to make it 21 for both men and women.

The NFHS-5 said about two-fifths of women married before reaching the legal age in West Bengal (42 per cent), Bihar (40 per cent), and Tripura (39 per cent), and about one-third of them tied the knot before reaching the legal age of marriage in Jharkhand (35 per cent) and Andhra Pradesh (33 per cent).

But the report also said that early marriage has been declining over time. "Marriage before the legal age of 18 is 23 percent for women age 20-24, compared with 47 percent for women age 45-49. Similarly, for men, marriage before the legal age of 21 years has dropped from 27 per cent for men aged 45-49 to 18 per cent for men aged 25-29," it said. The median age at first marriage for women aged 20-49 slightly increased from 19 years in 2015-16 to 19.2 years in 2019-21. For men aged 25-49, the median age at first marriage slightly increased between 2015-16 and 2019-21 (from 24.5 to 24.9 years), the NFHS said.

It was also noted that women having 12 or more years of schooling marry much later than other women. "The median age at first marriage for women aged 25-49 increases from 17.1 years for women with no schooling to 22.8 years for women with 12 or more years of schooling," it said.

Economic Empowerment

India is one of the world's fastest growing economies, with women mainly from the middle class increasingly entering the workforce. Urban centres like Delhi and Bengaluru have seen an influx of young women from semi-urban and rural parts of the country, living alone and redefining themselves. However, the story of economic empowerment for women is not a singular narrative; rather it is located in a complex set of caste, class, religious, and ethnic identities. World Economic Forum ranked India at 135 out of 146 countries in its Global Gender Gap (GGG) Index for 2022. India's overall score has improved from 0.625 (in 2021) to 0.629, which is its seventh-highest score in the last 16 years. In 2021, India was ranked 140 out of 156 countries.

In terms of the "Economic Participation and Opportunity", that analyses the percentage of women in labour force, Wage Equality for similar work, Earned income; India ranks a lowly 143 out of the 146 countries. In 2021, India was pegged at 151 out of the 156 countries. India's score is much lower than the global average, and only Iran, Pakistan and Afghanistan are behind India on this metric.

The all-India female labour force participation rate (LFPR) in usual status has increased 2.3% in 2021 to 25.1% as compared to 22.8% a year ago, shows the Periodic Labour Force Survey (PLFS) annual report for July 2020-June 2021. However this is still less than the LFPR in usual status for persons of age 15-29 years in India which is 41.4%.

The diversity of women's economic opportunities between states is due to the cultural, religious, and ethnic diversity of each state. Northern states like

Self-help groups (SHGs) are a widely practiced model for social and economic mobility by NGOs and the government. SHGs provide women with the opportunity to manage loans and savings that can be used by members for varying needs.

Delhi and Punjab lag far behind on gender equality measures, including the alarming sex ratio between men and women (due to son preference and sex-selective abortion), low female literacy levels, and high rates of gender-based violence. In rural India, women's economic opportunities remain restricted by social, cultural, and religious barriers. Most notably, inheritance laws embedded in Hindu and Shariat civil codes continue to marginalize women in the household and the larger community. Rural women, particularly of lower caste and class, have the lowest literacy rates, and therefore do not have the capacity to negotiate pay or contracts and most often engage in the unorganised sector, self employment, or in small scale industry.

Self-help groups (SHGs) are a widely practiced model for social and economic mobility by NGOs and the government. SHGs provide women with the opportunity to manage loans and savings that can be used by members for varying needs. SHGs also are used to promote social change among the members and the community at large. Members of SHGs have used their experiences as leverage to enter other local institutions such as the Panchayat Khap. Rural, low caste, and tribal women also make up 70% of domestic workers in India, a sector which is largely unregulated and unorganised. India's growing economy has allowed for many upper and middle-class women to enter the workforce, and while poor rural women have little access to education and training, there is a high demand for domestic workers in urban hubs. Domestic workers are mostly illiterate, with little or no negotiating power for wage equity, and are highly vulnerable to exploitation and sexual and physical abuse.

Women are also very visible in the construction sector in India, and like domestic workers are largely unorganised and rely on daily wagers. Women construction workers are mostly poor and illiterate and have little negotiating power. This sector is also unregulated and highly vulnerable to exploitation. Women workers also earn significantly less than men, although women are the ones who do most of the backbreaking work like carrying bricks and other heavy materials on site. On the other end of the spectrum, while India has one of the highest percentages of professional women in the world, those who occupy managerial positions are under 3%.

Most women work in low administrative positions, and many of the young women migrating to urban centres mostly work in service and retail industries, although more and more women are entering the IT and other technical sectors.

Women are also involved in human development issues of child rearing, education, health, and gender parity. Many of them have gone into the making and marketing of a range of cottage products—pickles, tailoring, embroidery, etc. The economic empowerment of women is being regarded these days as a sine-quo-non of progress for a country; hence, the issue of economic empowerment of women is of paramount importance to political thinkers, social thinkers, and reformers.

RISK FACTORS IN WOMEN'S LIVES

Unfavourable Sex Ratio

India's overall sex ratio — women per thousand men — is now at a level seen in developed countries. For every 1,000 men, India has 1,020 women. If that's a reason to celebrate, there is a cause for concern, too, since the sex ratio at birth continues to be lower than what is naturally expected. The fifth National Family Health Survey (NFHS), from where this data comes, has also found that the sex ratio is better in rural areas compared to urban centres.

NFHS 2019-2021 indicates that India has made significant strides in the last five years — in 2015-16, the sex ratio was just 991. However, analysis also shows that 13 states and union territories still have more males than females. In a rural versus urban analysis, the sex ratio was found skewed in favour of males in rural areas of 14 states, while 22 states had a sex ratio favouring males in urban areas.

It has been observed that in backward states and districts, the female-male ratio is better as medical facilities are yet to become easily available. In districts where these are available, sex determination goes up and sex ratio declines.

India's Sex Ratio at Birth Has Been Moving Toward Balance in Recent Years

Sex ratio at birth, or the number of male births per 100 female births

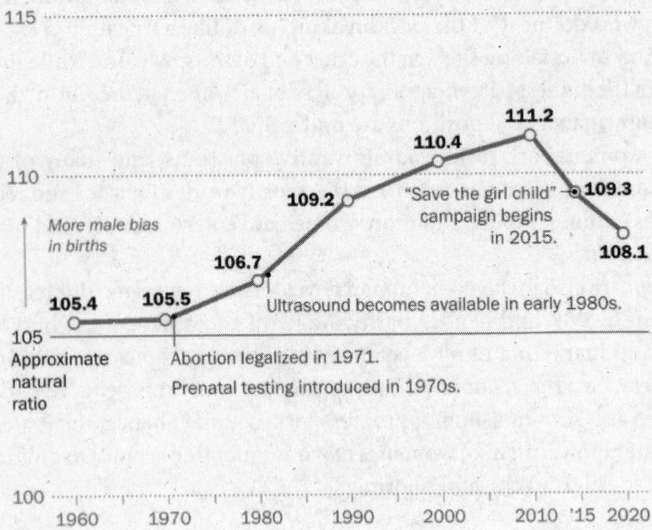

Notes: The natural sex ratio of birth is about 105 boys per 100 girls. Number in this chart generally describe the sex ratio of births in the previous five years, except for the 2001 and 2011 numbers, which are from the census and are based on a question introduced in 2001 measuring the sex of babies born in the previous year.

Sources: Census of India, 2001 and 2011; National Family Health Survey, 2015-16 and 2019-21. United Nations, Department of Economic and Social Affairs. Population Division,

"World Population Prospects 2019."

"India's Sex Ratio at Birth Begins to Normalize"

Source: Pew Research Centre

At the same time, the data suggests that India's artificially wide ratio of baby boys to baby girls – which arose in the 1970s from the use of prenatal diagnostic technology to facilitate sex-selective abortions – now appears to be narrowing.

The new data suggests that Indian families are becoming less likely to use abortions to ensure the birth of sons rather than daughters. This follows years of government efforts to curb sex selection – including a ban on prenatal sex tests and a massive advertising campaign urging parents to "save the girl child" – and coincides with broader social changes such as rising education and wealth. Among India's major religions, the biggest reduction in sex selection seems to be among the groups that previously had the greatest gender imbalances, particularly Sikhs.

Health

If health is defined 'as a state of complete physical, mental, and social well-being and not merely the absence of disease or infirmity', it follows that existence is a necessary condition for aspiring for health. The multiple roles of household work, child rearing, and paid work that women carry out has implications for their physical and mental health. A study on the impact of work and environment on women's morbidity in a sample population in Mumbai found that cohabiting women with children engaged in paid work had the highest morbidity rates (Madhiwalla and Jesani, 1997), higher than that of either single women or housewives. The types of morbidity experienced by the women included reproductive problems, aches, pain and injuries; weakness, fever, respiratory problems; problems in the gastro intestinal tract; skin, eye, and ear problems, and a residual category of 'other' problems.

The study also found, quite significantly, that degraded living environment, as in a slum, has deleterious effects on people's health and that the morbidity rates were highest for those adult women with children who were living in slums and were engaged in paid work. Another study of working and non-working women in the slums of Vadodara found that though working women contributed significantly to the household income, yet they had to face a burden of household work and childcare (in addition to their paid work). Such women put in more hours of work to fulfill their numerous responsibilities and had less leisure time. Women in both the categories had lower nutritional intake than what is recommended, with the working women faring worse than the housewives. Similarly, in the case of nutritional deficiencies such as anaemia, mottled enamel, etc., both the categories of women fared poorly, with the working women being worse off.

In India, a vast majority of the households rely on biofuels (wood, dung, etc.) for cooking. Cooking being a female preserve in the household domain, the pollutants arising from the burning of such biofuels affect women (and young children) disproportionately, with consequences on their health respiratory tract infections, blindness, and asthma being some of the diseases that affect them (Parikh, Smith, and Laxmi, 1999; also Gopalan and Saksena, 1999).

Domestic Violence

A longitudinal research study by BMC Women's Health analysing trends and lessons on domestic violence faced by Indian women from 2001 to 2018 has highlighted that India needs to focus on efforts to reduce the gaps in the administrative data which includes underreporting and almost stagnant data over the time. Between 2001 and 2018, the majority of the domestic violence cases were filed under 'cruelty by husband or his relatives', with the reported rate of this crime increasing by 53% over 18 years.

The cases of domestic violence further increased during the imposition of lockdown in response to the COVID-19 Pandemic. The National Commission for Women (NCW) that receives complaints of violence against women from across the country, has recorded an over two-fold increase in complaints since the imposition of the lockdown in the country. Data from National Legal Services Authority (NALSA) collected through 28 State Legal Services (SLAs) have observed an increase in cases of domestic violence during the lockdown. This is termed as 'shadow pandemic' or 'hidden pandemic' as per experts.

Dangers of HIV/AIDS

Intimate relationships may be fraught with other dangers. Sexual relationships with one's spouse are not without risks, its acuteness heightened in this age of HIV/AIDS. Across the country, sex within marriage is viewed as the man's right. Women may have some leverage in temporarily stalling off sex but to 'deprive' their husbands of it 'for too long' would invite social censure (George, 1997). If the man has been straying, then it puts the woman at risk, inspite of her being in a monogamous relationship. In fact, one of the tragic aspects of the HIV/AIDS epidemic in the country today is that it has spread to monogamous women in the rural interiors of the country, the infection having been contracted from the husband who has migrated to urban centres often in search of a livelihood. Transmission of the human immunodeficiency virus (HIV) in the country is overwhelmingly through sexual contacts, with other modes like perinatal transmission, blood and blood products, injection of drugs, etc. together accounting for less than 15% of the total infection (CBHI, 2003).

EDUCATION

The 15th official Census in India was calculated in the year 2011. In a country like India, literacy is the main foundation for social and economic growth. When the British rule ended in India in the year 1947 the literacy rate was just 12%. Over the years, India has changed socially, economically, and globally. After the 2011 Census, literacy rate India 2011 was found to be 74.04%. Compared to the adult literacy rate here the youth literacy rate is about 9% higher. Though this seems like a very great accomplishment, it is still a matter of concern that still so many people in India cannot even read and write. The numbers of children who do not get education especially in the rural areas are still high. Though the government has made a law that every child under the age of 14 should get free education, the problem of illiteracy is still at large. Now, if we consider female literacy rate in India, then it is lower than the male literacy rate as many parents do not allow their female children to go to schools. They get married off at a young age instead. Today, the female literacy levels according to the Literacy Rate 2011 Census are 65.46% where the male literacy rate is 82.14%. The literacy rate in India has always been a matter of concern but many NGO initiatives and government ads, campaigns, and programs are being held to spread awareness amongst people about the importance of literacy. Also, the government has made strict rules for female equality rights. India literacy rate has shown significant rise in the past 10 years. Kerala is the only state in India to have 100% literacy rate. It is followed by Goa, Tripura, Mizoram, Himachal Pradesh, Maharashtra, and Sikkim. The lowest literacy rate in India is seen in the state of Bihar.

It has been estimated that at the current rate of progress, India will attain universal literacy only until 2060. Though there has been seen a substantial increase in the number of literate women and this gap is narrowing, it still persists. Among such figures, there exists a ray of hope as well. According to the 2011 Census, since year 2011, 110 million additional women had become literate as compared to 107 men which means that the number of literate women is increasing.

Females constitute about 50% of country's human resource but lack of education snatches their chance to be a part of the progress and development of India. This means our pace of progress is less than the required pace. Even if females do not use education to work, total illiteracy has a huge negative impact on our society.

Region-based and State-based Disparity

There is a dramatic difference in the female literacy rate based on various regions in India. Female literacy rate in urban areas is higher as compared to rural India. In Rajasthan, most of the rural women are illiterate.

Kerala has the highest female literacy rate (92% as per 2011 Census) whereas Rajasthan (52.7% as per 2011 Census) has the lowest female literacy rate in India. States such as Uttar Pradesh (59.3% as per 2011 Census) and Bihar (53.3% as per 2011 Census) that are the most populated states in India show low levels of female literacy. This is directly related to the health and infant mortality. Kerala has the lowest infant mortality whereas states of Bihar and Uttar Pradesh have a high mortality rate.

Low Female Literacy Rate and Its Impact on Our Society

Low female literacy rate means an overall sluggish growth of India, as it impacts every arena of the development. India is struggling hard to stabilize its growing population through family planning programs. When a girl or a woman is not educated, it is not only she who suffers but the entire family has to bear the consequences of her illiteracy. It has been found out that illiterate women face more hardships in life than literate ones. They have high levels of fertility as well as mortality; they suffer from malnutrition and all other related health problems. In one of the surveys, it has been found out that infant mortality is inversely related to the mother's educational level. In such a scenario not only women but their kids also go through the same conditions.

Lack of education means lack of awareness. Illiterate women are not aware of their rights. They know nothing about initiatives taken by the government for their welfare. Illiterate women keep on struggling hard and bear harshness of life, family, and even their husbands.

Why is Female Literacy Rate Low in India?

The negative attitude of parents towards the girl child and her education is one of the major reasons of low female literacy rate in India. In most of the families, boys at home are given priority in terms of education but girls are not treated in the same way. Right from the beginning, parents do not consider girls as earning members of their family, as after marriage they have to leave their parents' home. So their education is just considered a wastage of money as well as time. For this reason, parents prefer to send boys to schools but not girls.

Poverty is the root cause of many problems in India and also of low female literacy rate. More than one-third of population in India is living below the poverty line. Though government is putting efforts to make the primary education free but still parents are not ready to send their girls to school. To this is connected the accessibility to schools. In most of the rural areas lack of easy accessibility to school is another reason for low female literacy rate. Even if schools are there, then lack of adequate school facilities becomes a hurdle. Some of the schools are really in pathetic conditions and do not have even basic facilities.

Another barrier to female education in India is the lack of female teachers. As India is a gender segregated society, it is a very important factor in the low female literacy rate in India. But in spite of all reasons, women must understand and realize that education can actually end the vicious cycle of poverty which is their misfortune, so that they can live a life with pride. In case of any misfortune in life, it is education that would help her, not anything else. The government should really work towards the number, distance, and quality of schools in rural as well as urban India. We should encourage the girl child in getting education to create a balanced and an educated society.

Factors Responsible for Poor Female Literacy Rate

Historically, a variety of factors have been found to be responsible for poor female literacy rate, viz.

- Gender based inequality.
- Social discrimination and economic exploitation.
- Occupation of girl child in domestic chores.
- Low enrolment of girls in schools.
- Low retention rate and high dropout rate.

GOVERNMENT STRATEGIES FOR INCREASING FEMALE LITERACY IN THE COUNTRY

The main strategies adopted by the Government for increasing female literacy in the country include:

- National Literacy Mission for imparting functional literacy
- Universalisation for Elementary Education
- Non-Formal Education

CONTRIBUTION OF LITERACY CAMPAIGNS TO FEMALE LITERACY

The provision of educational opportunities for women has been an important part of the national endeavour in the field of education since India's

Independence. Though these endeavours did yield significant results, gender disparity persists with uncompromising tenacity, more so in the rural areas and among the disadvantaged communities. It is with this concern that the Government of India launched the National Literacy Mission in 1988 for eradication of adult illiteracy. Since women account for an overwhelming percentage of the total number of illiterates, the National Literacy Mission is for all practical purposes a Mission of imparting functional literacy to women. *Total literacy campaigns launched since 1988 are making efforts to:*

- Create an environment where women demand knowledge and information, empowering themselves to change their lives.
- Inculcate in women the confidence that change is possible, if women work collectively.
- Spread the message that education of women is a precondition for fighting against their oppression.
- Highlight the plight of the girl child and stress the need for Universalisation of elementary education as a way of addressing the issue.

Some of the significant ways in which the literacy campaigns have contributed to the promotion of female literacy and women's empowerment are as follows:-

Heightened Social Awareness

Literacy campaigns have heightened social awareness among women regarding the importance of education, both for themselves as well as for their children. Large numbers of women have been participating whole-heartedly in the literacy campaigns as learners and volunteers. Because of the campaign mode and creation of a positive environment for literacy, women receive a social sanction to participate in the literacy programs. As women came out of their homes and take part in the campaigns with great enthusiasm, they acquire a heightened sense of self-awareness and desire to gain knowledge of host of women's issues.

Increased School Enrolment

The literacy campaigns have also motivated and encouraged women learners to educate their children, particularly girls by enrolling them in formal schools. An evaluation study of the literacy campaign in Birbhum District shows that the biggest achievement of the adult literacy program in Birbhum has been its impact on girls' education.

Table 1. Indian States Ranking by Literacy Rate

S.No	State	Literacy Rate (2011 Census)	Male Literacy Rate (2011 Census)	Female Literacy Rate (2011 Census)
1	Andaman & Nicobar Islands	86.3%	90.1%	81.8%
2	Andhra Pradesh	67.7%	75.6%	59.7%
3	Arunachal Pradesh	67.0%	73.7%	59.6%
4	Assam	73.2%	78.8%	67.3%
5	Bihar	63.8%	73.5%	53.3%
6	Chandigarh	86.4%	90.5%	81.4%
7	Chattisgarh	71.0%	81.5%	60.6%
8	Dadra & Nagar Haveli	77.7%	86.5%	65.9%
9	Daman & Diu	87.1%	91.5%	79.6%
10	Delhi	86.3%	91.0%	80.9%
11	Goa	87.4%	92.8%	81.8%
12	Gujarat	79.3%	87.2%	70.7%
13	Haryana	76.6%	85.4%	66.8%
14	Himachal Pradesh	83.8%	90.8%	76.6%
15	Jammu and Kashmir	68.7%	78.3%	58.0%
16	Jharkhand	67.6%	78.5%	56.2%
17	Karnataka	75.6%	82.8%	68.1%
18	Kerala	93.9%	96.0%	92.0%
19	Lakshadweep	92.3%	96.1%	88.2%
20	Madhya Pradesh	70.6%	80.5%	60.0%
21	Maharashtra	82.9%	89.8%	75.5%
22	Manipur	79.8%	86.5%	73.2%
23	Meghalaya	75.5%	77.2%	73.8%
24	Mizoram	91.6%	93.7%	89.4%
25	Nagaland	80.1%	83.3%	76.7%
26	Orissa	73.5%	82.4%	64.4%
27	Puducherry	86.5%	92.1%	81.2%
28	Punjab	76.7%	81.5%	71.3%
29	Rajasthan	67.1%	80.5%	52.7%

S.No	State	Literacy Rate (2011 Census)	Male Literacy Rate (2011 Census)	Female Literacy Rate (2011 Census)
30	Sikkim	82.2%	87.3%	76.4%
31	Tamil Nadu	80.3%	86.8%	73.9%
32	Tripura	87.8%	92.2%	83.1%
33	Uttar Pradesh	69.7%	79.2%	59.3%
34	Uttarakhand	79.6%	88.3%	70.7%
35	West Bengal	77.1%	82.7%	71.2%
-	INDIA	74.04%	82.14%	65.46%

Increase in Self-Confidence and Personality Development

The literacy classes conducted under literacy campaigns have given women an opportunity to break the isolation which is socially structured into their lives, giving them a chance to meet other women and learn collectively, rather than learn singly as individuals. The newly acquired literacy skills have enhanced their ability to solve family problems and learn new skills.

Gender Equity and Women's Empowerment

Total literacy campaigns have provided illiterate adult women, who have been denied access to formal schooling, with a great opportunity for reading, writing, increasing awareness levels, and skills training. Literacy campaigns have thus actively promoted gender equity and have sought to empower them as to decision-making about themselves, their families, and their communities. The impact of literacy on women's life has often been dramatic. Experiences of Puddukottai in Tamil Nadu (where women learnt how to bicycle and acquired ownership right in stone quarries) and Nellore in Andhra Pradesh (where a lesson in the literacy Primer inspired women to launch anti-arrack agitation that later engulfed the entire district and the state) have shown how women have been empowered at individual and collective levels as a result of their participation.

Status in the Family

Literacy campaigns have played a significant role in improving the status of women within their own families. Whereas traditionally, women had little say in the family decision-making, they, through participation in literacy programs, have begun to express their newly found self-belief in having a say both within and outside the family.

Educational Equality

Another area in which women's equality has shown a major improvement as a result of adult literacy programs is the area of enrolment of boys and girls in schools. As a result of higher participation of women in literacy campaigns, the gender gap in literacy levels is gradually getting reduced. Even more significant is the fact that disparity in enrolment of boys and girls in neo-literate households is much lowered compared to the non-literate householders.

Women as Entrepreneurs

Participation of women is literacy campaigns have opened several opportunities for neo-literate women to step out of the households and involve themselves in some enterprise or a new vocation. The Dumka campaign in Bihar has demonstrated how the literacy campaign has helped women to take charge of their lives. They have formed a group called 'Jago Behna' (Awake sister), which tries to sensitize the women to the need of collective action against social ills. These women have also set up 'Didi Bank' (Sister Bank) which promotes the habits of thrifts and savings. Here, women have also learnt to maintain the hand pump, thereby breaking their dependence for repair on mechanics from outside the village.

Household Savings and Access to Credit

In almost all the districts, the literacy campaigns have gone beyond the transaction of mere literacy skills and have served to enhance knowledge and skills for better management of expenditure and improving earning capacities. In several districts, the women participants in literacy campaigns have begun to set aside their earnings not only in regular banks but also in special thrift societies. Such societies, as for example in Dumka, are run by the women themselves.

Health and Hygiene

Literacy campaigns in most districts have taken up health and hygiene issues as an integral component of adult education programs. Literacy campaigns have helped to spread knowledge about healthcare and nutrition, thereby enabling mothers to keep their family in better health and to care better for their children. Literacy campaigns have also disseminated information for creating awareness about problems of early marriage, spacing, and small family norms.

WOMEN'S EMANCIPATION

The world over women are struggling to break the shackles that bind them and challenging the unequal distribution of power in society. Transforming the existing egalitarian pattern of gender relationships necessitates leadership in the state, markets, and civil society—the key centres of power in the present globalizing economy. It is, therefore, imperative for women to be in the corridors of power and have the power to negotiate a better deal for themselves, if they are to influence policy decisions which have an impact on them. Empowerment of women in all spheres, in particular the political sphere is critical for their advancement and the foundation of a gender-equal society. Women's political empowerment is premised on "three fundamental and non-negotiable principles: (a) the equality between women and men; (b) women's right to the full development of their potential; and (c) women's right to self representation and self-determination".

Involvement of women in the political arena and in decision-making roles is an important tool for empowerment as well as monitoring standards of political performance." Gender Justice Judicial activism in recent years had led to ensuring greater equality for women before the law. Review of legislation from a gender perspective has begun to bring greater equality for women. Greater awareness among women; a stronger recognition of women's rights, sustained public advocacy, and effective judicial activism are beginning to show some results. The Supreme Court's landmark judgement in 1997 on a writ petition by some women's groups seeking the enforcement of the fundamental rights of working women has paved the way for their greater protection from sexual harassment. The Supreme Court in 1997, also announced a set of guidelines for sexual harassment for the first time. Court judgements have also started invoking international conventions like CEDAW to make a stronger case for women's justice. Institutions like the National Commission for Women and the National Human Rights Commission are carrying out detailed investigations of injustice against women.

Steps Taken to Empower Women

In India, numerous steps have been undertaken to provide constitutional safeguards and institutional framework for activities for women welfare. The development of women has been the central focus in development planning since Independence. There have been various shifts in policy approaches during the last 40 years from the concept of 'welfare' in the 70s to 'development' in the '80s, and now to 'empowerment' in the '90s and afterwards. Now the emphasis is on the inclusion of women in decision-making and their participation at the policy formulation levels. The Government of India declared the year 2001 as Year for the Empowerment of Women, but the struggle to reach this stage has been long and arduous. The concern for women's political equality in India first emerged as a political issue during the national movement in which women were active participants. As early as 1917, Indian women raised the issue of representation in politics, which at a time meant a demand for universal adult franchise. By 1929 women had the right to vote on the basis of wifehood, property, and education. Under the Government of India Act, 1935, all women over 21 could vote provided they fulfilled the conditions of property and education. Post-Independence, women continued to play a significant role in less conventional political activities such as environmental movement, anti-alcohol agitation, peace movement, and even revolutionary activities, which equally affect power relationships as they have the capacity to influence the state. Yet, politics proved to be a very inhospitable terrain for women and continues to be the male bastion into which the entry of women is severely restricted. It was only with the setting up of the Committee on the Status of Women in India (CSWI) September, 1971 that the demand for greater representation of women in political institutions in India was taken up in a systematic way. The 73rd amendment, among other things, handed over the reins of power to the people at the panchayat level with a 33 per cent reservation of certain seats and key positions within the panchayat to women. The amendment also made it mandatory for all states to hold gram panchayat and municipal elections and empowered these bodies to undertake development activities at the local level. However, as per the information available with the Ministry of Panchayati Raj, 21 States have made provision of 50% reservation for women in Panchayati Raj Institutions in their respective State Panchayati Raj Acts. In respect of remaining States, Constitutional provision as prescribed in Article 243D applies.

About three years after women started occupying the seats of power, changes can already be seen. Many panchayats have performed well despite financial constraints. On an average, around Rs 200 per person reaches every gram panchayat (Rs 1.5 lakh per gram panchayat in Haryana, Rs 2.3 lakh in Himachal Pradesh Rs 90,000 in Uttar Pradesh, Rs 6.5 lakh in Madhya Pradesh, Rs 66 lakh in Kerala) to undertake development work in the village. Since most of this money to panchayats is already tied and committed for certain infrastructure and other development activities, panchayats do not have much autonomy in defining the programme priorities. However, the Kerala's People's Plan (KPP) allots, on an average, Rs 30 lakh per gram panchayat for unlisted projects giving scope for local initiative.

By and large, women sarpanches or members attend panchayat or block level meetings by themselves and are not represented by their male relatives," says Chandan Dutta of the Delhi-based non-governmental organisation (NGO), Participatory Research in Asia. There has also been a perceptible improvement in administration at the gram panchayat level mainly because women sarpanchs hold meetings during the day and no dubious deals are struck late at night. They are also more accessible than men who are often not around. Due to these factors there is much more honesty and transparency in local administrative matters.

Women are also making substantial contributions in giving suggestions for raising educational standards, addressing water sanitation and fuel problems - areas which were generally not discussed by men. A woman panchayat member from Yavatal district of Maharastra organised a camp for women to discuss issues like dowry and also convinced women to implement improved stove and biogas systems.

Reservation of Women in Parliament

Despite the share of women legislators in the Lok Sabha peaking at 14.39% as of June 2019, India is still worse than 140 countries in the representation of women in Parliament. The global average for the share of women parliamentarians stood at 24.6%. Rwanda has the highest proportion of women in Parliament (over 60%). India ranks 141st out of 191 nations as per the Women in Politics Report released by the World Bank.

Women in Lok Sabha

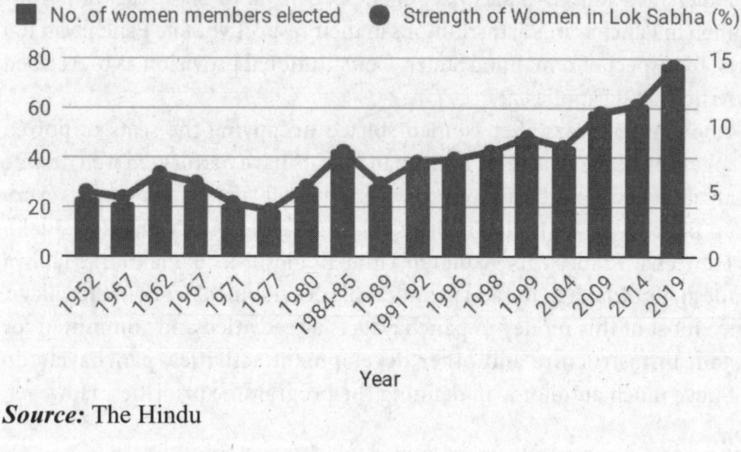

Source: The Hindu

The first Lok Sabha in 1951 had 22 women MPs. The current Lok Sabha has 78. In the span of 59 years and 17 Lok Sabha elections it amounts to a three- fold increase in the number of women MPs that made their way to the lower house of the parliament. From 5% in 1951, women MPs constitute 14% of the Lok Sabha today.

The rise in numbers has been steady through the years. The notable exceptions have been the dip in numbers during the 6th Lok Sabha in 1977, the 9th Lok Sabha in 1989 and most recently the 14th Lok Sabha in 2004.

From 1991 onwards to the present Lok Sabha, the rise in women's representation has been constant albeit disproportionate to their population. The 1991 figures show a jump from 5% in the previous Lok Sabha to 7% and the steady increase from thereon (except for 2004). It would be interesting to understand the factors for this watershed year and continuous rise and also the fall in numbers during 2004.

The other interesting story from the numbers over the years emerges from the relative success rate of women contestants as opposed to the male contestants. Consistently, the success rate of women has been higher over the years than men. Success rate is the number of winners against the total contestants in that category.

Women have had a greater success rate than men in every single election except the last general elections in 2019. In some years, the difference has been quite stark. In 1971, the success rate for men was 18%, whereas it was 34% for women, which is twice that of men.

For the current Lok Sabha, the success rate was 15.7% for men and 10.7% for women. This could mean one of the two things: Either women had a greater chance of winning from the seats that they stood from or that tickets were being given to women who had a greater chance of success.

Women's Economic, Social, and Cultural Rights

The movement to assure women's economic, social, and cultural rights (ESCR) as basic human rights is just emerging in India. The movement aims to locate women's rights within the larger human rights framework, and by doing so moves away from looking at women's issues only within the framework of violence against women and reproductive rights. ESCR attempts to look at the broader issues facing women, namely poverty, housing, unemployment, education, water, food security, trade, etc. While the human rights movement on ESCR is largely contained at the international policy level, there are emerging social movements around the world. In the Indian context, projects like the Programme on Women's Economic, Social, and Cultural Rights (PWESCR), for example, is creating linkages between the international human rights movement and the local articulation of women's rights. PWESCR aims to build a women's rights movement in India that creates equality in all spheres of women's lives. By empowering women economically and socially, ESCR provides for a broader discourse on rights that moves women's rights from a victim-centered approach to one that cuts across other fundamental human rights issues.

Women's economic opportunity in India is a rapidly changing landscape. Women are increasingly entering the workforce—particularly women professionals—and are creating change, but there remains a large number of invisible women workers in unorganised and volatile sectors. Implementation of national and state level policies lags behind in ensuring that women workers have equal pay and are free from exploitation.

POVERTY ALLEVIATION/INCOME GENERATION ACTIVITIES FOR WOMEN

The Constitution of India grants equality to women in various fields of life. In the past, the position of women was miserable in the society and even women were not ready to undertake any assignment or job due to many reasons like fear, shyness, male dominance in the society, and Purdah system but time has changed now. Women of today are not like the early days. Now, they are always ready to come forward and want more economic independence, their own identity, achievements, equal status in the society, and greater freedom. Government of India has provided for Self-Help Groups (SHGs) to them so that proper attention should be given to their economic independence through self employment, entrepreneurial development, and well-being that ultimately leads to its contribution. SHGs have been emerged as a powerful instrument in order to alleviate poverty and for the empowerment of women in the rural economy. SHGs through the network of commercial banks, co-operative banks, regional rural banks, NABARD, and NGOs has been largely supply driven and a recent approach in the provision of financial services to the poor and further upgrading their status in the society. In this way, SHGs are important not only to reduce rural poverty and to promote rural savings, but also to increase gainful employment.

Women and Self-Help Groups

Self-help groups (SHG) can act as a bridge between women entrepreneurs who have the will to begin an enterprise but do not have the resources to fulfil their dream, and the finances needed for it. An SHG comprises a small group of women who come together to make regular monetary contributions. Emerging as important micro-finance systems, SHGs work as platforms that promote solidarity among women, bringing them together on issues of health, nutrition, gender parity and gender justice. SHGs have already made a significant contribution in developing entrepreneurship aptitudes among rural women by enhancing their skills and giving them a chance to engage in various entrepreneurial activities.

Self-help groups (SHG) can act as a bridge between women entrepreneurs who have the will to begin an enterprise but do not have the resources to fulfil their dream, and the finances needed for it. An SHG comprises a small group of women who come together to make regular monetary contributions. Emerging as important micro-finance systems, SHGs work as platforms that promote solidarity among women, bringing them together on issues of health, nutrition, gender parity and gender justice. SHGs have already made a significant contribution in developing entrepreneurship aptitudes among rural women by enhancing their skills and giving them a chance to engage in various entrepreneurial activities.

Self-help groups are exceedingly relevant today because their provision of micro-loans helps overcome regional imbalances as well as information asymmetries, thus offering a level playing field in terms of access to resources for women. The multi-faceted IFMR study conducted by the ministry of rural development evaluated the impact that SHGs have had on livelihoods, and thereby on consumption, expenditure and savings patterns in households whose women are part of it. The study found that women aided by SHGs were 10% more likely to save on a regular basis, resulting in economic empowerment, while working towards a better future for the next generation.

SKILL DEVELOPMENT

The 11th Five Year Plan (2007–12) has recognised India's massive need to skill millions of formal and informal workers in the next ten years. In response, the government developed an ambitious scheme "of increasing the proportion of formal and informal skilled workers in its total workforce from a mere 2% now to 50% by 2022, thus creating a 500 million strong resource pool." Women form a significant proportion of this workforce in India, however, they are largely concentrated in the informal sector, engaged in vocations characterised by low earning, low productivity, poor working conditions, and lack of social protection. Both, women and men, whether urban or rural, are majorly unskilled compared to having some skills. There are higher number of unskilled workers in rural than in urban areas, and more number of women do not have any skills, compared to men with no skills. Low social value is attached to girl's education, and as they are considered secondary income earners, lower importance is given to training of girls for employment. The gender roles defined for women, expect them to primarily devote their time to household chores and child rearing, while time devoted to skill training and economic activities is conditional and limited. Hence, a sustainable skill development programme would aim to take on board, both women's as well as men's concerns and experiences. These should form an integral part of the design, implementation, monitoring, and evaluation of policies and the programmes.

Provision of modern skill training programmes may substantially help in increasing the productivity of this workforce. It demands action in the form of policy change, and local level initiatives and building of institutes that are sensitive to the needs and work conditions experienced by women and men separately. However, it is to be noted that the initiatives required to skill the workforce, cannot be assumed to be the same for both men and women, as women and men face very different social and economic circumstances in India. The key strategy for women's empowerment and gender equality is to combine policy and institutions at the local level.

ROLE OF MINISTRY OF WOMEN AND CHILD DEVELOPMENT (MWCD)

The Department of Women and Child Development, Government of India, came into existence as a separate Ministry with effect from 30th January, 2006. Earlier, it was a Department under the Ministry of Human Resources Development since 1985. The Ministry was constituted with the prime intention of addressing gaps in State action for women and children for promoting inter-Ministerial and inter-sectoral convergence to create gender equitable and child-centred legislation, policies, and programmes.

Vision and Mission

1. Promoting social and economic empowerment of women through cross-cutting policies and programmes, mainstreaming gender concerns, creating awareness about their rights, and facilitating institutional and

legislative support for enabling them realize their human rights and develop to their full potential.

2. Ensuring development, care, and protection of children through cross-cutting policies and programmes, spreading awareness about their rights, and facilitating access to learning, nutrition, institutional, and legislative support for enabling them to grow and develop to their full potential.

Mandate

The broad mandate of the Ministry is to have holistic development of women and children. As a nodal Ministry for the advancement of women and children, the Ministry formulates plans, policies, and programmes; enacts/amends legislation, guides, and coordinates the efforts of both governmental and non-governmental organisations working in the field of women and child development. Besides playing its nodal role, the Ministry implements certain innovative programmes for women and children. These programmes cover welfare and support services, training for employment and income generation, awareness generation, and gender sensitisation. These programmes play a supplementary and complementary role to the other general developmental programmes in the sectors of health, education, rural development, etc. All these efforts are directed to ensure that women are empowered both economically and socially and thus become equal partners in national development along with men.

Policy Initiatives

For the holistic development of the child, the Ministry has been implementing the world's largest and most unique and outreach programme of Integrated Child Development Services (ICDS) providing a package of services comprising supplementary nutrition, immunisation, health checkup and referral services, and pre-school non-formal education. There is effective coordination and monitoring of various sectoral programmes. Most of the programmes of the Ministry are run through non-governmental organisations. Efforts are made to have more effective involvement of NGOs. The major policy initiatives undertaken by the Ministry in the recent past include universalisation of ICDS and Kishori Shakti Yojana, launching a nutrition programme for adolescent girls, establishment of the Commission for protection of Child Rights, and enactment of Protection of Women from Domestic Violence Act.

Organisation of Autonomous Bodies Under MWCD

The Ministry of Women and Child Development has 6 autonomous organisations working under its aegis, viz.

- National Institute of Public Cooperation and Child Development (NIPCCD)
- National Commission for women (NCW)
- National Commission for Protection of Child Rights (NCPCR)
- Central Adoption Resource Agency (CARA)
- Central Social Welfare Board (CSWB)
- Rashtriya Mahila Kosh (RMK)

NIPCCD and RMK are societies registered under the Societies Registration Act, 1860. CSWB is a charitable company registered under section 25 of the Indian Companies Act, 1956. These organisations are fully funded by the Government of India and they assist the Department in its functions including implementation of some programmes/schemes. The National Commission for Women was constituted as a national apex statutory body in 1992 for protecting and safeguarding the rights of women. The National Commission for Protection of Child Rights is a national level apex statutory body constituted in the March 2007 for protecting and safe guarding the rights of children.

Subjects Allocated to the Ministry

- Welfare of the family
- Women and Child Welfare and Coordination of activities of other Ministries and Organisation in connection with this subject
- References from the United Nations Organisations relating to traffic in Women and Children
- National Nutrition Policy, National Plan of Action for Nutrition, and National Nutrition Mission.
- Charitable and religious endowments pertaining to subjects allocated to this Department
- Promotion and development of voluntary effort on the subjects allocated to this Department

Implementations of the Ministry

- Immoral Traffic in Women and Girl Act. 1956 (as amended upto 1986).
- The Indecent Representation of Women (Prevention) Act, 1986 (60 of 1986).
- The Dowry Prohibition Act. 1961 (28 of 1961)
- The Commission of *Sati* (Prevention) Act, 1987 (3 of 1988), excluding the administration of criminal justice in regard to offences under these Acts.
- Implementation of the Infant Milk Substitutes, Feeding Bottles and Infant Food (Regulation of Production, Supply and Distribution) Act, 1992 (41 of 1992).
- Coordination of activities of Cooperative for Assistance and Relief Everywhere (CARE)
- Planning, Research, Evaluation, Monitoring, Project Formulations, Statistics and Training relating to the welfare and development of women and children, including development of gender sensitive data base.
- United Nations Children's Fund (UNICEF)
- Central Social Welfare Board (CSWB)
- National Institute of Public Cooperation and Child Development (NIPCCD)
- Food and Nutrition Board (FNB)
- Nutrition Extension
- Womens Empowerment and Gender Equity
- National Commission for Women.
- Rashtriya Mahila Kosh (RMK)
- The Juvenile Justice (Care and Protection of Children) Act, 2000 (56 of 2000)
- Probation of Juvenile offenders
- Issues relating to adoption, Central Adoption Resource Agency and Child Help Line (Childline)
- The Children Act, 1960 (60 of 1960)
- The Child Marriage - Restraint Act, 1929 (19 of 1929)

7

EFFECTS OF GLOBALISATION ON INDIAN SOCIETY

"Global interaction, rather than insulated isolation, has been the basis of economic progress in the world. Trade, along with migration, communication, and dissemination of scientific and technical knowledge, has helped to break the dominance of rampant poverty and the pervasiveness of 'nasty, brutish and short' lives that characterised the world. And yet, despite all the progress, life is still severely nasty, brutish and short for a large part of the world population. The great rewards of globalised trade have come to some, but not to others."
Nobel Laureate and Economist Amartya Sen

DEFINITION AND CONCEPT OF GLOBALISATION

Globalisation can simply be defined as the growth and acceleration of economic and cultural networks which operate on a worldwide scale and basis. It is a process of interaction and integration among the people, companies, and governments of different nations, a process driven by international trade and investment and aided by information technology. From time immemorial, countries have been doing trade with one another. This process however has got an unprecedented boost in the last two decades. This has been primarily credited to the policies of International Monetary Fund, World Bank, and the World Trade Organisation who have been the working on a broad agenda of developed countries like USA, Germany, China etc. They are believed to entice underdeveloped countries to adopt globalisation by opening up their local markets to world trade. Development of advanced means of communication and transport, internationalisation of financial markets, and tremendous mobility of goods, and manpower have further boosted the recent process of globalisation.

Globalisation initially started as trade relations only. But the process has gradually incorporated national and regional economies, societies, and cultures through global network of trade, communications, and migrations. It is believed that there are above 200 million migrants around the world today who moved from underdeveloped countries to developed countries. In addition, there is a large transnational workforce. These phenomena have changed the sociocultural face of various countries the world over. This process has had its effect on the environment, on culture, on political

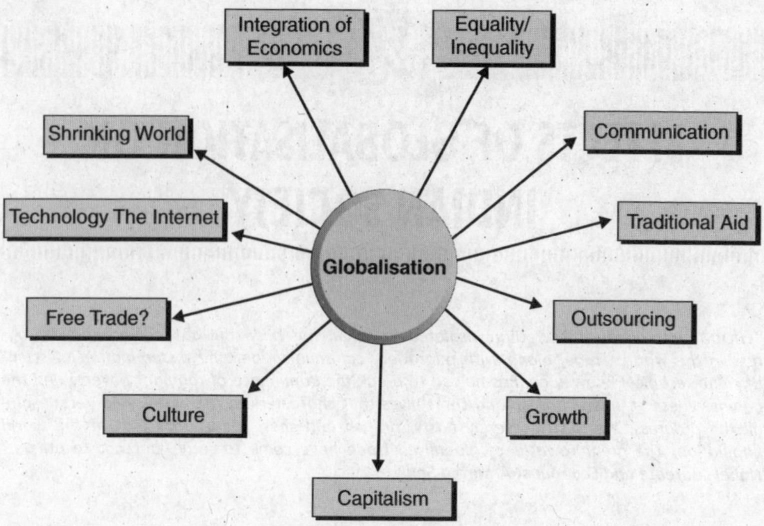

systems, on economic development and on physical well-being of humans in societies around the world.

People have travelled for thousands of years such as through the famed Silk Road across Central Asia that connected China and Europe during the Middle Ages is for trade and commerce. What marks a difference technological developments of the past few centuries have spurred increases in cross-border trade, investment, and migration to such a large extent that many observers believe the world has entered a qualitatively new phase in its economic development.

GLOBALISATION AND PUBLIC POLICY

The Reforms of 1991

The new model of economic reform of India is commonly known as the LPG or Liberalisation, Privatisation, and Globalisation. The economy of India had undergone significant policy shifts in the beginning of the 1990s after the 1991 liberalisation. The primary objective of this model was to make the economy of India the fastest developing economy in the globe with capabilities that help it match up with the biggest economies of the world. Thus, many interlinked reforms took place in policies related to business, manufacturing, and financial services industries targeted at boosting the economy of the country.

The economic liberalisation in India denotes the continuing financial reforms which began since July 24, 1991. Privatisation refers to the participation of private entities in businesses and services and transfer of ownership from the public sector (or government) to the private sector as well. Globalisation stands for the consolidation of the various economies of the world. Before the sweeping wave of globalisation, India had socialistic economic strategies. In 1991, the country experienced a balance of payments crisis due to the Gulf War and the segregation of the erstwhile Soviet Union. The country had to make a deposit of 47 tonnes of gold to the Bank of England and 20 tonnes to the Union Bank of Switzerland. This was necessary under a recovery pact with the IMF or International Monetary Fund. Furthermore, the International Monetary Fund forced India to undertake a sequence of systematic economic restructuring. This was the situation that led the then Prime Minister, P V Narasimha Rao initiating the unprecedented economic reforms. Dr Manmohan Singh, the then Finance Minister of the Government of India played a key role in implementing these reform policies. *The recommendations of the Narasimha Rao Committee were as follows*:

- Introduction of the Security Regulations (Modified) and the SEBI Act of 1992 which rendered the legitimate power to the Securities Exchange Board of India to record and control all the mediators in the capital market.
- Removing the Controller of Capital matters in 1992 that determined the rates and number of stocks that companies were supposed to issue in the market.
- Initiating the National Stock Exchange in 1994 in the form of a computerised share buying and selling system. This impacted the restructuring of the other stock exchanges in the country. By the year 1996, the National Stock Exchange became the biggest stock exchange in India.
- Making available the equity markets of the country for investment through overseas corporate investors by 1992. The companies were allowed to raise funds from overseas markets through issuance of Global Depository Receipts (GDRs).
- Promotion of Foreign Direct Investment (FDI) as means for raising the highest cap on the contribution of international capital in business ventures or partnerships to 51% from 40%. In high priority industries, 100% international equity was allowed.
- Cutting down duties from a mean level of 85% to 25%, and withdrawing quantitative regulations. The Rupee or the official Indian currency was turned into an exchangeable currency on trading account.

- Reorganisation of the methods for sanction of FDI in 35 sectors. The boundaries for international investment were defined.

The outcome of this bold restructuring can be estimated by the fact that the overall amount of overseas investment (comprising portfolio investment, FDI, and investment collected from overseas equity capital markets) rose to $5.3 billion in 1995–1996 in the country) from a pitiable US $132 million in 1991–1992. Narasimha Rao did away with the License Raj, leaving just 18 sectors which required licensing. Control on industries was moderated.

The wave of reforms, thus, brought about a sea change in public policies of India that has had a lasting impact on the lives of its citizens.

GLOBALISATION AND INDIA

Globalisation, liberalisation, and privatisation are the three pivotal elements of the New Economic Policy (NEP) introduced in 1991. Globalisation has enabled the increasing integration of Indian economy with the world economy through the reduction in import duties and export restrictions, promotion of the foreign investment, and permission for the flow of foreign technology and skills. Liberalisation has, to a large extent dismantled bureaucratic regulations and control on private enterprises. Privatisation has involved the private sector in the ownership and operation of state-owned undertakings. This consequently leads to denationalisation of important state-owned sectors of the Indian economy. The primary aim of these economic reforms policies was to achieve higher rate of national per capital income, full employment, self-reliance, and reduction of inequalities and poverty. Thus, globalisation impacts individuals, institutions, societies, and nations.

However, social observers often express that globalisation usually benefits people who are at the helm and not so much as those at the bottom and those who make livelihood through traditional means of production. Tom McCallie Executive Director of the Maclellan Foundation lists changes which are taking place, such as nation states to networks, export-led to consumer-driven, farms to super cities, labour intensive to high-tech, male dominance to emerging women, West to East, etc. These are the world trends, markedly impacting Asia, and especially the people of India and China. These cause certain challenges in future in areas like urbanisation, anarchy and crime and increased inequality of income. This will result in decentralised and diminished government power, migration of the people, environmental pressures, information explosion, and increased use of English. In "New Horizons", Manohar Samuel, in his article, "contemporary India and popular culture", speaks of great changes that occurred in India's socio and cultural aspects. Modern India is emerging with its liberalisation and market reforms, as one of the dynamic major Asian economies. It is leading in several areas—its indigenous-built communications satellites have been successfully launched, it has the best manpower for computer software in the world, its telecommunication technology has successfully reached the most remote rural areas, and it has a strong army too. Yet, it is considered as one of the poorest countries in the world, with a population touching 1.25 billion and it is a country with a high illiteracy rate. This has led to the over-exploitation of natural resources of this country, damage to the environment, pollution, and other evils. The impact of globalisation on Indian society can be gauged through the following observation by Stephen Cohen, "India is an ancient state, but a modern civilisation" (Cohen 2001:36). That is, globalisation has touched every aspect of Indian life, yet the country has been able to maintain its uniqueness. India's traditional acceptance of diversity is still influenced by a lot of different religions, languages, and traditions. Additionally, due to globalisation, the western values are gaining acceptance in India like never before.

GLOBALISATION AND ITS IMPACT ON THE ECOSYSTEM

According to the National Footprints Accounts (2014), India has an ecological footprint of 1.12 global hectares (gha) per person and a biocapacity of 0.45 gha per person which means it is a 'biocapacity debtor' or an 'ecologically deficit country' with there being a 148 per cent more demand than supply on its natural resources. There are ways in which ecologically deficit countries can balance themselves including by increasing their net imports over exports, minimising the overuse of their ecosystems and using the global commons by carbon debiting. The footprint of the richest 1% (inclusive of the wealthiest) of Indians is two-thirds that of the average citizen of a rich country and over 17 times that of the poorest 40% of people in India. Thus, a person who owns a car and a laptop in India consumes roughly the same resources as 17 poor Indians. Such a person consumes roughly the same resources as 2.3 average "world citizens" (the world per capita income being about $10,000 per person per year).

According to the Ministry of Environment & Forests (MoEF) State of Environment Report 2009, the "food security of India may be at risk in the future due to the threat of climate change leading to an increase in the frequency and intensity of droughts and floods, thereby affecting production of small and marginal farms." A significant decrease in crop yields is expected across the country. While India's present share of global carbon emissions is about 8%, as a rapidly growing economy it is rising every year. India's per capita emissions are expected to triple by 2030 if present trends continue.

India derives more than half its energy from coal. According to Coal India, which handles most of India's coal mines, our usable coal reserves are not as large as was previously believed. At current rates of growth these are likely to last just about 80 years. At projected rates of growth, they will finish in just 3–4 decades. And yet, the budget for non-conventional energy sources in India is only 1.28% of the total energy budget.

Impact on Water Supply

Chronic water shortages are affecting ever more regions of the country. India has the highest volume of annual groundwater overuse in the world. Water mining is taking place at twice the rate of natural recharge in many parts of the country. As aquifers have begun to dry up, water tables have dropped, sometimes (as in Punjab) at the rate of 3–10 feet per year! As temperatures rise on account of climate change, the per capita availability of water in India is expected to fall from 1,820 cubic metres per annum in 2001 to 1,140 cubic metres per annum in 2050. The number of rainy days every season could fall by 15, even as the intensity of rain increases on the rainy days. 2009 was one of the worst drought years in India in the past several decades. The overall shortfall of monsoon rains was over 20%, and significantly more in some of the agricultural regions of the country like Western UP and Punjab. This has had significant consequences for agriculture. Topsoil is critical to agricultural productivity. According to the Indian Council of Agricultural Research (ICAR), 16 tons of topsoil per hectare are being lost annually, or about 5 billion tons across the country. It takes millennia for the topsoil to form.

Impact on Forests

Between 1990 and 2000, the annual rate of afforestation was 0.57% every year. This fell to 0.05% between 2000 and 2005. Less than 12% of India's land mass is under "dense" or "moderately dense" forest. An equal area is "open forest" or "scrub". Of the total forest land diversion that has taken place since 1980–81, about 55% has been after 2001; about 70% of the forest land diverted for mining since 1980–81, came between 1997 and 2007. Globalisation has once again led to rapid deforestation and land degradation, phenomena that were more under control in the 1980s. India is one of the most biodiverse parts of the world, with over 130,000 plant and animal species, and immense diversity in crops and livestock. According to the MoEF, at least 10% of both flora and fauna in the country find themselves on the list of "threatened species", without taking account of climate change.

But if a 2°C warming happens, India will lose 15–40% of its species. "The creation of valley bottom reservoirs in wilderness areas has brought on the destruction of some of finest forests and biodiverse-rich unique ecosystems. Deforestation due to hydropower and mining projects is perhaps the greatest threat to biodiversity in India." Many of the country's numerous sacred groves, or other community conserved areas, protected traditionally by rural communities have come under threat because of the onslaught of economic growth. Around 70% of the Indian population depends on land-based occupations, forests, wetlands, and marine habitats and are thus directly dependent on local ecosystems for their basic subsistence requirements with regard to water, food, fuel, housing, fodder, and medicine. Around 10,000 species of plants and a few hundred animal species are involved in this direct relationship of biodiversity and livelihood. Ecological destruction directly affects these people's lives and livelihoods.

Impact on Marine Environment

India's 7500-km-long coastline has 12 major and 185 minor ports, and dozens of oil refineries and petrochemical or other hazardous industries along the coast. Many more are in the pipeline, with consequences for marine ecosystems and beaches. According to the Central Pollution Control Board, the 187 coastal towns and cities release 5.5 billion litres of wastewater into the ocean every day. 250 million people live along the Indian coastline, many of them in fishing villages which number 3,600. There are also over 4,000 sq. kms of mangrove forests, crucial in protection against cyclones. Traditional livelihoods like fishing and sensitive marine ecosystems are both coming under severe threat as India's economic growth makes ever greater demands on resources.

Impact on Hazardous Waste

India has become the largest producer of e-waste after China and the United States. More than 95 per cent of this waste is handled by the informal sector, which only adds to the problem. According to a Central Pollution Control Board report, in financial year 2019-2020, India generated 1,014,961.2 tonnes of e-waste for 21 types of electrical and electronic equipment (EEE).

The enormous generation of e-waste is not a new issue, but it has resurfaced in the discourse of climate change. According to a survey, 78 per cent respondents agreed with the statement: "COVID-19 caused unnecessary short-term investment in technology, which leave us at risk with data being stored on a wide range of devices."

Over the last few years the MoEF has issued permits to several companies to import thousands of tons of toxic e-waste into India. Import of several kinds of hazardous and toxic wastes has risen phenomenally in the globalisation phase. Plastic wastes, for instance, jumped from 101,312 tonnes in 2003–04 to 465,921 tonnes in 2008–09. Thousands of tonnes of metal waste imported into the country includes the remains of wars in Africa and west Asia, with unexploded devices blowing up every once in a while in recycling units.

According to the Environmental Action Group *Kalpavriksh*, the Indian government clears 3 mining, industrial, or infrastructure projects a day! It has over 6,000 projects to monitor through 6 regional offices and a staff of 2–4 officers per office for the task. Projects granted environment clearances are monitored once in 3–4 years. All this makes compliance with necessary environmental laws all too rare. And to make clearances easier, there have been over 30 changes (mostly dilutions) of relevant notifications (Environment Impact Assessment, and Coastal Regulation Zone, both under the Environment Protection Act) in the last decade or so. Despite impressive growth of several sectors in India, the share of the country's budget going directly into environmental work and regulation has remained extremely low (well below 1%).

ECONOMIC DIMENSIONS OF GLOBALISATION

Globalisation is believed to have set its foot in India when the oil crisis in 1970's and various other factors had created financial emergency around 1990. At this time foreign currency reserves were reduced to only 3 weeks of imports. A stagnant economy, mounting fiscal deficits, in international trade, and high rate of inflation during the preceding many years were the factors that lead to such a crisis. Fiscal deficit had touched 8.4% of GDP during 1990–91.Current account deficit was about 3.3% of GDP while rate of inflation was as high as 10%. In such a situation, some drastic structural changes in Indian economic policies was inevitable. At this point, the Indian Government had no option but to accept the precondition of joining the stream of globalisation so as to be able to avail loan/grant facility from the World Bank. For this, it agreed to reduce quantitative restrictions imposed through a licensing system. It also agreed to reduce custom duties in phases to levels acceptable to the WTO.

However, realising that globalisation alone may not help the ailing Indian economy, the then Government of India decided to go for privatisation of its economy and to adopt liberalised economic policies. *Some steps towards these structural changes were:*

- Virtual abolition of Industrial Licensing of the Licence Raj
- Free access to foreign technology
- Abolition of Government control over capital issues and creation of SEBI to encourage equity culture in India
- Sharp reduction in industries reserved for the public sector
- Decision to go for partial disinvestment in public sector enterprises

Some Positive Effects of Globalisation on the Indian Economy

Policies of privatisation and liberalisation of economy, along with the process of globalisation, had a cascading effect on the Indian economy. Fiscal deficit immediately came down to 5.9% in 1991–92 itself. The real GDP increased at an annual rate of about 6%. Some of the positive developments that happened right after this were that many new companies were formed by Indian entrepreneurs across different industrial segments in view of liberalised economic policies announced by Government and a large number of high paying job opportunities became available in India. This resulted in sharp growth in Middle Income Group which, in turn, fuelled domestic consumption. Liberalised policies on foreign direct investment (FDI) and Foreign Institutional investment (FII) helped in faster developments in telecommunication, roads, ports, airports, insurance, and other major sectors.

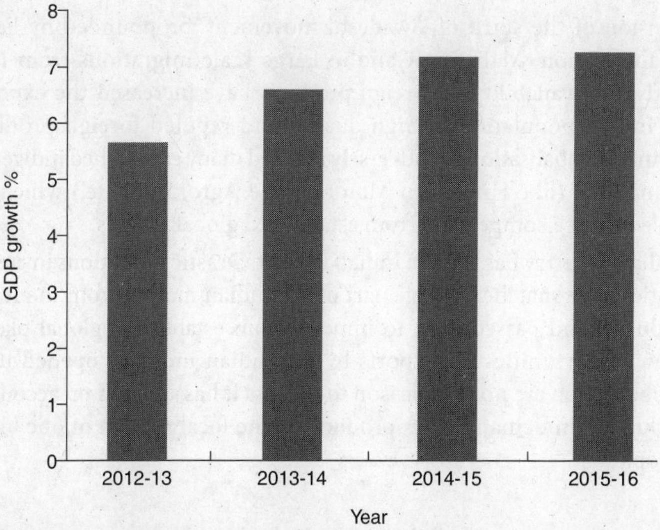

The Indian economy recorded the most impressive growth rates in its history during 2003–08, averaging 8–9% per annum. However, this performance was adversely affected by the great financial crisis that began in the West in 2007–08. During 2008–12, India's GDP growth rate fluctuated between 6.7–8.4% p.a. After the Eurozone crisis of 2012, and partly also on account of the stagnation in manufacturing and agriculture within the Indian economy, growth rates have fallen to even lower levels. It slipped to 5.3% in the fourth quarter of 2011–12, lowest in nearly 9 years. Farm output also exhibited a similar trend and expanded by just 1.7% during the quarter, compared to 7.5% during 2010–11. The graph given in this section displays the average GDP growth rate from 2012-16.

Some Negative Effects of Globalisation on the Indian Economy

Despite some positive trends and growth, there have been some not-so-encouraging effects of globalisation on the Indian economy too. *A few such developments are:*

- Indian economy and world economy have become interdependent. As a result, it has become difficult for the Government of India to insulate its economy from the world economy. Government is no more the sole driver of the Indian economy. Rather, Indian economy is increasingly influenced by international policies and international economic conditions. Direction and depth of all economic activities in India is now governed largely by the global economy.
- Erosion of the spirit of 'Swadeshi movement' propounded by Father of the Nation, Mahatma Gandhi. Large scale migrations from India and easy availability of foreign products have increased the exposure of Indian population to high quality and reputed foreign products/ brands. Globalisation has adversely affected many established indigenous companies (like Hindustan Motors, Parle Agro, BPL, etc.) which had failed to face competition from established global players.
- Indian industry has lost the Indian market. Drastic reductions in custom duties have snatched a large part of the Indian market from the Indian industry and passed it on to imports from established global players. New opportunities for exports by the Indian industry opened up by globalisation are no comparison to the loss it has suffered on account of reduction in demand of its products in the local market of one billion people.

- Indian industries' transformation from labour intensive processes to capital intensive processes. For surviving the competition brought about by globalisation, Indian industries have adopted global technologies and automatic machinery. This has resulted in high rate of unemployment in India. Unemployment is the biggest challenge for Indian government today.

A globally connected world also means that any global threat would mean the shattering of the increasingly connected economies together. The outbreak of the recent COVID-19 pandemic is a testimony of the same. From the disruption of the global supply chain to the debacle of the tourism sector and manufacturing sector and a more entrenched dependencies among the developed countries over the developed ones are some of the repercussions of the pandemic that have impacted the entire globe. the pandemic has only exposed the fragility of the world order resulting from the impact of globalisation.

Globalisation can be called a double-edged weapon. It did help the Government of India to tide over its serious foreign exchange problem but also lead to handing over control of the economy to foreign players at the cost of the local industry.

SOCIAL AND CULTURAL DIMENSIONS OF GLOBALISATION

Introduction

Globalisation has ushered in an unprecedented transmission and exchange of ideas, meanings, and values around the world. This process has brought common consumption of cultures accross the world influenced diffused by the Internet, popular culture media, and international travel. The dissemination of cultures enables individuals to take part in extended social relations that cut across national and regional borders. Globalisation has increased crosscultural contacts. But on the flip side, it has decreased the uniqueness of communities. The emergence of certain cuisines such as like McDonald's and Starbucks is a visible aspect of cultural globalisation. Globalisation is expanding scope for art, music, cinema and theatre. UNESCO report showed that cultural exchange is becoming more frequent from Eastern Asia, but Western countries are still the main exporters of cultural goods. China, India are some of largest exporters of cultural goods, after the UK and US.

Positive Impact for India

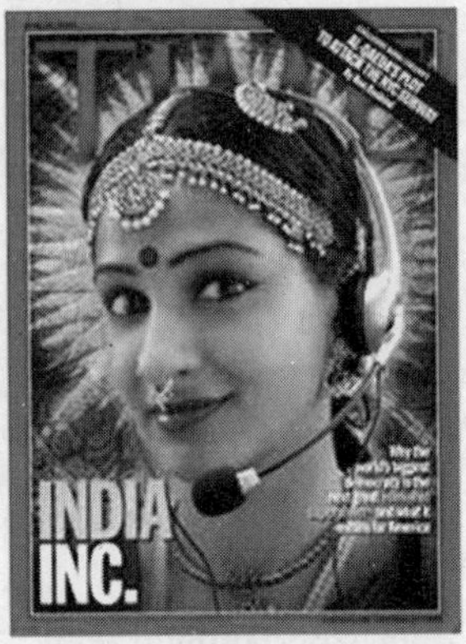

Globalisation ushered in improved economic conditions for the Indian society. It brought along with it an increased recognition of uniform human rights, unprecedented mobility, and interaction of people from different countries. These have had irreversible impact on the local cultures of people. Transnational workforce and large scale immigrants, a product of globalisation, are dispersing different cultures in various countries leading to a unified world culture that consists of a mixture of various regional cultures. Global population is getting closer to sharing similar social values, aspirations, attitudes, and lifestyles. Local culture, spiritual practices, and core social values have been getting reframed and a new meaning is being given to human life. Globalisation is responsible for changing people's outlook and lifestyle.

Negative Impact for India

The movements of people from rural to urban areas have accelerated, and the growth of cities in the developing world, especially, is linked to poor quality of life. Family disruption and social and domestic violence are increasing. Concepts of national identity and of family, job, and tradition are changing rapidly and significantly. There is also a concern that competitiveness introduced by globalisation is leading to more individualistic societies. Rapid changes are breeding fundamentalism, a desire for the past, and less tolerance for differences in religion and culture. The nation state is losing influence relative to global economic pressures. Countries are moving away from welfare oriented social policies. All of these changes increase the likelihood that vulnerable people will be exploited, and threats to the human rights of less able people will increase. It is believed by economists that the sub prime crises of 2008 was an example of the rapid spread of adverse human consequences because of the interdependence of economies and people. Thousands of people lost prosperity and livelihoods, and education and health services were among those cut across many regions. The effects, including social unrest and poverty, are still evident. Domestic violence and suicide increased in this period and illicit drug trade has grown in recent years to form a significant proportion of the total business volume in the world. All over the world, multinational companies are taking the lead in establishing themselves and creating a major presence in almost every part of the world. Coca Cola, McDonalds, and Nike are examples of such growth and proliferation. Slowly but steadily, the food that we eat, the clothes we wear, and the lifestyle we lead begins to change to become a part of global consumerism.

GLOBALISATION AND ITS EFFECTS ON AGRICULTURE

Introduction

Globalisation in the context of Indian agriculture is basically about adhering to the agreements with GATT and WTO in the traditional agricultural economy. There are three elements of this change, namely, (a) abandonment of channelising the trade to determine the value or the nature of the importance and exports (except onion, pulses, and edible oils), (b) dismantling of most of the quantitative restrictions on agriculture, and (c) reduction in tariffs. Thus, the Indian agricultural economy is by and large freely exposed to the world market forces which are mainly dominated by the economies of the developing countries.

Agrarian Structure and Indian villages

74% of the India's population lives in villages and their livelihood mainly depends on agriculture and the related activities. The village economy has been independent throughout the ages and even the industrial development has not reduced its importance. It played a crucial role in the economic development of India by providing food and raw materials, employment to 2/3 of workforce, capital for development, and surplus for national development. The Indian agrarian structure is dominated by 90% of small and marginal farmers (*Buggi et al.*, 2001). The extent of landholdings is associated with caste and social status. The small and marginal farmers and agricultural labourers constitute the vast majority of the rural society.

Impact and Implications

Globalisation resulted in the neglect of agriculture that adversely affected the vulnerable classes of rural society in their employment conditions, income and consumption pattern, their education, and health status. The small and marginal farmers are affected by a reduction in the fertiliser and chemical subsidies and in the budget of poverty alleviation programmes as well as by the shift of area under food production to export oriented commercial crops. The disintegration of rural economy brought about by globalisation lead to the disintegration of village communities, their society, culture, and religious aspects (A. Maria Alphorsal, *et al.* 2003).

Further, in the process of globalisation, the rural poor in developing countries would experience the dislocation of their economy in its totality for the first time in the history of their existence. This transformation is going to bring all the differences in future to come. The rapid changes in the size and nature of the economy would not allow the small and marginal farmers to make a gradual adoption. Lack of government intervention could make things worse. The absence of any clear cut vision about the adverse consequences of globalisation on the rural society, would ultimately result in the disintegration of the culture and traditions of the poor.

OVERALL IMPACT OF GLOBALISATION

Introduction

Indian society is drastically changing after globalisation and urbanisation. These forces have brought about remarkable changes in our culture. Economic policies formulated and executed by the government, have played an important role in the determination of levels of income, savings, investments, and employment in the society. However, it will be difficult for India to adopt to global changes without dealing with domestic problems like control of corruption, inequal distribution of resources, terrorism, providing employment to rural educated people, and work for the rural poor, empowering women and marginalised people, and providing reasonable price and market facilities for the farmers. In this backdrop, India must guard itself to not lose sight of its national interest.

Globalisation resulted in the neglect of traditional agriculture that adversely affected the vulnerable classes of rural society in their employment conditions, income and consumption pattern, and their education and health status. The small and marginal farmers are affected as there is a reduction in the fertiliser and chemical subsidies and shift of area under food production to export oriented commercial crops. The disintegration of rural economy brought about by globalisation lead to the disintegration of village communities, their society, culture, and religious aspects. Globalisation has also been attributed to commodification, and modern-day slavery of women in Asia, particularly in India. Globalisation has increased the migration to urban areas by the poor women in search of jobs. Hence, the rural people are shifting to cities and towns in search of labour for their livelihood.

Even though globalisation has brought a dynamic change to the economic life of India, it has also brought about polarisation of wealth and opportunities. India will gain, in true sense, if the national policies take adequate measures to maintain a balance. The dichotomy between urban and rural society must diminish to the extent of vanishing altogether. Modern industries could be split into various components which require simple industrial skills to be manufactured in rural areas by all those concerned through training, in addition to their own traditional skills. Planning for rural and urban growth should always ensure the vanishing of the urban–rural gap.

Positive Impacts of Globalisation

- Improved economic transactions resulting in rapid development of the capital market.
- Introduction of new modes of communication and technologies such as telecommunication, introduction of satellites, mobiles, etc.
- Modernisation of living standards.
- Bringing in of different ideologies and thought processes amongst people.
- Strengthening of democratic ideas and processes.

Negative Impacts of Globalisation

- Due to massive and rapid flow of capital amongst countries, it has introduced unfair and unequal distribution of income.
- Nations are losing identities because of too much exchange of trade, money, etc. and hence, independent domestic policies are lost.
- There is pressure of productivity and performance.

Rising Protectionism/De-globalisation

Protectionism is the economic policy of restricting imports from other countries through methods such as tariffs on imported goods, import quotas, and a variety of other government regulations. Unilateralism and protectionism prevent free trade and restrict economic flow. In India also, government actions and statements are inclining more towards the view that the Covid-19 pandemic has brought India's capabilities and need for more domestic production rather than unchecked globalization.

Globalization had already begun to plateau or stagnate since the 2008-09 global financial crisis (GFC). This is reflected in Brexit and US' America First Policy.

Further, trade wars and the halting of WTO talks is another recognition of the retreat of globalization. These trends pave the way for an anti-globalization or protectionism sentiment, which may further amplify due to the spread of the Covid-19 pandemic.

In India also, there were many actions associated more with protectionism that the government had initiated in recent times. Some instances include not opening up for imports, particularly after the Indian Government failed to agree on terms for a mini trade deal with the US; walking out of the 15-nation Regional Comprehensive Economic Partnership of Asian countries; and launch of the "Aatmanirbhar Bharat (Self-Reliance) initiative", after the beginning of the pandemic, was also perceived internationally as a protectionist move.

Many experts are suspicious of this new trend and rather suggest that contemporary issues are more interconnected and necessitate collective and globally coordinated actions. Thus, the shift towards protectionism is rather a dangerous trend. The issues of health hazards, rising inequality, climate change and climate-induced disasters require a seamless transaction of ideas, funds, technology and resources. At the same time, a balance needs to be found to keep the core interests of individual countries (especially the less developed countries) uncompromised. No model of development should lead to dependency and rather aim for an inclusive and just social order the world over.

8

PROBLEMS OF THE AGED

"The best people are the good old wrinkled people with a sparkle in their eye, a wink when you walk by or a toothless smile saying you are doing just fine...." —*Robert Wesley Miller*

INTRODUCTION

The law in India defines a "senior citizen" as any person being a citizen of India, who has attained the age of sixty years or above. The citizens of India are enjoying a longer life as a result of increased life expectancy, increased standard of living, as well as medical advancement. The longevity of life, if not planned well for retirement, could lead to a high fiscal burden for the individual and for the government on account of providing health care in the absence of proper insurance and inefficient public healthcare system. Despite the efforts by the Government to introduce new policies, the elderly lack the security needed in old age. Reports of financial deprivation, abandonment,

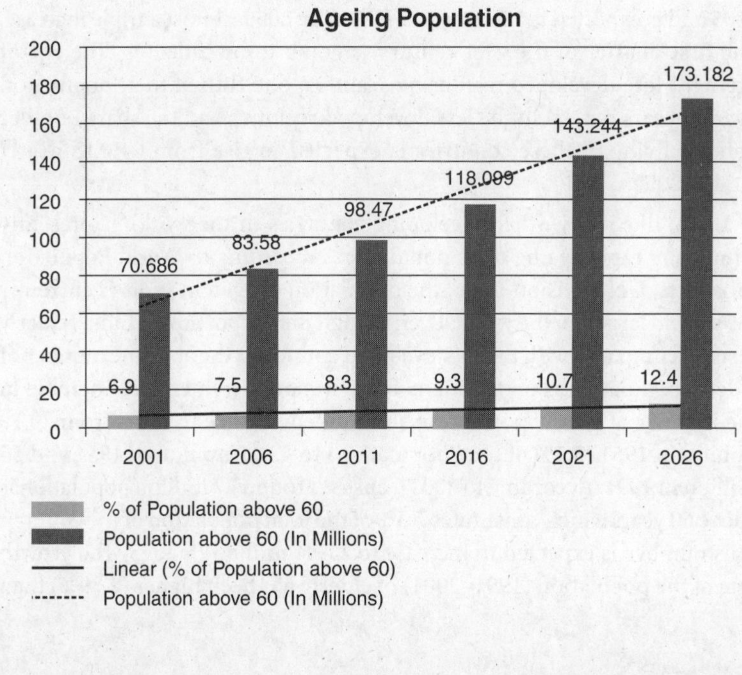

and humiliation have been increasing. India's elderly population (aged 60 and above) is projected to touch 194 million in 2031 from 138 million in 2021, a 41 per cent increase over a decade, according to the National Statistical Office (NSO)'s Elderly in India 2021 report.

NATURE OF THE PROBLEMS OF THE AGED

The process whereby the proportion of children in the population decreases and those of elderly persons increases is known as the "ageing of population". Population ageing is a global issue, which has been recognized to have implications on the healthcare and social welfare systems. The global population of elderly has constantly been increasing during the second half of the last century. This has been possible due to easy availability of life saving drugs, control of famines and various communicable diseases, better awareness and supply of nutrition and health facilities, and overall better standard of living than in the past. These achievements have resulted in drastic reduction in mortality rates and substantial increase in the life expectancy at birth and the overall longevity of people. This phenomenon has been experienced by developed countries in the mid of the 20th century. During the last thirty years, this has been emerging as a significant issue in the developing countries also.

The number of people 60 years and over in the globe was 673 million in 2005 and is expected to increase to 2 billion by 2050, almost a triple increase. The first quarter of the 21st century is going to be called as 'The age of ageing'. More developed regions have almost one-fifth of their population over 60 years but 8% in the less developed regions. And the share of older persons living in these countries is expected to rise from 64% to nearly 80% in 2050.

India, like many other developing countries in the world, is presently witnessing rapid ageing of its population. According to World Population Prospects, UN Revision, 2006, the population of aged in India is currently the second largest in the world. Even though the proportion of India's elderly is small compared with that of developed countries, the absolute number of elderly population is on the high. There has been tremendous increase in the number of elderly population since independence in India from 20.19 million in 1951 (5.5% of total population) to 43.17 million in 1981 and 55 million in 1991. According to 2001 Census , around 77 million population is above 60 years which constitutes 7.5% of the total population of the country. This number is expected to increase to 177.4 million in 2025. The growth rate of the population (1991–2001) of elderly has been higher (2.89%) than overall growth rate (2.02%) of the total population. The percentage share of the elderly population in the total population is said to rise from 8.6 per cent in 2011 to 10.1 per cent in 2021 and projected to touch 13.1 per cent in 2031, according to the National Statistical Office (NSO)'s Elderly in India 2021 report.

Defining the Concept of Ageing

Ageing is a continuous, irreversible, universal process, which starts from the conception of the individual till the death. However, the age at which one's productive capabilities declines and one tends to get physically and economically dependent can probably be treated as the advent of the aged stage of life. Old age is the final phase of the human life cycle, which is again universally true. The use of the words 'elderly', 'older persons', and 'senior citizens', in both popular and scholarly work gives the impression that they are a homogenous group. However, the fact is, there is considerable variation between and among various categories of older people and also between societies. As such it is difficult to provide a clear definition. Different writers have viewed ageing in different contexts as the outcome of biological, demographic, sociological, psychological, or other processes. *The WHO defines those aged 60–74 years as elderly and the various categories it defined are as follows:*

1. Young Old—between the ages of 60–75 years.
2. Old-Old— between the ages of 75–85 years.
3. Very Old—85 years and above

In the Indian context, the age of 60 years has been adopted by the Census of India for the purpose of classifying a person as old, which coincides with the age of retirement in the government sector.

Change in Social Structure and Institutions

Indian society is undergoing rapid transformation under the impact of industrialization, urbanization, technical and technological change, education, and globalization. Consequently, the traditional values and institutions are in the process of evolution. As a result, there has been an erosion of the intergenerational family structure that used to be the hallmark of traditional Indian families. With the advent of industrialization, mass production by the factories has corroded the simple family production units. Economic transactions are now between individuals. Individual jobs and earnings have given rise to income differentials within the family. Push factors such as population pressure and pull factors such as greater economic opportunities and modern communication have brought in migration, especially from rural to urban areas mostly among the youth.

With the rapid disintegration of joint families and increasing influence of newer lifestyles, the care of the elderly has emerged as an important issue in India. Providing care for the aged has never been a problem in India where a joint family system was dominant. However, with a growing trend towards nuclear family set-up, the vulnerability of the elderly is rapidly increasing. The coping capacities of the younger and elder family members are now being challenged under various circumstances resulting in neglect and abuse of elderly in many ways, both within the family and outside.

Sociologically, ageing marks a form of transition from one set of social roles to another. In an agriculture based traditional society, where children followed their parent's occupation, it was natural that the expertise and knowledge of each generation were passed on to the next, thus conforming value to old age roles. However, this is no longer true in the changed societal environment, in which improved education, rapid technical change, and new forms of organization have often rendered the expertise, knowledge, experience, and wisdom of older persons obsolete. This has ensued a feeling of loss of status,

With the rapid disintegration of joint families and increasing influence of newer lifestyles, the care of the elderly has emerged as an important issue in India. Providing care for the aged has never been a problem in India where a joint family system was dominant. However, with a growing trend towards nuclear family set-up, the vulnerability of the elderly is rapidly increasing.

worthlessness, and loneliness. The growth of nuclear families has also meant a need for changes in role relations. Neither having authority in the family, nor being needed, they feel frustrated and depressed. If the older person is economically dependent on the children, the problem is likely to become even worse. Nuclear households, characterized by individuality, independence, and desire for privacy are gradually replacing the idea propounded by the joint family set-up that considers family as a unit and demands deference to age and authority. When children migrate, old parents are often left behind in the village, causing problems of loneliness and lack of care.

Thus, the changing structure and function of family are altering the capacity of the family to provide support to the elderly.

Dimensions of the Age Problem

Often, old age ushers in disadvantages to an individual as the physical and mental capabilities begin to weaken. The disabilities that a person experiences in the course of ageing are multiple in nature. For some, ageing enhances status and enriches life satisfaction, but for many others, it may be difficult and problematic. On one hand, getting old provides opportunity to relax, enjoy and do things they always wanted to do, but never had the time for when they were young. On the other hand, old age also implies increasing physical, mental, and psychological disabilities. Such disabilities are the result of many factors. With the increasing age and decreasing health, the older person begins to depend unknowingly (physically and psychologically) on either the kinship group or the existing social support network.

Economic Problems

Economic dependence is one of the major factors that very often affects the well-being of older persons. Economic dependence is manifested in two ways: first, the status of economic dependence may be caused by retirement for a person employed in the formal sector. Secondly, for a person in the rural or urban informal sectors, it may result from their declining ability to work because of decreased physical and mental abilities. Sometimes, older persons are also faced with economic dependence when management responsibilities for matters relating to finances, property, or business are shifted to children, pushing the older person into a new status of economic dependence.

Psychological Problems

The common psychological problems that most of the older people experiences are: feeling of powerlessness, feeling of inferiority, depression, uselessness, isolation, and reduced competence. These problems along with social disabilities like widowhood, societal prejudice, and segregation aggravate the frustration of the elderly people. Studies report that conditions of poverty, childlessness, disability, in-law conflicts, and changing values were some of the major causes for elder abuse.

Health Problems

Health problems are supposed to be the major concern of a society as older people are more prone to suffer from ill health than younger age groups. It is often claimed that ageing is accompanied by multiple illness and physical ailments. Besides physical illness, the aged are more likely to be victims of poor mental health, which arises from senility, neurosis, and extent of life satisfaction. Most of the surveys in India reveal that elderly in general and the rural aged in particular are assumed to have some health problems like cough, poor eyesight, anaemia, and dental problems. The proportion of the sick and bedridden among the elderly is found to be increasing with advancing age, the major physical disabilities being blindness and deafness. Besides physical ailments, psychiatric morbidity is also prevalent among a large proportion of the elderly. Given the prevalence of ill health and disability among the elderly, there is also lack of the provision of medical aid, and proper familial care, in addition, while public health services are insufficient to meet the health needs of the elderly.

Almost eight out of ten older people in India live in rural areas. According to 2001 Census , 78% of elderly people in India resided in rural areas. Women comprise a slightly higher proportion than men, basically due to higher female expectancy at birth. Pervasive poverty and inequalities of income, coupled with a very inadequate safety net, has meant that majority of older persons become marginalized or even destitute. The poor among elderly people have been losing out even as economic development is taking place in the country as a whole.

This is a bigger problem in the case of women. Not only do women live longer but most of them are widows. They face serious discrimination with respect to their rights and are overburdened with familial responsibilities. This adversely affects their health, nutrition, and mental well- being. Irrespective of economic, marital, or educational status, elderly women face an emotional void in their life. This condition is explained by the 'empty nest syndrome'. The 'empty nest' period may indeed bring in depression in the course of their diminishing role in the family. Extra provisions of care and support are required to redeem them from their miserable plight. Approximately 99% of India's elderly population lives below the poverty line and 50% of them are widows. They are especially vulnerable to poverty, inadequate care, and neglect in old age. The tradition of women marrying men older than them by several years, the increasing life expectancy of women, social disapproval of widow remarriage, patrilineal inheritance, and problems of finding employment all render widows more vulnerable than most other groups in the society. Their situation become worse when they own very little or no assets of their own and do not have an independent source of income. Single persons, particularly women are more vulnerable in old age as few people are willing to take care of non-lineal relatives.

Problems Faced by Individual Aged

S.No.	Problem	Need
1	Falling health	Health security
2	Economic insecurity	Economic security
3	Isolation	Inclusion
4	Neglect	Care
5	Abuse	Protection
6	Fear	Reassurance

S.No.	Problem	Need
7	Boredom (idleness)	Engagement
8	Low self-esteem	Self confidence
9	Loss of control	Respect
10	Lack of preparedness for old age	Preparedness

Demographic and Socio-Economic Changes and the Aged

According to the 2001 Census, the total number of older persons in India was approximately 70.6 million and is expected to cross 173 million by 2026 as the life expectancy at birth is projected to increase to 69.8 years for males by 2021–25 (from 61.6 years in 1996) and 72.3 years for females (from 62.2 years in 1996). At the same time, the total fertility rate (TFR) declined to 3.2 per woman in 2001 and is expected to drop further, to replacement level, by 2021–25. However, this demographic transition is not taking place uniformly across all the states in the country.

The evolving population dynamics in India is significant that is arising out of the joint effect of declining fertility and increasing longevity and consequent shifting of the population age structure. Until recently, India, like other developing countries, had a young age structure with the median age remaining at about 20 years from 1961 to 1981, and increasing marginally to 22.5 years in 2001. However, the projections suggest that the country is gradually but surely transitioning away from a young age structure with a steady increase in the median age to 31 years by 2026. The index of ageing is the shift in the balance between the child and older populations and is expressed as the number of persons above 60 years for every 100 children below the age of 15 years. In India, the index of ageing increased slowly between 1961 and 2001, but is expected to increase more rapidly in the following 25 years. The UN population projections show that soon after the year 2050, the elderly population in the country will outnumber children (United Nations, 2010). This tipping point is likely to occur in India approximately five years ahead of the less developed regions as a whole.

DEMOGRAPHIC CHARACTERISTICS OF THE AGED

The population dynamics fuelling India's growth and changing age structure are rooted in the combined impact of increasing life expectancy and declining fertility. Life expectancy at birth in India climbed from 37 years in 1950 to 65 years in 2011, reflecting declines in infant mortality and survival at older ages in response to public health improvements. By 2050, life expectancy at birth is projected to reach 74 years. Fertility rates in India have declined to 2.6 children per woman, less than one-half the early 1950s rate of 5.9 children per woman. As India's population ages, the nation will face a shrinking pool of working-age people to support the elderly population. India's national trends mask tremendous regional variation. Fertility rates in India's southern states of Kerala and Tamil Nadu were a low 1.7 children per woman in 2009, while the fertility rates in the northern states of Bihar and Uttar Pradesh were twice as high. These stark regional differences will mean that the impact of a shifting age structure and population aging will not unfold uniformly throughout the country.

Growth of the Population of the Aged

Ageing of population is affected due to downward trends in fertility and mortality. Low birth rates coupled with long life expectancies, increase the population of the aged. It is observed that percentage of aged 60 or more is rapidly swelling and even the percentage of persons above age 80 is going up over the years. Simultaneously, the ratio of people of "working age" (15–59 years) to those of elderly population is shrinking—and even within the working age group, average age is also increasing. For the developing countries like India, the ageing population may pose mounting pressures on various socio-economic fronts including pension outlays, health care expenditures, fiscal discipline, savings levels, etc.

By 2026, north India population would be younger compared to the south. In India another paradoxical problem will arise in due course of time—by the year 2026 Kerala will have highest educated working people with average age hovering above (median age) 35 years whereas Uttar Pradesh will have uneducated and less educated working population with average age below 30 years. Although projections indicate that India's population above 60 years will be double in size between 2001 and 2026, the elders will account for 12.17% of the overall population in 2026, and being a vast country India may face the problems differently in rural and urban parts.

India will have another kind of a problem as despite rapid and consistent economic growth, it will have a huge ageing population who may be far poorer than their counterparts in the West.

In India, though percentage-wise greying population is not very rapid, but due to its huge size, planning for the elderly is a big challenge for the policy makers. The problems faced by the females are more critical compared to that of men due to low literacy rate, customary ownership of property by men, and majority of women not being in labour force during their prime age with only very few in the organized sector. Educating the masses with high investment in human resource development can overcome these problems up to a great extent.

As a by-product of the decadal Population Census operation, some important information is obtained on the share of elderly people in the total population and its change over time and across states, the size of the grey population and its sex ratio for various sub-populations, their literacy, and activity patterns. The Sample Registration System also undertaken by the Office of the Registrar General and Census Commissioner, India gives valuable data on life expectancy, age-specific death rates, etc. The last few rounds of the National Family Health Surveys provided data on the socio-economic and health condition of the elderly persons at the national and state level in India.

Dependency Ratio

The ratio of the dependent population to that of the working age population is defined as the dependency ratio and is an important indicator of the economic burden carried by each worker. The young age dependency ratio reflects the dependency burden from children below 15 years of age. Similarly, old age dependency is the ratio of persons aged 60 years and above to the working age population. In 2001, the total dependency ratio (from both the young and the old age-groups) was significantly high (73%) but is expected to fall to 56 by 2026. The young age dependency ratio is generally much higher than the old age dependency ratio since the population age structure in India has been young. As per the recent estimates, old-age dependency ratio (OADR) in India estimated as ratio of population 60+ to that of 15-59 years is found to be 0.14 and the old-age economic dependency ratio (OAEDR) is much higher at 0.23. Both OADR and OAEDR is highest in Kerala followed by Punjab and Haryana among the major states in India. Elderly dependency is high in most of the states and the economy is not prepared to bear the burden. While the young age dependency ratio is expected to decrease by 25 percentage points to 36.3 by 2026, the old age dependency ratio shows an increasing trend and is expected to increase by about 7 percentage points during the same period.

The 52nd National Sample Survey also assessed the problems faced by elderly men and women in obtaining the basic necessities of life such as food, clothing, and medical care. All the elderly were asked: "Are your day-to-day requirements on the following (food, clothing and medicines) adequately met?" In rural areas, around 3% of the females had difficulty in obtaining adequate food, 5% had difficulty in purchasing clothing, and 10% had difficulty in purchasing necessary medicines. The proportions are lower for males compared to females and lower in urban areas compared to rural areas. Nine percent of elderly males and 11% of elderly females in rural areas faced difficulties with regard to access to one of the three basic needs. The figures were 4% and 5% respectively for urban areas. Among rural females, Andhra Pradesh, Assam, Bihar, Tamil Nadu, and West Bengal reported that more than 10% of elderly had problems in adequately meeting at least one of their basic needs. A few states such as Gujarat, Karnataka, Kerala, Madhya Pradesh, and Maharashtra reported percentages between 5 and 10. Rural females are at a disadvantage compared to their urban counterparts. Large variations existed between states among rural females—from 3% in Punjab to 20% in Assam.

Sex Ratio

The growing number of women in older ages compared to men is an important concern for policy relevant research. The sex ratio shows an increasing trend from 94 women per 100 men in 1991 to 105 in 2011 and a projected 105 by 2026. Among the oldest -old, the sex ratio is expected to be as high as 136 women per 100 men by 2026. This trend poses more specific challenges relating to very old women who are also likely to be widowed. A major transition into old age occurs due to the loss of spouse that contributes to a feeling of increased insecurity among both men and women.

Widowhood

Widowhood is defined as the status of an individual who was legally married to someone who subsequently died. As per the 2011 census, there are 5.6 crore widowed persons in India. Women outnumber men accounting for

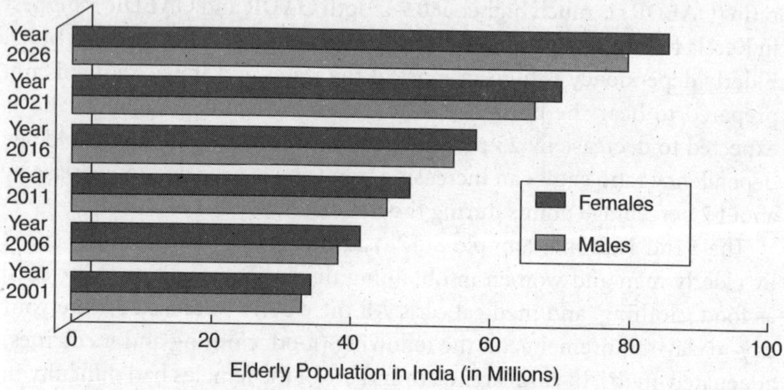

Source: *Report of the Technical Group on Population Projections constituted by the National Commission on Population, May 2006 published by the Office of the Registrar General, India.*

nearly 78% of total widowed population. Between 2001 and 2011, 89.71 lakh widowed persons were added.

Several factors may explain the imbalanced gender ratio among the widowed. Firstly, women experience greater longevity than men. The life expectancy in India has increased from 62.3 years for males and 63.9 years for females in 2001-2005 to 67.3 years and 69.6 years respectively in 2011-2015. Secondly, wives are generally younger than their husbands, a fact that increases their probability of surviving their spouses even without the differences in longevity.

The widows, as per Census data, can be seen from the age-group perspective also. 0.45% of the total widows are the Child Widows in the age group of 10-19 years. 9.0% are in the age group of 20-39 years, 32% in the age group of 40-59 years and 58% are above 60 years. Widows in different age groups face specific challenges pertaining to loss of adolescence, access to employment, skill development, property rights, shelter, access to healthcare etc. Further, it is indeed a matter of concern that we still have 1.94 lakh child widows despite the Prohibition of Child Marriage Act, 2006.

Major Concerns of Older Women

Destitution, alienation, isolation, and marginalisation in old age is among the most common issues that are affecting older women constantly. Older women, who are still living with their sons or daughters and grandchildren are also suffering from emotional alienation. Due to fast changing socio-economic scenario of the country, fast paced modern lifestyle, and rapid urbanization across the country, younger generations hardy interact with their elderly family members. Popularity of nuclear family system has virtually crushed strong traditional bonds between grandchildren and grandmothers.

Social Insecurity

Older women, who live in cities, are prone to social alienation/marginalization in comparison to older women of villages. Joint family system (to a certain extent) is still alive in rural areas. Older women, who live in semi urban situations/industrial townships find it difficult to cope with old age, particularly after their children have grown up and husbands retire. Due to lack of social protection, older women are forced to lead a life full of distress. Ignored by their own kith and kin, they do not expect any kind of social security from others.

Financial Insecurity

With increased lifespan of older women in old age, their financial needs are emerging as a major concern. However, today, many older women have property/money but they cannot possibly use the money or take financial decisions on their own. Social traditions do not allow them to use their ancestral property for their own welfare. They may be rich or poor; but they always have to act according to others' directives. Since they are habitual of sacrificing their own interests for the good of other family members throughout their life, in old age they do not want to ask for their share.

Medical Problems

Due to negligence, lack of awareness, financial support, and religious mindset of women, older women often have to face acute health problems. Since most of the older women are living within the four walls and barely come out in open public places, most of their health problems remain unnoticed. Their family ignores these—saying that in old age diseases are common. Older women living alone could not share their pain, since there is no one to lend them patient hearing. Above all, many times, due to lack of health awareness, older women themselves ignore symptoms of diseases. Most of them believe more in divine powers instead of medical science. In India, there are still a few religious sects that do not allow its followers to take particular medicines.

Emotional Insecurity

In old age most of the older women face family problems like uncomfortable relations with son and daughter-in-law, limited interaction with children, grandchildren, etc. Their daughters-in-law do not like their interference in family matters, children are busy with their jobs, and their husbands invariably have mood swings after retirement and mostly restrict their free movements.

Most old women are self conscious. In old age, women turn towards religious rituals and activities, pilgrimage, etc. after losing their life partner or any other family members. Many are from orthodox/religious background and have been following religious lifestyle since childhood. Since women have been emotionally attached to their near and dear ones throughout their life, in old age when they are not with them, they miss it a lot. Emotional support is much needed in old age.

ECONOMIC CHARACTERISTICS OF THE AGED

Economic status is a significant indicator to assess well-being of the elderly. Some of the aspects are mentioned below.

Work Participation

Place of residence	Gender	Population Census 2001	NSSO survey (2007–08)
Rural	Male	66	66
	Female	25	23
	Person	45	45
Urban	Male	44	39
	Female	09	07
	Person	26	23
Rural+Urban	Male	60	59
	Female	21	19
	Person	40	39

Percentage of elderly population working

A number of surveys indicate that about 60% of the elderly depend on others for their day-to-day maintenance while less than 20% elderly women and majority of elderly males, were economically independent. Amongst the economically dependent, 85% of men and 70% of women were supported by their children. Of the economically independent elderly, more than 90% supported one or more dependents. The table above shows that nearly 40% of elderly with 60 % being males were working and the proportion was higher in rural areas as 66% of rural men were working compared to 39% of urban men. The workforce participation of the oldest elderly (80 years and above) also is relatively high with 13% among men and 3% among women. It was reported that a majority of the elderly work due to economic necessity and not by chance or choice. India does not have a population-wide mechanism of providing social security because of which people work as long as possible to support themselves. A large population of the elderly continue to participate in the workforce with nearly 95% of them being self-employed. Also related to this is the issue of employer attitudes towards older workers. So, another reason for high self employment is that the elderly are discouraged by the employers because of declining health and energy. Majority of the elderly in India are reported in bad condition in terms of deprivation, though there is significant disparity across states, gender, and sector in case of different aspects of deprivation (Prasad, 2011). In most of the cases in India, women are disadvantaged compared to men, especially in urban areas. In India, number of female workers per 1,000 males is generally very low and therefore dependency is high. Further, women tend to live longer than men and have different medical requirements. That phenomenon also impacts the economic status of the elderly women in the family and they continue to be dependent on the male members in the family.

Economic Status

Asset Ownership by the Elderly

The ownership of assets is an important indicator of the financial well-being of individuals. Assets in the form of land, housing, and cash can provide a source of income for the elderly through rents, interest, dividends, etc. This source of income is advantageous as it has the potential of providing income for elderly persons without involving much labour. It also has the advantage of acting as collateral for loans. Further, asset ownership endows the elderly with status within the household as well as in society, especially in the case of women. Finally, the elderly who hold assets such as land in rural areas are more likely to co-reside with their children since land is usually passed down through the generations. Unlike assets belonging to the household, personal assets are the resources that the elderly can fall back on in times of need and which give them security.

Land

About 40% of all elderly reported that they own land which is either inherited (28%) or acquired (12%). More than half of all men but only about one-fourth of all women possess this asset, with more elderly inheriting it than acquiring it. About 38% of all men and 19% of all women own inherited land, while only 19% of men and 6 % of women own self acquired land. There is also a significant difference by place of residence—more land of both types is held by the elderly in rural areas since livelihoods are more dependent on agriculture and therefore land is an important resource. Thus, 45% of the elderly men in rural areas reported owning inherited land and 20% reported owning self acquired land compared to about 14% each in the case of elderly men in urban areas. It is interesting to note that 23% of the elderly women in rural areas also reported owning inherited land.

HEALTH CONDITION OF THE AGED

The First National Sample Survey (NSS) conducted during the second half of 1980s, focussed on the elderly and indicated that 45% of the elderly suffered from some chronic illness like pain in the joints and cough. Other diseases noted in the NSS survey included blood pressure, heart disease, urinary problems, and diabetes. The major killers among the elderly consisted of respiratory disorders in rural areas and circulatory disorders in urban areas. Another rural survey reported that around 5% of the elderly were bedridden and another 18.5% had only limited mobility. Given the prevalence of ill health and disability among the elderly, it was found that dissatisfaction existed among the elderly with regard to the provision of medical aid.

Schemes/ Provisions made by the Government to Improve the Condition of the Aged Persons

Ministry of Women & Child Development

The Government has been looking at the special position of widows and has initiated a number of interventions. Many state governments have formulated widow remarriage schemes. State governments have also formulated schemes for pensions to widows and for assistance to widows for the marriage of their daughters. Under MNREGA, special provisions have been made to identify widowed women who can then qualify as a household so that they are provided 100 days of work the death.

The Union Ministry of Women and Child Development has been giving emphasis to the issues related to widows for the last two years. One major issue faced by the widow is that after the death of her husband, she has to run from pillar to post to get her entitlements which often get delayed shows as she is unable to prove that her husband has died. Accordingly, the Ministry has undertaken a special drive with the state governments so as to ensure that the name of the widow is mandatorily mentioned in the death certificate of a man.

Keeping in view such circumstances, a new shelter home for widows is being established in Vrindavan, Uttar Pradesh which will have facilities for 1000 widows. This will be the largest ever Home for widows established or funded by the Government. It will be a Home with a difference since here widows will be able to learn and get skill development to enable them to use their time productively. The shelter home will give a new life to widows.

The recently announced Draft National Policy for Women places special emphasis on widows as a special category who need assistance, care and protection. The new policy will also bring about convergence on the issues of widows with single women as these cannot be addressed in isolation without referring to the issues concerning the broad category of single women which includes widowed, divorced, separated or never married. This will enable special attention to be given on the larger issue of vulnerability, both socio-economic, physical and psychological which single women including widows have to face.

However, there are certain challenges that require constant attention of the government. Effective implementation of Maintenance and Welfare of Parents and Senior Citizens Act, 2007 can automatically ensure a safety net of family care for widows. Universal coverage of pension for widows can bring sustenance and respectability for widows. It is important to encourage and incentivize couples to include the name of the wife into the title of her husband's land and property. This will be a protection for widows after death of her husband. There is a need to provide age relaxation for widows to sit for competitive exams for government and PSU jobs.

Ministry of Social Justice and Empowerment

The Umbrella Scheme of Atal VayoAbhyudayYojana, being run by Department of Social Justice and Empowerment, has the vision to create a society where senior citizens live a healthy, happy, empowered, dignified and self-reliant life alongwith strong social and inter-generational bonding. The Umbrella Scheme has the following welfare schemes for senior citizens:

1. Integrated Programme for Senior Citizens (IPSrC)

The Ministry of Social Justice and Empowerment implements a Central Sector Scheme namely Integrated Programme for Senior Citizens (IPSrC) under which grants in aid are given for running and maintenance of Senior Citizens Homes/ Continuous Care Homes, Mobile Medicare Units etc. to the Implementing Agencies (IAs) such as Registered Societies/ Panchayati Raj Institutions (PRIs) / Local bodies; Non-Governmental/Voluntary Organizations.

2. State Action Plan for Senior Citizens (SAPSrC)

Appreciating the critical and significant role of States/UTs, each State/UT is expected to plan and strategize taking into account their local considerations and frame their own State Action Plans for the welfare of their senior citizens. This State Action Plan may comprise a long-term strategy for five years as well as Annual Action Plans. Department of Social Justice and Empowerment releases funds to the States/UTs for formulation and implementation of their State Action Plans.

3. RashtriyaVayoshriYojana (RVY)

RashtriyaVayoshriYojana (RVY) is a Central Sector Scheme funded from Senior Citizens' Welfare Fund. Under the Scheme of RVY, aids and assistive living devices are provided to senior citizens belonging to BPL category or those senior citizens who earn less than 15000/- per month and suffer from age related disabilities such as low vision, hearing impairment, loss of teeth and loco-motor disabilities. The aids and assistive devices viz. walking sticks, elbow crutches, walkers/crutches, tripods/quadpods, hearing aids, wheelchairs, artificial dentures and spectacles are provided to eligible beneficiaries, free of cost. The Scheme is being implemented by Artificial Limbs Manufacturing Corporation of India (ALIMCO) which is a Public Sector Undertaking under the Ministry of Social Justice and Empowerment.

4. Livelihood and Skilling Initiatives for Senior Citizens

It aims to supplement the efforts of the senior citizens by providing them opportunities to enhance their earning and sense of self-respect. To encourage senior citizens of the country to form Self Help Groups for keeping themselves engaged for carrying out activities that may result into marketable products. This scheme has two programmes:

Senior Able Citizens for Re-Employment in Dignity (SACRED) portal – The portal allows bringing people together by virtual matching of preferences by providing the Senior Citizens a platform to connect with the private enterprises for certain positions. For this, the Ministry dedicated the SACRED portal (http://sacred.dosje.gov.in) to the Nation on 01.10.2021 on the occasion of the International Day of Older Persons.

Action Groups Aimed at Social Reconstruction (AGRASR Groups): The Senior Citizens are encouraged to form Self-Help Groups (SHGs), which will provide them with a platform to share the time constructively with each other. To attain financial assistance under the scheme SHGs will function as 'Action Groups Aimed at Social Reconstruction (AGRASR Groups)'.

5. Promoting Silver Economy

To promote out-of-the-box and innovative solutions for the commonly faced problems, innovative start-ups will be identified and encouraged for developing products, processes and services for the welfare of the elderly under this initiative. The selected start-ups/start-up ideas can be provided equity support of up to Rs.1 crore per project while ensuring that the total Government equity in the start-up should not exceed 49%. For this, the SAGE portal (http://sage.dosje.gov.in) has been launched on 04/06/2021.

6. Channelizing CSR funds for Elderly Care

This initiative is to channelize the CSR funds in an appropriate manner for elderly care projects. Under Schedule VII of Section 135 of the Companies

Act, setting up old age homes, day care centres and such facilities for Senior Citizens are approved items for CSR funding.

7. National Helpline for Senior Citizen (14567)-Elderline

The Ministry has set up the National Helpline for Senior Citizen for senior citizen to address the grievance of the elders. The helpline has been launched across the country and has been dedicated to the Nation by the Hon'ble Vice President of India on the occasion of the International Day for Older Persons i.e. on 01st October, 2021. The Elder line offers services to the senior citizens through toll free number 14567.

8. VayoshreshthaSamman- A Scheme of National Award for Senior Citizens

National Award for Senior Citizens 'VayoshreshthaSammans' are conferred to eminent and outstanding institutions or organizations and individuals from different categories. The VayoshreshthaSamman Awards are given on 1th October every year by Hon'ble President of India in a function organised at VigyanBhawan, New Delhi. The Awardees are given a Certificate, a Memento and also Cash Award in some of the categories.

9

MIGRATION

"As we encounter each other, we see our diversity—of background race, ethnicity, belief—and how we handle that diversity will determine in the end whether we will be able to rise successfully to the great challenges we face today."

—*Dan Smith*

INTRODUCTION

Migration is often defined as a move from an origin to a destination, or from a place of birth to another destination across international borders. Measures of global bilateral flows are often based on movements from a country other than a migrant's usual residence for a period of at least a year, so that the country of destination becomes the migrant's new country of usual residence. In developed countries, the idea of the migrant as a permanent, or at least long-term mover, is often institutionalized through flow data that admit people as immigrants as opposed to those who enter through a variety of non-immigrant or temporary migration channels. Thus, migration is often seen as a permanent move rather than a series of backward or onward movements. Studies of contemporary international migration show high rates of immigration to developed countries. For example, in 2010, the United States accepted 1.04 million persons under permanent immigrant categories while admitting 2.82 million temporary workers and their families. Australia admitted 213,409 migrants through permanent channels in 2010–2011, while temporary entry arrivals amounted to 504,671 persons. Canada admitted 280,681 persons in its immigrant channel against 383,929 persons in non-permanent categories.

Sociological Significance of Migration

Migration has played a significant role throughout history in shaping the world as we know it today. The phenomenon of migration has been indispensable to human histories, cultures, and civilizations. The connection between religion and migration is a cross-cutting issue throughout the history of major religions such as Christianity (the spread of Catholicism by Portuguese and Spanish during the 11th and 12th centuries), Islam (the first and second migration during Prophet Mohamed's time), and Judaism (the migration of Jewish from Eastern to Western Europe and overseas, and to the United States of America during the 19th century). Religion has been playing a fundamental role in not only triggering massive population movements, but also in influencing the lives and conditions of migrants in their displacement. Today, the 'meeting point' between religion and migration is at the core of contemporary migration debate. During the Age of Discovery (15th–17th century) many Europeans, with the Portuguese and Spanish leading the way, undertook maritime travels and explored the Americas, Africa, Asia, and Oceania. This transoceanic migration led to their discovery of new lands, the expansion of trade relations, and the development of the economies of both the countries of origin and destination. Commercial and strategic factors influenced migration in that period, as many European countries were competing to colonize strategic regions and territories. At the same time, in order to tackle labour shortages, the slave trade was introduced at various times throughout history, and subsequently abolished in the mid 19th century. A second wave of labour came from Europe, especially England, Spain, and Portugal, to what was then called "the new world" (i.e. USA, Canada, Australia, and southern Africa).

Migrants have been essential for the development of many modern states, have shaped labour dynamics around the globe, and have been a cornerstone for the global economy.

A great wave of migration subsequently took place in central Europe after World War I when populations resettled after the creation of many new States, especially following the dissolution of the Austro-Hungarian Empire. Another migration period of note was from about 1935 until after World War II when population movements occurred inside Europe. Migration at that time began with the expansion of Hitler's Germany and later through forced or inevitable evacuations with people attempting to escape from the war and the relocations which followed in its wake. Migrants have been essential for the development of many modern states, have shaped labour dynamics around the globe, and have been a cornerstone for the global economy.

In recent years, discussions have taken place on the linkage between migration and development in a number of forums and especially since the UN General Assembly High Level Dialogue on Migration and Development (GFMD) in 2006. Migration is a phenomenon, whose benefits can be maximised when countries of origin form dialogues and partnerships with countries of destination. Mexico, for example, as the 2010 Chair of the GFMD focused on improving the collaboration between countries of origin and destination and introduced the concept of shared responsibility, collective benefits, and partnerships. The linkages between migration and development are now recognized as being strong and diverse. However, there is an inherent vulnerability in being a migrant, which can be more problematic in some situations than others. Migrants, by definition, are 'outside their places of habitual residence' and often countries of origin (many times also away from their families), in a place where they might not understand the language and/or culture. They usually lack their familiar or community support mechanisms and can be exposed to racism, xenophobia, and discrimination.

CONCEPT OF MIGRATION

Migration can be defined as "a process of moving, either across an international border, or within a State and includes any kind of movement of people, it includes refugees, displaced persons, uprooted people, and economic migrants". Migration is certainly not a recent phenomenon; on the contrary, it has been part of the human history since its very beginning. People have migrated from one continent to the other, from country to country, or internally inside the same country.

According to International Organization of Migration, there are about one billion migrants around the world. This number includes 214 million international migrants and 740 million internally displaced persons. In an increasingly interconnected and interdependent world, with improved means of transportation and communication, international migration has been growing in not only magnitude but also scope, complexity, and impact. Today, most countries are simultaneously countries of origin, transit, and destination of migrants. Countries in both less and more developed regions face various challenges and opportunities associated with migration. Much of the growth in international migration has been regular migration, typified by the mobility of workers and their family members. The magnitude of undocumented migrants or migrants in irregular situations has also increased, while there are growing concerns that dislocations caused by environmental degradation and climate change could add to involuntary movements of people across international borders in the coming decades.

There has been a growing consensus that migration is an integral feature of global development. It is generally recognized that, if properly managed, migration can contribute to poverty reduction and improvements in human well-being in both sending and receiving countries. In sending countries, emigration can boost development through the beneficial use of remittances and diaspora investments, the alleviation of labour market pressures, and the contributions of the diaspora through knowledge, technology, and skills transfer. Returnees can also contribute to their countries of origin through innovation and investment capacities acquired abroad. Destination countries, on the other hand, can benefit from immigration through the alleviation of labour shortages, stimulation of job growth, and innovative behaviour of immigrants. International migration also contributes to social, cultural, and value exchanges between origin and destination countries. However, if not well managed, international migration can also have negative consequences, such as the loss of valuable human resources and skills in countries of origin or rising xenophobia, which can lead to poor integration, discrimination, exploitation, or even abuse in countries of destination.

FORMS OF MIGRATION

Migration of people, from one place in the world to another, occurs for the purpose of taking up permanent or semi permanent residence, usually across a political boundary. Example of "semi permanent residence" would be the seasonal movements of migrant farm labourers. People either move by choice—voluntary migration, or are forced to move—involuntary migration. Migration occurs at a variety of scales: intercontinental (between continents), intracontinental (between countries on a given continent), and interregional (within countries). One of the most significant migration patterns has been rural to urban migration—the movement of people from the countryside to cities in search of opportunities.

TYPES OF MIGRATION

Internal Migration

Moving to a new home within a state, country, or continent.

External Migration

Moving to a new home in a different state, country, or continent.

Emigration

Leaving one country to move to another (e.g., the Pilgrims emigrated from England).

Immigration

Moving into a new country (example, the Pilgrims immigrated to America).

Population Transfer

When a government forces a large group of people out of a region, usually based on ethnicity or religion. This is also known as an involuntary or forced migration.

Impelled Migration (also called "reluctant" or "imposed" migration)

Individuals are not forced out of their country, but leave because of unfavourable situations such as warfare, political problems, or religious persecution.

Step Migration

A series of shorter, less extreme migrations from a person's place of origin to final destination—such as moving from a farm, to a village, to a town, and finally to a city.

Chain Migration

A series of migrations within a f amily or defined group of people. A chain migration often begins with one family member who sends money to bring other family members to the new location. Chain migration results in migration fields—the clustering of people from a specific region into certain neighbourhoods or small towns.

Return Migration

The voluntary movements of immigrants back to their place of origin. This is also known as circular migration.

Seasonal Migration

The process of moving for a period of time in response to labour or climate conditions (e.g., farm workers following crop harvests, or working in cities off-season).

TERMS ASSOCIATED WITH THE PEOPLE WHO MIGRATE

Emigrant

A person who is leaving a country to reside in another.

Immigrant

A person who is entering a country from another to take up new residence.

Refugee

A person who is residing outside the country of his or her origin due to fear of persecution for reasons of race, religion, nationality, membership in a particular social group, or political opinion.

Internally Displaced Person

A person who is forced to leave his or her home region because of unfavourable conditions (political, social, environmental, etc.) but does not cross any boundaries.

Migration Stream

A group migration from a particular country, region, or city to a certain destination.

CHARACTERISTICS OF MIGRATION

In India, there are two main sources of data on population mobility. They are the Census and the National Sample Survey (NSS). However, these surveys may not reflect some migration flows, such as temporary, seasonal, and circulatory migration due to empirical and conceptual difficulties. Since such migration and commuting is predominantly employment oriented, the data underestimate the extent of labour mobility. Furthermore, migration data relate to population mobility and not worker mobility, although economic theories of migration are primarily about worker migration. Migration surveys give only the main reason for migration, and that too only at the time of migration.

Population Mobility

In India, studies show that the proportion of migrants of both sexes, in both rural and urban areas, increased during the last decade of the 20th century. Migration in India is predominantly short distance, with around 60% of migrants changing their residence within the district of enumeration and over 20% within the state of enumeration while the rest move across the state boundaries. A significant proportion of women migrate over short distances, mainly following marriage. For inter-state migration, it is observed that developed states show high inter-state immigration while poor states, except Madhya Pradesh, show low rates of total and male immigration.

Migration for Work

The primary motive for migration, recorded by the census as well as the NSS, is an important indicator of how mobility is influenced by conditions of the labour market. The proportion migrating for economic reasons is greater among long-distance migrants; most male migrants moving between states did so for economic reasons. An analysis of the occupational division of migrant workers (other than cultivators and agricultural labourers) shows that among males, 43% are engaged in production related work. In the tertiary sector, significant proportions of male migrants are engaged as sales workers, followed by clerical and related work. All the western states have a significant proportion of male migrants in secondary activity and in the southern and north-eastern states, they are mainly engaged in the tertiary sector. In the case of female migrant workers, 40% are in production related works and a significant proportion are in technical and professional activities. In the urban areas, the NSS shows a significant transition towards regular employment and self-employment among males, with a small decline in the percentage of casual labour. In the rural areas, there is an increase in all three categories including casual labour, but the most significant shift is towards self-employment. In the case of female migrants, however, along with an increase in the percentage of workers to population in all three categories after migration, there is also an increase in casualization both in rural and urban areas, but quite significantly in the former.

Short Duration Labour Migration

Short duration migration lack stable employment and sources of livelihood at home and belong to the poorer strata. These migrants find work in agriculture, seasonal industries, or are absorbed in the amorphous urban economy, either as casual labourers or as self employed. They may move from one type of job to another or even from rural to urban areas. There is another category of poor and destitute migrants who have virtually no assets in the areas of origin and have lost all contact with their origin. Thus, not all poor migrants would fall in the category of seasonal/short term migrants. The National Commission of Rural Labour (NCRL) made a quick estimate of such labourers based on their numbers in industries employing migrant workers. According to the NCRL, there were approximately 10 million seasonal/circular migrants in the rural areas alone. This included an estimated 4.5 million inter-state migrants.

REASONS FOR MIGRATION

People move for a variety of reasons. Some are termed as ***push*** factors and some as ***pull*** factors. Push factors are the reasons why people leave an area. Pull factors are the reasons why people move to a particular area.

Push and Pull Factors

Push Factors	Pull Factors
lack of services	higher employment
lack of safety	more wealth
high crime	better services
crop failure	good climate
drought	safer, less crime
flooding	political stability
poverty	more fertile land
war	lower risk from natural hazards

Migration usually happens as a result of a combination of these push and pull factors. *Several types of push and pull factors may influence people in their migration:*

1. Environmental (e.g., climate, natural disasters)
2. Political (e.g., war)
3. Economic (e.g., work)
4. Cultural (e.g., religious freedom, education)

Other Factors

Place Utility

The desirability of a place based on its social, economic, or environmental situation, is often used to compare the value of living in different locations. An individual's idea of place utility may or may not reflect the actual conditions of that location.

Intervening Opportunities

Opportunities nearby are usually considered more attractive than equal or slightly better opportunities farther away, so migrants tend to settle in a location closer to their point of origin if other factors are equal.

Distance

As distance from a given location increases, understanding of that location decreases. People are more likely to settle in a (closer) place about which they have more knowledge than in a (farther) place about which they know and understand little.

Economic Factors

Jobs and Education

The dictionary defination of an economic migrant is someone who goes to a new country because living conditions or opportunities for jobs are not good in their own country. This word is used by governments to show that a person is not considered a refugee (someone who has been forced to leave their country for political reasons). When Poland and seven other Eastern European countries joined the EU in 2004, the UK received many economic migrants. There were 500,000 workers from Eastern Europe in 2009. Some come for seasonal jobs while qualified migrants look for more stable jobs.

Migration is affected by several complex economic factors. Better quality of life, a chance at financial stability, and access to education are just some of the factors that contribute to immigration around the world. New immigrants are not the only ones who experience economic change when wide-scale migration hits; it also changes the economic landscape of their new home country and its inhabitants.

Salary

Wealthy industrialised countries offer far higher basic wages than developing and third-world economies. In addition, first-world economies also have a statutory minimum wage ensuring that even migrant workers from less developed economies receive a high basic wage. Migrants used to a lower standard of living will also be able to survive on less, enabling them to save or send money to their family back home. This can result in wage deflation, resulting in native workers being priced out of the marketplace, particularly in the manufacturing and agricultural sectors.

Welfare System

Economies with a highly developed welfare state, such as a benefit system for the unemployed and state-funded health care, are attractive to foreign migrants who are able to access quality services without having to pay exorbitant fees. In addition, immigrants with children may elect to take advantage of a subsidised education system of a far higher quality than even private institutions in their own countries. The economic consequences for the host country are potentially serious as large scale migration can strain welfare services. In reality, however, immigration to first-world countries almost always results in a net increase in tax revenues even taking into account increased pressure on the welfare state.

Economic Policy

The strictness of a given economy's immigration criteria have a significant impact on the amount and type of immigration they receive. Countries with a strict points-based system receive more skilled and highly skilled workers than low-wage manufacturing and agricultural labourers. In addition, a country signed up to a particular economic area may have little control over immigration. Countries within the European Economic Area (EEA), for example, are unable to prevent large scale immigration as there are no barriers to entry for any worker travelling between countries within the EEA.

Sociocultural and Political Factors

Family Conflict and Quest for Freedom

Sociocultural and political factors play important roles in migration. Sometimes, family conflicts and the quest for independence also cause migration, especially of those in the younger generation. Improved communication facilities, such as transportation, impact of television, good network communication, the cinema, the urban oriented education, and resultant change in attitudes and values also promote migration. Likewise, conducive or non-conducive political atmosphere encourage or discourage migration from one region to another.

According to the Organization for International Migration, there are approximately 192 million people who live outside their place of birth. A majority of these people are migrant workers and they make up 3% of the world's population. Human beings have always migrated from one place to another in search of better economic opportunities. But apart from economic factors, there are political factors that cause people to move from their home country to another country. War, persecution, and the absence of political rights are the predominant political factors in migration.

State Persecution

State persecution involves the harassment, discrimination, and torture of people who disagree with their government, have minority religious beliefs, or ethnic backgrounds. Because conditions in their country are unsafe, these people are forced to migrate to safer countries. Asylum seeking is a direct result of the outflow of political migrants from an oppressive state to a more democratic country. For example, in the year 2002, United Kingdom received the highest asylum applications: 555,310 or 15% of the total global asylum applications. These numbers which remain reflect the rise in claims of persecutions in countries such as Iraq, Zimbabwe, Somalia, Afghanistan, and China.

Lack of Political Liberties

The lack of political liberties and rights, and endemic corruption act as push factors for migrants seeking greater freedoms. Even though they are not persecuted in their places of birth, concerns that limit people's freedoms causes them to leave. If the political environment is hostile, then the economic situation is likely to be poor. This triggers migration for political and economic reasons. Most migrants leave for more democratic countries where they can pursue better careers, education, and freedom.

War

According to the National Geographic's Earth Pulse, there are approximately 42 million people worldwide who have been forced to migrate due to war. War and armed conflict have diverse causes but all these factors are influenced by political issues. War migrants not only migrate to the usual countries such as United States, United Kingdom, Canada, and Australia, they also migrate within their own geographical areas such as within their continent. Most war migrants become refugees or asylum seekers. Refugees International indicates that by the end of 2015, there were 65.3 million refugees globally.

Cultural-Political Factors

Political instability caused by cultural diversity causes people of a certain cultural affiliation to move within the country or away from their country altogether. As a result of wars or ethnic strife, ethic groups that were initially living apart can be forced within the same geographical boundaries. An influx of one cultural group can displace another group. Governments can also force cultural groups to move from one place to another (within or outside the country) to gain political advantage in having less cultural diversity.

CONSEQUENCES OF MIGRATION

There are conflicting views. One view is that migration adversely affects the welfare of the source areas because of increasing rural to urban migration in spite of rising urban unemployment, increasing environmental problems, overgrowing of population, and the shortage of urban amenities. Although the available urban opportunities and the rising wage levels in urban areas continue to be the main source of attraction for the migrants, the urban problems and the problem of shortage of labour in rural areas are aggravated more by the accelerating rural to urban migration. It is due to this reason that migration is viewed as adversely affecting the welfare of both the rural as well as the urban areas. The other view is that migration directly or indirectly takes care of the welfare of rural areas, and positively affects urbanisation, cultural transformation, and development.

Migration is a function of certain objective social conditions operating at the rural source and at the urban destination. Those conditions are generally referred to as rural push and urban pull factors of migration. The interplay of these push–pull factors plays an important role in determining the flow of out- or in-migration.

Migration is both a separative and additive process. It separates people from the place of origin and adds them to the place of destination. These functions of migration have important social consequences. The immediate effect of migration is the separation of individual migrants from the origin areas.

ECONOMIC ASPECTS OF MIGRATION

Source Country

Economic costs include

- The loss of young adult labour force
- The loss of those with skills and entrepreneurial talents, which may slow economic development
- Regions where out-migration takes place may suffer from a spiral decline that is difficult to halt
- The loss of labour may deter inward investment by private organisations, increasing dependence on governmental initiatives

Economic benefits include

- Reduced under-employment in the source country
- Returning migrants bring new skills to the country, which may help to revitalize the home economy

- Many migrants send remittances home and much of this money is reinvested in the some economy in projects such as new buildings and services
- There is less pressure on resources in the area, including basic supplies such as food essential services such as healthcare

Destination Country

Economic costs include

- The costs of educating the migrants' children have to be borne
- There is an over-dependence of some industries on migrant labour, e.g., the construction in the UK
- Much of the money earned, including pension payments, is repatriated to the country of origin
- Increased numbers of people add to the pressure on resources, such as health services and education

Economic benefits include

- Economic migrants tend to take up the less desirable jobs
- The host country gains skilled labour at a reduced cost
- The 'skills gap' that exists in many host countries is filled by qualified migrants
- Costs of retirement are transferred back to the source country

SOCIAL AND PSYCHOLOGICAL ASPECTS OF MIGRATION

Source Country

Social costs include

- The perceived benefits of migration encourage more of the same generation to migrate, which has a detrimental effect on social structure
- There is a disproportionate number of females left behind
- The non-return of migrants causes an imbalance in the population pyramid
- Returning retired migrants may impose a social cost on the community if support mechanisms are not in place to cater for them

Social benefits include

- The population density is reduced and the birth rate decreases, as it is the younger adults who migrate

- Remittances sent home by economic migrants can finance improved education and health facilities
- Returning retired migrants increase social expectations in the community, for example, the demand for better leisure facilities

Political effects include

- Policies to encourage natural increase
- Policies to encourage immigration to counteract outflow or to develop resources
- Requests for international aid

Destination Country

Social costs include

- The dominance of males is reinforced, especially in countries where the status of women is low—for example, in the Persian Gulf states
- Aspects of cultural identity are lost, particularly among second-generation migrants
- Segregated areas of similar ethnic groups are created, and schools are dominated by migrant children

Social benefits include

- Creation of a multi-ethnic society increases understanding of other cultures
- There is an influx of new and/or revitalized providers of local services—for example, spas, gymnasium, Turkish baths and local corner shops
- There is a growth of ethnic retailing and areas associated with ethnic food outlets—for example, the 'Curry' culture in Britain came from Asian Indian Migrants.

Political effects include

- Discrimination against ethnic groups and minorities which may lead to civil unrest and extremism
- Call for controls on immigration
- Entrenchment of attitudes which may encourage fundamentalism

PROBLEMS OF REFUGEES AND DISPLACED PERSONS

Refugee and human displacement have been a feature and consequence of conflict within and between societies. One key change in the twentieth century was the move by governments towards regulating migration, in particular immigration, and towards defining those who were to be granted the special status of refugees. The question of how governments regulate immigration and define categories of immigrants has, over time, led people to view migration as an issue related to the security both of the state and of existing citizens and legal residents. Simultaneously, there has been an evolution of security analysis that can shed new light and renewed attention upon the importance of refugees and human displacement in international relations and security. There have also been changes in the nature of the state, in socio-economic organization within states and at the international level, and in demography that indicate particular patterns contemporary forced migration.

Many scholars have opined that changes in economic environment and the reduction of state involvement have contributed to poverty and inequality, which may be an underlying cause of migration. In the developing world, traditional social support mechanisms have been dented by the modernisation of economic production. In many societies, localised high population density, in conjunction with environmental degradation and resource shortages, has rendered areas untenable for human support. Urbanisation, coupled with changes in social and economic organisation that have reduced the viability of rural lifestyles, has encouraged the movement of people into unsustainable urban lifestyles. All have been offered as underlying explanations for migration. The broader context for migration flow is often identified as being a consequence of globalisation, technological progress, and interdependence: easier and cheaper transportation across greater distances, a greater awareness of better opportunities "elsewhere", and a reduction of physical boundaries to movement in some regions of the world.

Irregular Migration and Refugees

- The actual number of migrants in irregular situation is difficult to determine, but it is believed to be significant. Irregular migration is a major concern for countries of origin, transit, and destination of international migrants.
- In 2011, out of 146 countries with data, three out of four Governments viewed irregular migration in their countries as a major concern. Governments of 22 of the 25 countries with the largest migrant stocks regarded irregular migration as a major concern. A growing number of Governments have responded to address irregular migration by reforming their immigration laws, promoting the return of irregular migrants, and implementing regularization programmes.
- Smuggled migrants and victims of trafficking are extremely vulnerable to severe infringements to their human rights. The exact number of victims

of human trafficking is not known. For example, in 2012, the International Labour Organization estimated that globally 20.9 million people were victims of forced labour, which included victims of human trafficking.

- Refugees and asylum seekers constitute an important component of migration flows. By the end of 2015, an estimated 50 million people were refugees, including 20.2 million fleeing wars and persecution the most since 1992. Today one in every 122 humans is someone who has been forced to flee their homes.

MIGRATION POLICY

International Migration

As the world's largest origin for international migrants, India has a rich history of immigration and emigration. The massive India diaspora, which can be found across the globe, includes millions of descendants of migrants and has taken shape mostly since the start of the colonial era, when large numbers of Indians were forcibly relocated to work on plantations and construction projects.

More recently, the Middle East and Western countries have been top destinations for Indians abroad. Slightly more than half of India's 17.9 million emigrants in 2020 lived in Persian Gulf countries, with nearly 3.5 million in the United Arab Emirates alone. Many have moved abroad for employment purposes; India is a significant source for low- and semi-skilled workers, as well as professionals in the health-care and science, technology, engineering, and math (STEM) fields

Over time, the Indian government has built multiple systems for engaging with its emigrant population and the many descendants who call India their ancestral home. Money sent as remittances represents a prime tactic for improving financial conditions and diversifying risk, particularly in rural households. The estimated U.S. $87 billion in official remittances received in India in 2021 represented the world's largest such flow and amounted to nearly 15 percent of all global transfers to low- and middle-income countries, according to the World Bank. India has also sought to capitalize on the skills and training well-educated workers acquire abroad, including by easing the path for them and their descendants to return to India or otherwise invest in its development. As an example, many college-educated emigrants who gained experience in Silicon Valley and other tech hubs subsequently used their ties to create a thriving information technology sector in Bangalore.

Many Indians have also emigrated for study. Nearly 589,000 Indians studied abroad in 2019, according to the Ministry of External Affairs, with slightly less than one-third of them going to the United States. Significant numbers also have gone to Australia, Canada, and other countries. However, Indian international enrollment dropped to 261,000 in 2020, amid the start of the COVID-19 pandemic. Many international students from India come from urban areas, the upper and middle classes, and various castes, with backgrounds in economics, engineering, management, and medicine.

Reverse Migration

Many challenges in the urban landscape like congestion, accommodation difficulties, rising uncertainties in the employment opportunities, socio-cultural alienation etc have also frequently triggered reverse migration. This is called so as in this process, the initial migrants who had come from the rural to urban areas in hope of better livelihood opportunities, finally decide to make their way back to the villages because of the above-mentioned reasons.

There was a sharp increase in reverse migration in response to the COVID-19 pandemic that had crippled the social order across the globe, with India being no exception. The sudden lockdown and deprivation from job, along with the general environment of fear and anxiety that nudges one to spend time with the emotional security of family, had forced many migrants to reverse migration.

Thus, during Covid–19 pandemic period since March, 2020, Union Government has taken several additional measures for the benefits of workers, such as; creation of 39.51 lakh new job opportunities by crediting Rs.2583 crores in EPF accounts under Atmanirbhar Bharat Rozgar Yojana (ABRY), benefits of Rs.2567 crores to retain 38.91 lakh low wage employees under Pradhan Mantri Garib Kalyan Yojana (PMGKY), financial assistance of Rs.7413 crore to Building & other Construction Workers (BOCW), unemployment benefit under Atal Beemit Vyakti Kalyan Yojana (ABVKY), Pradhan Mantri Garib Kalyan Rojgar Abhiyan (PMGKRA) generating 50.78 crore mandays with Rs.39,293 crores, working capital loan to street vendors under PM-SVA Nidhi Scheme, free food grain of 5 kg per person per month to all Targeted Public Distribution System (TPDS) beneficiaries and special training programme under Pradhan Mantri Kaushal Vikas Yojana (PMKVY) Scheme as a part of Garib Kalyan Rojgar Abhiyaan (GKRA) in the districts having high concentration of returnee migrants. In addition, the Government launched an initiative called SWADES (Skilled Workers Arrival Database for Employment Support) to conduct a skill mapping exercise of the returnee migrant workers from abroad under the Vande Bharat Mission. For facilitating employment opportunities, details of SWADES have been integrated with Skill India's ASEEM Portal.

Ministry of Labour & Employment has also launched e-SHRAM portal, a National Database of the Unorganised Workers on 26th August, 2021. It has been made available to the States/UTs for registration of unorganised workers including migrant workers on e-SHRAM portal. The main objective of the e-SHRAM portal is to create a national database of unorganised workers seeded with Aadhaar. It is also to facilitate delivery of Social Security and welfare Schemes to such workers.

10

CHILD ABUSE AND CHILD LABOUR

"Child slavery is a crime against humanity. Humanity itself is at stake here"— Kailash Satyarthi, Indian Child Rights and Education Activist (awarded Nobel Peace Prize 2014)

CHILD POPULATION AND THE WORKING CHILDREN

Defining what age a person is or ceases to be a child is a constant debate in India. The Census of India considers children to be any person below the age of 14, as do most government programmes. Biologically, childhood is the stage between infancy and adulthood. According to the United Nations Convention on the Rights of the Child (UNCRC) (1992), 'a child means every human being below the age of eighteen years unless, under the law applicable to the child, majority is attained earlier'. This definition of child allows for individual countries to determine according to the own discretion the age limits of a child in their own laws. But in India, various laws related to children define children in different age limits.

Child labour has been a persisting quandary that has been staring at the face of the nation. Although child labour is considered as old as mankind it was during the second half of the twentieth century, in the wake of industrial revolution, that policymakers and the public attempted to take stock of the causes and consequences of child labour. An international consensus developed on the elimination of the practice based upon the desire to protect children and favour their mental and cognitive development.

Childhood is viewed as a very happy stage which requires care and protection along with training for physical and mental growth. A child is a 'national asset' and future of the nation. Unfortunately, in developing countries like India, many children struggle for even day-to-day sustenance. The reasons are various. The common causes are marked as poverty, illiteracy, unemployment, and over population.

Following are statistics related to children in India according to the 2011 Census:

Percentage of Adults and Children

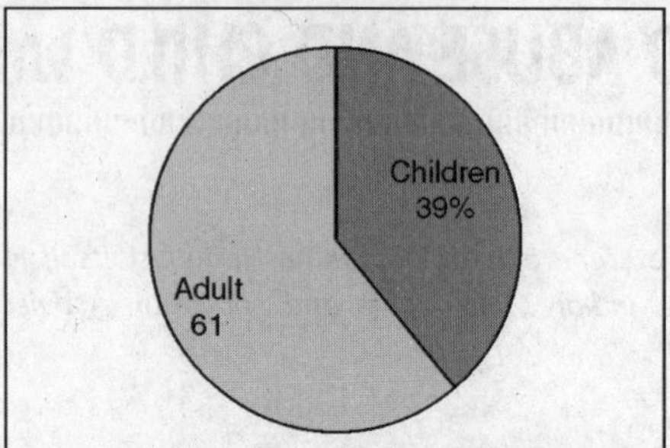

Age Group of India's Children

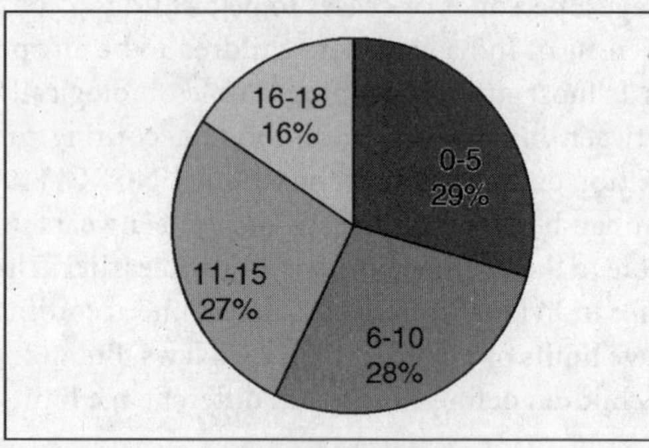

Age Group vs Gender of India's Children

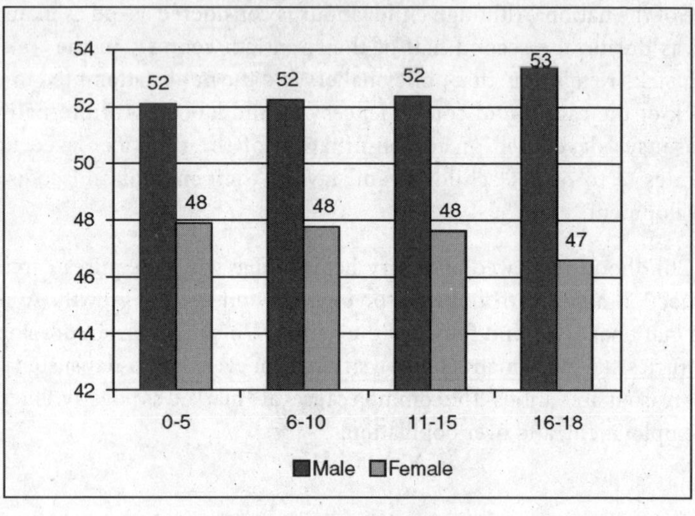

Gender of India's Children

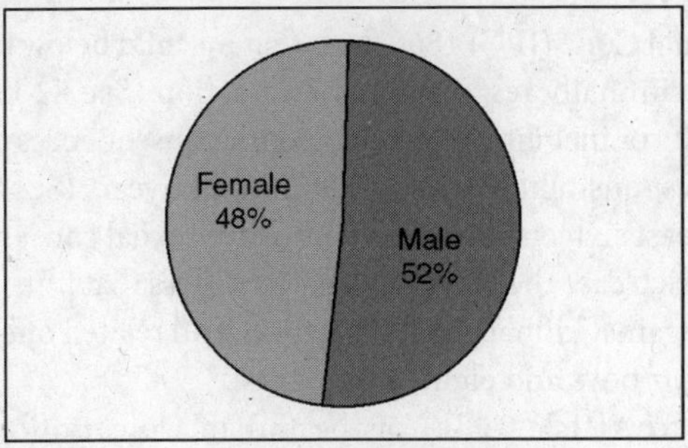

Rural–Urban Distribution of Indian Children Population

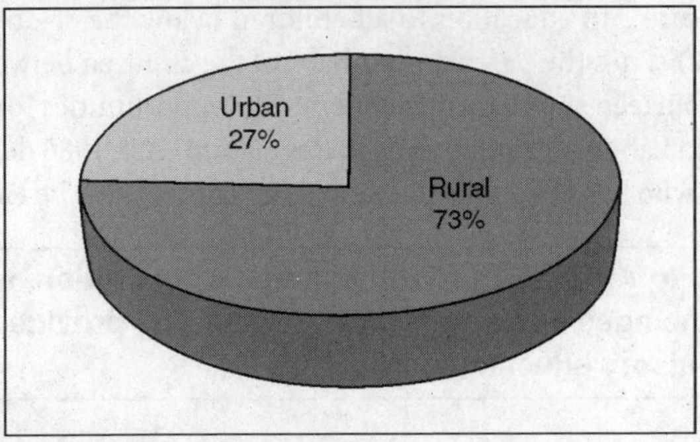

State-wise distribution of India's Child Population

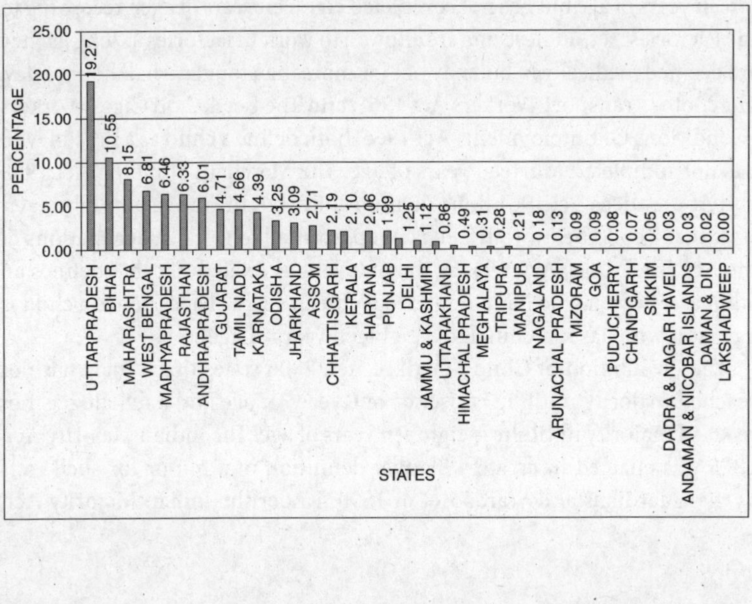

Child Protection and Child Rights in India

The Indian Penal Code (IPC) 1860 finds that no child below the age of seven may be held criminally responsible for an action (Sec 82 IPC). In case of mental disability or inability to understand the consequences of one's actions, the criminal responsibility age is raised to twelve years (Sec 83 IPC). A girl must be of at least sixteen years in order to give sexual consent, unless she is married, in which case the prescribed age is no less that fifteen. With regard to protection against kidnapping, abduction, and related offenses, the given age is sixteen for boys and eighteen for girls.

According to Article 21 (a) of the Indian Constitution, all children between the ages of six to fourteen should be provided with free and compulsory education. Article 45 states that the State should provide early childhood care and education to all children below the age of six. Lastly, Article 51(k) states the parents/guardians of the children between the ages of six and fourteen should provide them with opportunities for education.

The Child Labour (Prohibition and Regulation) Act, 1986 defines a child as a person who has not completed fourteen years of age. The Factories Act,

---

According to Article 21 (a) of the Indian Constitution, all children between the ages of six to fourteen should be provided with free and compulsory education.

1948 and Plantation Labour Act, 1951 states that a child is one that has not completed fifteen years of age and an adolescent is one who has completed fifteen years of age but has not completed eighteen years of age. According to the Factories Act, adolescents are allowed to work in factories as long as they are deemed medically fit but may not for more than four and half hours a day. The Motor Transport Workers Act 1961, and The Beedi And Cigar Workers (Conditions Of Employment) Act 1966, both define a child as a person who has not completed fourteen years of age. The Merchant Shipping Act 1958 and Apprentices Act 1961 don't define a child, but the provisions of the Act state that a child below fourteen is not permitted to work in occupations of the Act. The Mines Act, 1952 is the only labour related Act that defines an adult as a person who has completed eighteen years of age (hence a child is a person who has not completed eighteen years of age).

The Prohibition of Child Marriage Act, 2006 states that a male has not reached majority until he is twenty-one years of age and a female has not reached majority until she is eighteen years of age. The Indian Majority Act, 1875 was enacted to create a blanket definition of a minor for such Acts as the Guardians and Wards Act of 1890. Under the Indian Majority Act,

1875 a person has not attainted majority until he or she is of eighteen years of age. This definition of a minor also stands for both the Hindu Minority and Guardianship Act, 1956 and the Hindu Adoption and Maintenance Act, 1956. Muslim, Christian, and Zoroastrian personal law also upholds eighteen as the age of majority. The first Juvenile Justice Act, 1986 defined a boy child as below sixteen years of age and a girl child as below eighteen years of age. The Juvenile Justice (Care and Protection of Children) Act, 2000 has changed the definition of child to any person who has not completed eighteen years of age.

Because of its umbrella clauses and because it is the latest law to be enacted regarding child rights and protection, many are of the opinion that the definition of child found in the Juvenile Justice Act, 2000 should be considered the legal definition for a child in all matters.

CHILD PROTECTION AGAINST CHILD ABUSE

The United Nations Conversation Rights of Child (UNCRC), (1989) is the most widely endorsed child rights instrument worldwide.

1. In the UNCRC, Article 19.1, Child Protection has been defined as "States Parties shall take all appropriate legislative, administrative, social and educational measures to protect the child from all forms of physical or mental violence, injury or abuse, neglect or negligent treatment, maltreatment or exploitation, including sexual abuse, while in the care of parent(s), legal guardian(s) or any other person who has the care of the child."
2. Failure to ensure child right to protection adversely affects all rights. Child protection is critical to the achievement of Millennium Development Goals (MDG). These MDGs can't be achieved unless child protection is an integral part of the programmme and strategies are in place to protect children from child labour, street children, child abuse, child marriage, violence in school, and various forms of exploitation.
3. Several well developed countries of the world have well developed child protection systems, primarily focused at mandatory reporting, identification, and investigations of affected children, and often taking coercive action. The burden of high level of notifications and investigations is not only on the families, but also on the system, which has to increase its resources.
4. In these contexts, the problems of child protection in India, with huge populations, and additional socio-economic constraints, need serious and wider consideration.

India's Problems

In India, the number of children needing care and protection is huge and increasing. Uncontrolled families, extreme poverty, and illiteracy result in provision of very little care to the child during the early formative years. Even services that are freely available are poorly utilised. The urban underprivileged, migrating population (a very sizable number) and rural communities are particularly affected. In large cities, there are serious problems of street children (abandoned and often homeless) and child labourers, employed in menial work. Children in difficult circumstances such as children affected by disasters, those in conflict zones, refugees, and those afflicted by HIV/AIDS need appropriate care and rehabilitation. For example, in India, there are about 440 million children; about 40% of them are vulnerable or experiencing difficult circumstances. Twenty seven million babies are born each year. A large majority of these births are among the underprivileged section of the population, mostly unplanned, and where the parents cannot provide proper care to their children. The situation of the newborns and the periods of infancy and early childhood are particularly

Maternal undernutrition, unsafe deliveries, low birth weight babies and poor newborn care, lack of adequate immunizations, poor nutrition, and neglect of early development and education are major issues that need to be appropriately addressed.

critical and the morbidity and mortality rates continue to remain very high. Maternal undernutrition, unsafe deliveries, low birth weight babies and poor newborn care, lack of adequate immunizations, poor nutrition, and neglect of early development and education are major issues that need to be appropriately addressed.

Child rearing practices reflect social norms and very often adverse traditions are passed from one generation to the next, especially in illiterate and poorly informed communities, and are extremely resistant to change. As per Government of India (2007) survey, the prevalence of all forms of child abuse are extremely high [physical abuse (66%), sexual abuse (50%), and emotional abuse (50%)]. In these contexts, India must also seek its own insights and way forward plans to protect their children.

There are wider implications of the term "protection". The term "protection" readily relates to protection from all forms of violence, abuse, and exploitation. However, from India's perspective, the Indian Child Abuse Neglect & Child Labour (ICANCL) group has strongly propagated the view that "protection" must also include protection from disease, poor nutrition, and illiteracy, in addition to abuse and exploitation. The 9th ISPCAN Asia Pacific Conference of Child Abuse & Neglect (APCCAN 2011) conference outcome document "Delhi declaration" reconfirmed and pledged a resolve to stand against the neglect and abuse of children. It also promised to strive for achievement of child rights and the building of a caring community for every child, free of violence and discrimination. It urged and asserted the urgent need to integrate principles, standards, and measures in the national planning process to prevent and respond to violence against children. The UNCRC does not absolve either family or community or society at large. But it firmly puts the onus on the State. Governments are the ultimate duty bearer. In India, the State should ensure that all vulnerable children have access to school, basic health care, nutrition, besides social welfare and juvenile justice systems. These child protection systems can contribute to break down the cycle of inter-generational poverty and exploitation.

CONCEPT, CAUSES, EFFECTS, TYPES, AND INCIDENCE OF CHILD ABUSE

What is Child Abuse?

Any kind of harsh or ill-treatment of children is child abuse. WHO (1999) defines child abuse or maltreatment as "all forms of physical and/or emotional ill-treatment, sexual abuse, neglect or negligent treatment, or commercial or other exploitation, resulting in actual or potential harm to the child's health, survival, development or dignity in the context of a relationship of responsibility, trust or power". Globally, child abuse constitutes four types of maltreatment: physical abuse, sexual abuse, emotional and psychological abuse, and neglect. India is home to almost 19% of the world's children. More than one-third of the country's population, around 440 million, is below 18 years. Sixty years of child welfare and child development programmes have still not been able to control the severe forms of abuse such as female foeticide and infanticide, girl child discrimination, child sexual abuse, kidnapping children for organ sale, and exploitative child labour. The shocking and shameful incident of the sexual abuse, rape, and murder of children in Nithari village of Noida (UP) has been one of the worst forms of child abuse and neglect in recent years. Unfortunately, this incident is not a rare situation. Such grievous crimes are being committed on children and many of them continue to remain unreported. The reasons for under-reporting of abuse are closely linked with the causes of child abuse.

Causes of Child Abuse

Neglect is the root cause of most cases of abuse. Neglect is seen at all levels—family, civil society, and the State. There is a huge gap between coverage of children through various programmes of the government and NGOs, and facilities for children vis-a-vis the population of Indian children. Children are facing higher threats of vulnerability because of the State's inability to provide basic health and educational facilities. Further, some of the cultural practices and beliefs surrounding childcare within the family are responsible for child abuse. Abuse often takes place in the "private" domain of family life. Even today children are considered to be the property of their parents and other caregivers. Child abuse is an outcome of dysfunctional adult–child relationship or sometimes even child–child relationship. Most adults are not even willing to consider violation of children and basic child rights as child abuse. This adds to the complexity of the issue.

Impact of Child Abuse

Every episode of child abuse of any degree and form has serious implications on the child's health, growth, development, and well-being. Children without family or family support are some of the worst affected such as children in institutional care, children living on the streets, bonded child labour, and other trafficked children. Child abuse has another dimension as well. One of the grave consequences of child abuse is that abuse often leads to victims becoming perpetrators in later life. According to Sirpal (1996) "delinquency may not result so much from abuse as from the chain of events that follow abuse. Abuse may lead to changed environments or family conditions that may in turn affect the child's subsequent behaviour and involvement in delinquency".

Child Abuse within the Family

Haranath (1995) in his study on the background characteristics of 82 boys in a juvenile home in Andhra Pradesh found that 62% of children had left their homes due to parental abuse and neglect. This fact gets substantiated by the findings of the recent national study and is also reflected in The World Report on Violence and Health (2002). When abuse happens within the family, children can rarely protest, report, or get any help. However, apart from the family there are several societal factors and systemic consequences that result in child abuse and neglect.

Types of Child Abuse

The Study on Child Abuse: India 2007 by the Ministry of Women and Child Development (2007) highlights the serious issue of child abuse and neglect in the Indian context. This study and the proposed initiative to introduce an integrated child protection programme are significant in many ways. It indicates the State's willingness to seriously address the growing atrocities, abuse, and neglect of children, and move towards more effective measures for child protection. It includes nationwide empirical data on the nature and extent of child abuse in different settings and recommends immediate and appropriate responsive actions that can be undertaken by families, community, government, and civil society organisations.

The study includes a large sample of 12,447 child respondents, young adults, and other stakeholders across 13 states of India. It covers children in the age group of five years to 18 years and young adults from the age group of 18 to 24 years. It has a fair representation across gender, mother tongue, caste, and religion. The children in the sample came from five different evidence groups: children in family environment but not going to school, children in schools, children in institutions, children at work, and children on streets. It is important to note that four of these groups are children in especially vulnerable situations, and to that extent, the estimate of the incidence of abuse may be on the higher side. The study highlights various forms of abuse experienced by the children and includes physical, sexual, and emotional abuse. In addition, it also covers the neglect experienced by girls. The study indicates a phenomenal percentage of abuse experienced by Indian children. *Some of the major findings are listed here:*

Physical Abuse

(i) Two out of every three children were physically abused,
(ii) Out of 69% of physically abused children in 13 sample states, 54.68% were boys,
(iii) The states of Andhra Pradesh, Assam, Bihar, and Delhi have almost consistently reported higher rates of abuse in all forms as compared to other states,
(iv) Out of those children physically abused in family situations, 88.6% were physically abused by parents, and
(v) 65% of school-going children reported facing corporal punishment, i.e., two out of three children were victims of corporal punishment.

Sexual Abuse

(i) 53.22% children reported having faced one or more forms of sexual abuse;
(ii) Andhra Pradesh, Assam, Bihar, and Delhi reported the highest percentage of sexual abuse among both boys and girls;

(iii) 21.90% child respondents reported facing severe forms of sexual abuse and 50.76% experienced other forms of sexual abuse while 5.69% reported being sexually assaulted; and

(iv) 7.50% abusers are persons known to the child or in a position of trust and responsibility in the child's life.

Emotional Abuse and Girl Child Neglect

(i) Every second child reported facing emotional abuse;

(ii) Equal percentage of both girls and boys reported facing emotional abuse;

(iii) In 83% of the cases, parents were the abusers; and

(iv) 48.4% of girls wished that they were boys.

Incidence of Child Abuse

The latest report released by the National Crime Records Bureau (NCRB) shows that 1,49,404 cases of crime against children were registered in 2021 of which 53,874 — 36.05 per cent — were under the Protection of Children from Sexual Offences Act (POCSO). There were 47,221 POCSO cases out of 1,28,531 cases of crime against children in 2020 (36.73 per cent) and 47,335 of 1,48,185 such cases in 2019 (31.94 per cent).

NCRB data on cases registered under POCSO show a steady increase in the rate (incidents per 1 lakh children): 12.1 in 2021 (53,276 girls, 1,083 boys); 10.6 in both 2020 and 2019.

Sikkim has the highest rate of sexual offences against children with 48.6 followed by Kerala (28.1), Meghalaya (27.8), Haryana (24.7) and Mizoram (24.6). The largest number of cases registered under POCSO in 2021 was in UP (7,129) followed by Maharashtra (6,200), Madhya Pradesh (6,070), Tamil Nadu (4,465) and Karnataka (2,813). In percentage terms, the top categories under crime against children during 2021 were kidnapping and abduction (45 per cent) followed by POCSO cases.

In all, there was a 16.2 per cent rise in cases of crime against children in 2021 from the previous year, according to the NCRB report. "The crime rate registered per lakh children population is 33.6 in 2021 in comparison with 28.9 in 2020," the report states.

Sikkim had the highest rate of crime against children amongst states at 72.4 followed by Madhya Pradesh at 66.7. Madhya Pradesh had the highest number of actual cases registered — 19,173 cases in 2021. The state also had the highest number of cases registered in 2020 with over 17,000 cases, followed by UP and Maharashtra. In 2019, Maharashtra had the highest number of cases at 19,592, followed by Madhya Pradesh and UP.

Haryana, Chhattisgarh, Telangana, Odisha and Assam were the other states with the high rates of crimes against children in 2021. Nagaland had the lowest rate of crime against children at 6.2 as well as the lowest number of cases registered in 2021 at 51. The state also had the lowest number of cases registered in 2019 with 59, as well as in 2020 with 31. Among union territories, Delhi had the highest rate of crimes against children in 2021 with 128.5 — also the highest in the country with over 7,000 cases registered last year.

The NCRB report states that 29,364 children were declared missing and since deemed as kidnapped. This number includes 12,347 minor girls for the purpose of "being compelled into marriage", the NCRB report found. It shows that 1,046 children were trafficked last year with Delhi, Bihar and Assam topping the list.

There were 982 cases registered under the Child Labour Act last year with the highest number of cases registered in Telangana (305) followed by Assam. The report states that 1,062 cases were registered under the Prohibition of Child Marriage Act last year with the top three states including Karnataka, Tamil Nadu and Assam.

THEORETICAL EXPLANATIONS OF CHILD ABUSE

Psychological Theories

Psychological theories focus on the instinctive and psychological qualities of those who abuse. It is abnormalities within the individual abuser that are responsible for abuse, for example, abusive parents may themselves have been abused in childhood (Corby, 2000).

Attachment Theory

Attachment theory derives from the work of Bowlby (1951) who carried out studies into the nature and effects of maternal deprivation on young children. He theorized that any significant separation of a child from the mother in the first five years of life could lead to a variety of psychological and social difficulties in later life since proper bonding and attachment to the mother was crucial if a child was to benefit from physical protection and psychological security. Until the mid 1980s, attachment theory was not directly applied to the problem of child abuse but poor attachment experiences are now seen to be a cause and a consequence of child abuse (Crittenden and Ainsworth, 1989). The theory has been criticized because the focus is almost exclusively on the mother–child relationship and insufficient account is taken of the total dynamics of the family. Neither does the theory adequately explain sexual abuse (Corby, 1993; 2000).

Psychodynamic Theory

Psychodynamic theory claims that abuse and neglect are associated with maternal deprivation. The primary carer, who has often suffered abuse herself, displays a lack of empathy, sensitive awareness, and response to her child (Steele and Pollock, 1974; Steele, 1987). There is significant overlap between psychodynamic theory and attachment theory. Although the primary caretaker is not always the mother, the main focus is again on the mother–child relationship, and the mother's psychological make up is key. Psychological treatment focusing on improving the parent's ability to relate to other people is seen to be the solution to the problem. The theory has been criticised because of its neglect of social and environmental factors and its inadequacy in explaining sexual abuse (Corby, 1993; 2000; Finkelhor, 1986).

Learning Theory

Learning theory stipulates that behaviour is shaped or learned by the interaction of an individual with his or her environment. Child abuse is, therefore, the result of having learned or experienced dysfunctional child care practices, or not having learned functional child care practices. For example, violent behaviour is learnt from observing aggressive role models, so that adults who have themselves experienced punitive treatment may rely on such methods to discipline their own children.

Cognitive Approaches

The essential feature of cognitive theory is that the way people perceive, order, construct, and think about the world is an important key to their behaviour. Lack of parenting skills to cope with particular stages of their child's development, leads to patterns of child maltreatment. Cognitive theorists point to the value of finding out how parents who have abused children perceive that child's behaviour and intervention must be focused on helping them to perceive their children differently and using techniques to improve self control and self esteem (Corby, 1993; 2000; Buchanan, 1996).

Social Psychological Approaches

Social psychological approaches fall between focus on the individual and focus on broader social factors. They focus on the dynamics of the interaction between abuser, child, and immediate environment (Corby, 2000).

Individual Interactionist Perspectives

Individual interactionist perspectives stress that behaviour is determined by interactions between people. Interactionists place greater attention on the dynamics of current relationships than on parental background or characteristics and take the child's contribution to situations of abuse much more into account and also that of the spouse or partner. They suggest that a climate of abuse can result from parents lacking skills to cope with difficult behaviour and from certain children continually exposing that inadequacy.

Family Dysfunction Theory

Family dysfunction theory maintains that family dynamics contribute to abuse and that abuse occurs because 'normal' family boundaries, hierarchies, and relationships have broken down. Family dysfunction theorists maintain that children are sometimes subject to violence by a parent as a means of 'getting at' the other parent or that a child may be a 'scapegoat', the bad one in the family and the reason for all the family's ills. With regard to physical child abuse, family dysfunction theory has not had widespread influence as an explanatory theory but family therapy techniques as a mode of intervention have attracted more attention. Family therapy thinking has had more impact in explaining child sexual abuse. It suggests that child sexual abuse serves the function of keeping together families that would otherwise collapse. A classic scenario is the abuse of a teenage girl by her father who is considered to be seeking emotional and sexual gratification because communication and sexual relations with his wife have broken down (Kempe and Kempe, 1978).

Sociological Perspectives

Sociological perspectives emphasize social and political conditions as the most important reason for the existence of child abuse. It is forces in society which are responsible for child abuse, not individual factors. Sociological perspectives do not provide clear indicators for practice in that they look broadly at the conditions that create the climate for child abuse rather than at how this works out in individual cases. They have, therefore, not had a major influence on child protection thinking in Britain except in relation to sexual abuse and gender issues (Corby, 2000).

The Social Cultural Perspective

The social cultural perspective suggests there are certain factors within society which may contribute to the occurrence of abuse, for example, a society that endorses the attitude 'spare the rod and spoil the child' sets the scene for a variety of unwanted forms of violence of which physical child abuse is one. From this perspective, child abuse is seen as similar to socially approved forms of violence rather than as a separate pathological phenomenon. The implications are that there is a need for change at a broad societal level to the way in which children are treated, in particular there is a need to encourage non-violent means of ensuring pro-social behaviour. The same sort of analysis can be applied to sexual abuse, i.e., because sexual exploitation of women is tolerated in advertising, prostitution, etc., and because children are sexualized in the media, a climate is set whereby sexual abuse results (Gil, 1970).

The Social Structural Perspective

The social structural perspective holds that child abuse is class related. It is the State, not the abuser that is responsible for abuse because it sanctions inequality, and low standards of health, housing, education, and leisure for the children of the poor (Parton, 1985). The approach does justice to the fact that physical child abuse has a close association with deprivation but does not address child sexual abuse or emotional abuse which is generally considered not to be linked to class and poverty. Neither does it adequately explain why most poor people do not abuse their children (Corby, 1993; 2000).

The Feminist Perspective

The feminist perspective has had a huge impact on the practice of child abuse. This perspective sees abuse as an extreme example of institutionalized male power over women and children, i.e., men sexually abuse children as a means of exerting power and control. Feminist commentators have provided a challenge to assumptions which equate abuse with maternal deficiencies, confuse the term 'parent' with mother, and lead professionals to ignore male caregivers. With regard to physical abuse, women have been as implicated as men, but feminists argue that given the fact that women are mainly responsible for the care of children, they actually inflict less physical abuse in proportion to the amount of time children spend in their presence. Children spend far less time with their fathers and so, they in fact, pose a greater risk. Similarly, mothers have been implicated in cases of neglect and emotional abuse to a greater extent than fathers because they are expected to be responsible for the care of their children. The role of men in neglect and emotional abuse has been ignored.

The Children's Rights Perspective

The children's rights perspective suggests that if children had the same rights in society as adults, rather than being the property of their parents, then they would be less likely to be the object of physical abuse and neglect. For example, we do not consider it proper to smack adults for misbehaving so neither should we smack children (Corby, 1993; 2000; Doyle, 1996; Goddard, 1996). The United Nations Convention on the Rights of the Child recognizes that the family has primary responsibility for the care and protection of children but states that there is also a need for legal protection (Buchanan, 1996).

Integrated Theories of Child Abuse

Virtually, all researchers point to the dangers of adopting single cause explanations of child abuse. The term 'child abuse' covers a range of behaviours and problems, so a search for a single or even a cluster of causes is likely to be in vain. Social work has been criticized for focusing too readily on problems and 'pathology' within individuals and families and not sufficiently taking into consideration the wider context within which individuals and families exist (Parton, 1997; Goddard, 1996; Corby, 1993; Gardner, 1993).

Finkelhor (1986) criticized single-factor theories for their inadequacies in explaining the diversity and complexity of child sexual abuse. He proposed an alternative integrated model which attempted to explain how it was that some adults became sexually interested in children and described the process whereby such offences were committed. *The model suggests that four preconditions need to be met before abuse occurs:*

- the potential offender needs to have some motivation to abuse the child sexually, e.g., there must be a degree of sexual arousal to a child;
- the potential offender has to overcome internal inhibitions against acting on that motivation, inhibitions which are built around notions of conscience, morality, and fear of the law;
- the potential offender has to overcome external impediments such as protective adults so that unimpeded access to a child can be achieved, for example, through baby sitting or organising children's activities; and
- the potential offender has to undermine or overcome the child's possible resistance through sophisticated seduction techniques.

Finkelhor's model has been criticized, however, because it seems to say more about how sexual abuse occurs than why it actually happens.

CONSEQUENCES OF ABUSE OF CHILDREN

Poor Physical Health

Ill health caused by child abuse forms a significant portion of the global burden of disease. Some of the health consequences have been researched, others have only recently been given attention, including psychiatric disorders and suicidal behaviour. Importantly, there is now evidence that major adult forms of illness—including ischaemic heart disease, cancer, chronic lung disease, irritable bowel syndrome, and fibromyalgia—are related to experiences of abuse during childhood. The apparent mechanism to explain these results is the adoption of behavioural risk factors such as smoking, alcohol abuse, poor diet, and lack of exercise.

Psychological Damage

Similarly, there are many studies demonstrating short-term and long-term psychological damage. Some children have a few symptoms that do not reach clinical levels of concern, or else are at clinical levels but not as high as in children generally seen in clinical settings. Other survivors have serious psychiatric symptoms, such as depression, anxiety, substance abuse, aggression, shame, or cognitive impairments. Finally, some children meet the full criteria for psychiatric illnesses that include post-traumatic stress disorder, major depression, anxiety disorders, and sleep disorders.

11

JUVENILE DELINQUENCY

"I think it's important for us as a society to remember that the youth within juvenile justice systems are, most of the time, youths who simply haven't had the right mentors and supporters around them—because of circumstances beyond their control."
—*Q'orianka Kilcher*

INTRODUCTION

The Juvenile Justice (Care and Protection of Children) Act, 2000 is the primary legal framework for juvenile justice in India. The Act provides for a special approach towards the prevention and treatment of juvenile delinquency and provides a framework for the protection, treatment, and rehabilitation of children in the purview of the juvenile justice system. This law, brought in compliance of the 1989 UN Convention on the Rights of the Child (UNCRC), repealed the earlier Juvenile Justice Act of 1986 after India signed and ratified the UNCRC in 1992. This act has been further amended in 2006 and 2010. In the wake of the Nirbhaya Delhi gang rape (16 Dec 2012), the law suffered a nationwide criticism owing to its helplessness against crimes where juveniles get involved in heinous crimes like rape and murder. In 2015, responding to the public sentiment, both the houses of Parliament in India further amended the bill that lowered the juvenile age to 16 and proposed adult-like treatment for juveniles accused of heinous crimes. The lower house, i.e. Lok Sabha passed the bill on May 7, 2015 and the upper house, i.e. Rajya Sabha on December 22, 2015. The bill was approved by President Pranab Mukherjee's assent on 31st December, 2015.

The Juvenile Justice (Care and Protection of Children) Amendment Act, 2021 was passed to amend various provisions of the Juvenile Justice Act, 2015. *Some of the key provisions of the Act includes:*

Crimes against children which are mentioned in the chapter "Other Offences Against Children" of the JJ Act, 2015 that allow an imprisonment between three and seven years will be deemed "non-cognisable".

The amendment provides strength to the provision of protection and adoption of children. There are many adoption cases pending before the court and to make proceedings of the court faster now the power is transferred to the district magistrate.

Amendment provides that the district magistrate has the authority to issue such adoption orders.

Concerns Associated with the Amendment

- Specifically, the amendment under challenge is the one to Section 86 of the JJ Act, according to which crimes under the special law, with punishment between three to seven years, have been reclassified as non-cognisable.
- Making these crimes non-cognisable along with several other serious crimes under the special law would make reporting an offence to the police even more difficult.
- While the victims themselves are unable to directly report them due to the imbalance in power, most such crimes are reported to the police by either parents or child rights bodies and Child Welfare Committees (CWC). Here parents are mostly not well aware with the digital norms and CWCs' first instinct in most cases is to "talk and arrive at a settlement" without having to escalate the matter to the police.

CLASSIFICATION OF JUVENILE DELINQUENTS

Juvenile means a person who is very young, teenager, adolescent, or underage. In other words, juvenile means children who have not yet reached the age of adults in the sense that they are still childish or immature. Sometimes the term "child" is also interchangeably used for the term "juvenile". As per the Juvenile Justice (Care and Protection) Act, 2000, a juvenile shall not be treated as an adult even if he/she is involved in any criminal acts for the purpose of trial and punishment in the court of law. In legal terms, a juvenile can be defined as a child who has not attained a certain age at which he can be held liable for his criminal acts like an adult person under the law of the country. Juvenile is a child who is alleged to have committed certain acts or omissions which are in violation of any law and are declared to be an offence. Juvenile is a child who unlike an adult person, having not attained prescribed age, cannot be held liable for his criminal act. The age criteria for being a juvenile vary from country to country and state to state. In ancient India, a parent was supposed not to punish a child who is under five years of age for any offence. As per the law prevailing then, a child of such tender age should be nursed and educated with love and affection only. After the age of five, punishment may be given in some suitable form such as physical chastisement or rebuke by the parents. Towards the latter half of the childhood, punishment should be gradually withdrawn and replaced

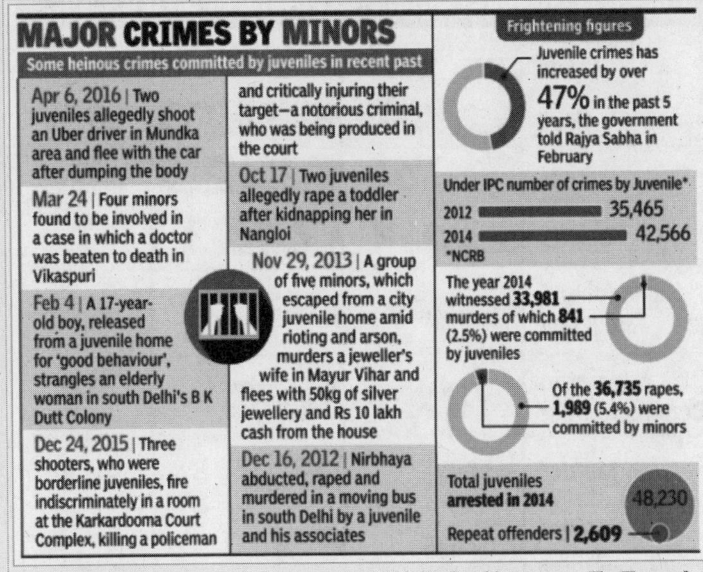

MAJOR CRIMES BY MINORS

Some heinous crimes committed by juveniles in recent past

Apr 6, 2016 | Two juveniles allegedly shoot an Uber driver in Mundka area and flee with the car after dumping the body

Mar 24 | Four minors found to be involved in a case in which a doctor was beaten to death in Vikaspuri

Feb 4 | A 17-year-old boy, released from a juvenile home for 'good behaviour', strangles an elderly woman in south Delhi's B K Dutt Colony

Dec 24, 2015 | Three shooters, who were borderline juveniles, fire indiscriminately in a room at the Karkardooma Court Complex, killing a policeman and critically injuring their target—a notorious criminal, who was being produced in the court

Oct 17 | Two juveniles allegedly rape a toddler after kidnapping her in Nangloi

Nov 29, 2013 | A group of five minors, which escaped from a city juvenile home amid rioting and arson, murders a jeweller's wife in Mayur Vihar and flees with 50kg of silver jewellery and Rs 10 lakh cash from the house

Dec 16, 2012 | Nirbhaya abducted, raped and murdered in a moving bus in south Delhi by a juvenile and his associates

Frightening figures

Juvenile crimes has increased by over 47% in the past 5 years, the government told Rajya Sabha in February

Under IPC number of crimes by Juvenile*

Year	Crimes
2012	35,465
2014	42,566

*NCRB

The year 2014 witnessed 33,981 murders of which 841 (2.5%) were committed by juveniles

Of the 36,735 rapes, 1,989 (5.4%) were committed by minors

Total juveniles arrested in 2014: 48,230

Repeat offenders | 2,609

Some heinous crimes committed by juveniles: 2012-16; Graphic courtesy: *The Times of India*, June 5, 2016

Source: inpaedia

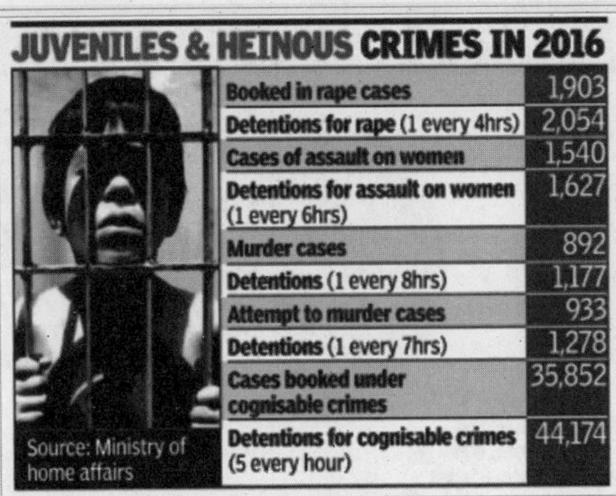

JUVENILES & HEINOUS CRIMES IN 2016

Booked in rape cases	1,903
Detentions for rape (1 every 4hrs)	2,054
Cases of assault on women	1,540
Detentions for assault on women (1 every 6hrs)	1,627
Murder cases	892
Detentions (1 every 8hrs)	1,177
Attempt to murder cases	933
Detentions (1 every 7hrs)	1,278
Cases booked under cognisable crimes	35,852
Detentions for cognisable crimes (5 every hour)	44,174

Source: Ministry of home affairs

Juveniles and heinous crimes in 2016

Source: inpaedia

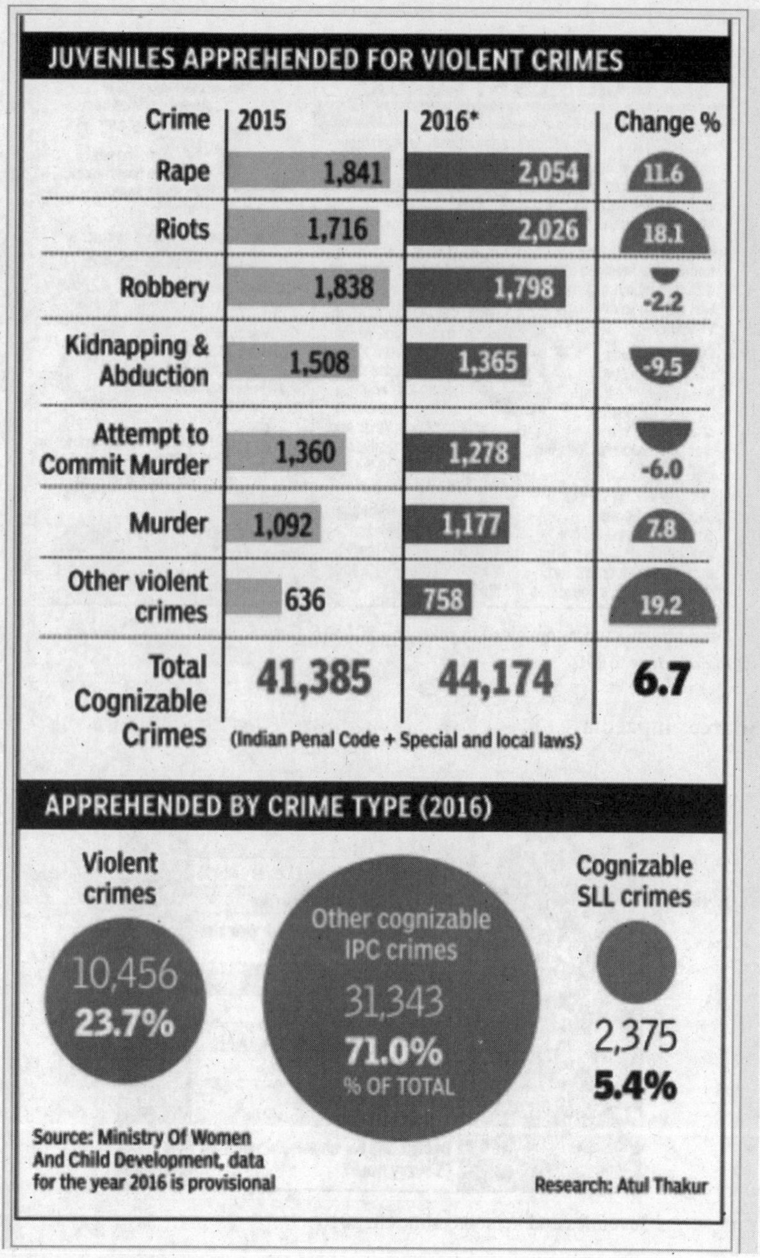

Source: inpaedia

by advice. From the age of sixteen upwards, sons and daughters should be treated as friends by the parents.

The term juvenile delinquency applies to violation of criminal code and certain patterns of behaviour that are not approved for children and young adolescents. It may be grouped as individual delinquency (in which only one individual is involved and the cause of the delinquent act is traced to an individual delinquent), group supported delinquency (committed in companionship and the cause is attributed not to the personality of the individual but to the culture of the individual's home and neighbourhood), organized delinquency, and situational delinquency. A delinquent young person is disobedient and wayward, cannot be controlled by the parents and teachers, is not amenable to any kind of discipline, is self-willed, and habitually acts in a manner injurious to the welfare and happiness of oneself and others.

Nature and Incidence

The National Crime Records Bureau's data shows that in the past decade, the rate of juvenile offences has steadily increased.

CHARACTERISTICS AND TYPES

Petty crimes in general and heinous crimes in particular are being committed regularly in India by children. Crimes such as theft, burglary, and snatching which are not so serious in nature but crimes such as robbery, murder, and rape, etc. which are relatively serious are on the rise in whole of the country. Among juveniles also there is a specific trend that juveniles between the age of 16 to 18 years are found to be more involved in heinous criminal acts. According to the National Crime Records Bureau, the data of 2013 shows that of the 43,506 crimes registered against minors under the Indian Penal Code (IPC) and the Special Local Law (SLL) by juveniles, 28,830 had been committed by those between the ages of 16 to 18. The statistics also show the number of juveniles found to be in conflict with law under the IPC and the SLL has risen 13.6% and 2.5% respectively in 2013, as compared with 2012.

The inhuman gang rape of a young girl on December 16, 2013, shocked the collective conscience of the nation. The brutality with which the heinous crime was committed was most shocking; it was later found out that among five accused, one was a minor and he was the most barbaric one. Again, in another brutal gang rape case which is known as Shakti Mill rape case, a minor was involved. These and several more recent events have triggered a public debate that the present Juvenile Justice (Care and Protection) Act, 2000 which treats persons below the age of 18 years as minor or juvenile, should be amended.

Some of the most common causes which are associated with juvenile crimes are: poverty; drug abuse; anti-social peer group; easy availability of firearms; abusive parents; single-parent child; nuclear family; family violence; child sexual abuse, and role of media. However, as far as India is concerned, poverty and the effect of media are generally considered to be the main reasons for juvenile delinquency.

It is extremely difficult to assess precisely the extent of the problem in any part of the country since accurate statistics are not available and are not an indicator of the true extent. This is because of the fact that a large number of such acts remain undetected or unreported. Nevertheless, it has been observed that delinquency rates are highest in all developed countries. It is in countries with the highest levels of technical and economic advancement that social change occurs most rapidly, and traditional social roles and institutional controls over child conduct tend to break down. *Different scholars have classified juvenile delinquents on a different basis. Hirsch classified them in six groups on the basis of kinds of offences committed:*

- Incorrigibility (for example, disobedience and keeping late hours),
- Truancy (staying away from school),
- Larceny (ranging from petty thefts to armed robbery),
- Destruction of property (both public and private),
- Violence against individual or community, and
- Sexual offences ranging from homosexuality to rape.

Eaton and Polk, classified delinquents into five groups according to the offence: minor violations (disorderly conduct and minor traffic violations), major violations including thefts, property violations, addiction, and bodily harm including homicide and rape. Trojanawicz classified them as accidental, ill socialized, aggressive, occasional, professional, and gang-organized.

Eaton and Polk classified the delinquents by the following types of offences they have been involved in:

(1) Minor violations which include disorderly conduct and minor traffic violations.
(2) Property violations which include all property thefts, except automobiles.
(3) Major traffic violations which include automobile theft and drunk driving and any other offence that would involve an automobile.
(4) Human addiction which includes sex offenses as well as alcohol and drug addiction.
(5) Bodily harm which includes homicide offenses that involve sexual deviation, such as rape, and generally, all other acts of violence against a person.

Kvaraceus classifies youngsters who become delinquent in relation to three major variables:

(1) The extent to which the individual engages in delinquent behaviour.
(2) The degree of demonstrable emotional pathology.
(3) The individuals' social class.

METHODS OF TREATING DELINQUENTS

The seriousness of offences committed by juveniles is taken into consideration under the Juvenile Justice JJ Act and Rules in the following ways: Juveniles who are not released on bail, are required to be first placed in the reception unit of an institution called the Observation Home (OH), pending inquiry. Here, along with age, physical, and mental status, the degree of offence allegedly committed is also considered in order to classify and segregate the juveniles so that all children residing there get the requisite care and protection while in the Home. Juveniles who are alleged to have committed a serious offence may also be housed in a place of safety instead of the OH during the period of inquiry. The state governments have been empowered to frame rules to provide for the classification and segregation of juveniles also in Special Homes (SH) (institutions where a juvenile may be placed as per a final order of the Juvenile Justice Board JJB) on the basis of age, the nature of offence committed, and their mental and physical status. The JJB can also pass a final protective custody order that a juvenile above 16 years of age who has committed an offence "so serious in nature" that it would not be in his interest or the interest of other juveniles in an SH to place him there and that none of the other measures specified would be suitable, be kept in a place of safety. Juveniles who have been found guilty of committing heinous or serious offences can, at the most be sent to an SH for a maximum period of three years. At the time of passing final orders, the JJB can also reduce the period of stay if it satisfied that it is necessary to do so having regard to the nature of the offence and the circumstances of the case.

Such juveniles, like all others, are entitled to be socially integrated/rehabilitated through adoption, foster care, sponsorship, and after care. After care organizations are mandated by law to take care of juveniles after they leave the SH for the purpose of enabling them to lead an "honest, industrious, and useful life". Such after care can be provided for a maximum of three years, and for a juvenile between 17 and 18 years of age, till he/she attains the age of 20 years. All juveniles in after care come under the jurisdiction of the JJB. The law demands that intensive individualised attention be provided to such juveniles. Probation officers, the key duty bearers in this regard, are required to undertake a number of responsibilities that are vital to achieve the goals relating to juveniles who commit serious offences including developing various kinds of care plans, facilitating after care, and mentoring, monitoring, supervision, and reporting the progress of each juvenile. Individual Care Plans (ICPs) must be prepared for all juveniles within one month of their admission into an institution in order to ensure they get individualized attention in their journey towards reformation, rehabilitation, social mainstreaming, and restoration back into the community. The JJBs are required to pass final orders based on these ICPs prepared by a probation officer or voluntary organization on the basis of interaction with the juvenile and his family where possible. Moreover, a Mental Health Care Plan, with recommendations from experts has to be maintained in every case file and integrated into the ICP of every juvenile.

An appropriate response to juveniles who commit serious crime requires a system that demands specialized customized responses based on the needs and circumstances of each juvenile, while also taking into consideration the impact on the victim of his crime (if any), and the wider interests of the society.

From the above analysis it is clear that juvenile law in India does indeed provide for a juvenile jurisprudence grounded system which focuses on reforming and rehabilitating juveniles who commit serious crime through services that are monitored and reviewed rigorously. It also retains the focus on the ends of justice, taking into account the interests of the victim and the wider society.

CUSTODY IN JUVENILE INSTITUTIONS

The Juvenile Justice (Care and protection of children) Act, 2000 seeks to consolidate and modify the law relating to juveniles in conflict with the law and children in need of care and protection, by providing for proper care, protection, and treatment by catering to their development needs, and by adopting a child-friendly approach in the adjudication and disposition of matters in the best interest of children. For the betterment of the children, the Juvenile Justice Act, 2000 has introduced Special Trial Process. Specific sections of the Juvenile Justice Act cater to specific situations as provided here.

Section/s of the Juvenile Justice Act	Action Recommended
Sections 9 to 12	Facilitate the Government to establish Juvenile Homes, Special Homes, Observation Homes, and After Care Organisations respectively for the Juveniles
Section 3	If an inquiry has been initiated against a juvenile and if during the course of which he ceases to be a juvenile then the inquiry may be continued as if he had been a juvenile
Section 4	The state government can constitute one or more juvenile welfare boards for discharging the duties conferred upon them in relation to the neglected juveniles under this Act.
Section 5	The state government to constitute one or more juvenile courts for exercising the power conferred upon such court in relation to delinquent juveniles under this Act
Section 6	This section provides that a person appointed as a member of the Board or as a Magistrate shall possess special knowledge of child psychology and child welfare
Section 7	This section asks the Board or the Juvenile Court to hold its proceedings in a room which is different from the ordinary setting if a civil or criminal court
Section 29	This section allows a guardian or parents who have a certain extend of control over the child to be present at the court thus providing the child with the mental support that he needs and destroying the feeling of loneliness that may engulf the child

PREVENTIVE PROGRAMMES

There may be two kinds of programmes for preventing the juvenile delinquency:

(i) Individual programme

Individual programme involves the prevention of delinquency through counselling, psychotherapy, and proper education.

(ii) Environmental programme

Environmental programme involves the employment of techniques with a view to changing the socio-economic context likely to promote delinquency.

ROLE OF POLICE

Introduction

The police has an important role in apprehending and protection of juvenile delinquents. The police has more contact with the juveniles than any other agency dealing with the juvenile delinquents. The police is a separate agency from the juvenile court and it is also guided and directed by the policies and philosophies of the Juvenile Court with which the police has to work. Thus, in order to understand the police's behaviour towards juveniles, it is essential to understand all the facts of the juvenile court. In America, the police have evolved a distinctive style and approach towards offenders

Unless specially trained police is deployed and mindset of police is changed to work and act as a friend of the people, particularly juveniles, noticeable and expected change in the working of the police cannot be brought about.

(juveniles as well as adults) and they have a unique effect on many of juveniles they contact. Moreover, the police have some kind of contact with those who are more misbehaving than the other delinquents. All the delinquent and misbehaving children are picked up and arrested by the police but less than half are referred to the juvenile court and other half are to be handled independently by the police. The police decide which children will be handled and how. In addition, police have many more informal functions and encounters with children on streets and in places where they (children) loiter and their main function is to protect them from harm and maintain law and order. In India also, police have an important role for protecting the children from harm and maintaining the law and order. It is necessary that sympathetic treatment should be given to such type of children who do commit mistake or offence so that they do not repeat such omission. Therefore, manner of handling of the juvenile by the police determines the child's subsequent behaviour to a large extent.

Constitution of Special Juvenile Aid Police Unit

India is a very wide country having many states and union territories. It has divergent problems so different ways and means are required to tackle this issue. Urban areas, cities, towns, industrial habitations, etc. face this problem more. In many states, only city police has a special wing but in the rural areas such trained police is not available. For instance, Mumbai has got a Juvenile Aid Police Unit established in October 1952 as a part of vigilance branch under the control of a Deputy Commissioner of Police (criminal branch) headed by a lady inspector. The Juvenile Aid Police Unit deals with the cases of pre-delinquent, delinquent, socially handicapped, and victimized children and enforces the provision of Bombay Children Act. Apart from it, there was a Bombay Railway Juveniles Guide Service especially for boys who had run away and were picked up in the railway station. In 1958, in Parele, a boys club has been established for children between ages of 10 to 16. Tamil Nadu also has such boys clubs. Chennai city has a Juvenile Aid Police Unit. Hyderabad has Juvenile Aid Bureau under a Deputy Superintendent of Police. There are male and female officers in this bureau who are specially trained in this work. Andhra Pradesh also has a police boys club. Bihar had 'Juvenile Aid Bureaus' at Ranchi and at Patna. Each Bureau had 8 members under one Inspector of Police. Delhi Police also established a 'Juvenile Aid Bureau'. Calcutta Police started a bureau in 1958 under inspector of police who worked under the Deputy Commissioner of Police, Detective Department. The officials in the bureau were not given any special training but were given only workable information. Unless specially trained police is deployed and mindset of police is changed to work and act as a friend of the people, particularly juveniles, noticeable and expected change in the working of the police cannot be brought about. Subsequent to the establishment of Juvenile Aid Police Unit in Bombay, Juvenile Aid Police units/bureaus were established at Kolkata in 1956, Hyderabad in 1958, Chennai in 1960, Calicut in 1970, and Bhilai, Indore, and Jabalpur in 1974. The third Five Year Plan took note of the good work done by these special police units and recommended their expansion for dealing with juveniles, including vagrants, delinquent children, and children in pre-delinquent stage. On the basis of their study on Juvenile Aid Police Unit in the country, Shukla and Malviya suggested that it is necessary to establish specialist units in all the big cities with a population of one lakh or more, where the problem has already assumed significant proportions and where it would be feasible to have a body of specially trained officers engaged in this task on a whole time basis. The specialist units should be a part and parcel of the general police function and their work should be fully integrated with normal police work at the level of the police station. The National Police Commission favoured a less aggressive approach in dealing with children of tender age. It recommended that juveniles becoming way-ward, taking drugs, and pilfering objects out of bravado and smartness could be warned on record and their parents duly advised. Persons in danger of falling into the clutches of criminals could be brought to notice of social welfare organizations. Counselling and warning should be deemed legitimate as police activities towards prevention of crime. The commission further recommended that the police be trained and equipped properly with service oriented functions, including the counselling of the persons in distressful situations, which the commission recognized as service par excellence. The commission recommended that police should make a start in the metropolitan cities with this activity of counselling. In regard to the role of police in the enforcement of social legislations, including Children Acts, the commission took the view that as the primary law enforcement agency available to the State, police cannot escape involvement in the enforcement of such laws; rather, police have a duty to enforce these laws. In taking this view, the Commission rejected the conservative view that police should have nothing to do with social and economic legislations because:

(1) the police are concerned with the basic criminal law only;
(2) due to deficiencies of manpower and equipment, they can barely manage to enforce the basic criminal law and cannot undertake a wider role;
(3) socio-economic reform is not the business of police; and
(4) greater efficiency would result from concentration on a narrow role.

The Commission endorsed a forward looking view and observed that:

(1) police are the primary law enforcing agency and must enforce all laws;
(2) social and economic legislations represent an attempt to fulfil the aspirations of the people as outlined in the preamble of the Constitution and the Directive Principles of State Policy, and therefore, police must lend a hand in this national effort;
(3) by enforcing these laws police would be acting as agents of social change, a role which is definitely better for their psychological health than the traditional negative and punitive role; and
(4) social legislations often aim at social defence which being preventive in approach is of direct concern to the police.

After having taken this positive view, the commission recommended that a separate police wing might be set up for the enforcement of all social legislation. The main reason advanced for this suggestion was that the enforcement of social legislation requires a certain operational approach and attitude of mind on the part of the enforcement personnel which can be brought about by specialization and training. The commission recommended the creation of special police squads for metropolitan and other important cities which should function under the supervision of the city Police Chief. This recommendation of the Commission endorses the idea of establishing special juvenile aid police that had been considered appropriate for dealing with the cases of delinquent and non-delinquent children needing police attention and care.

Special Training Programme for Police

A special unit of police is necessary for the big cities like Kolkata, Mumbai, Bengaluru, Chennai, and Delhi etc. at the police station level where one-to-one contact takes place between the police and the delinquent. There must be at least one Inspector of Police having interest in the field. He must have attended special courses on the issue. This aspect of special training of Liverpool model has been discussed and recommended by the Annual Conference of inspector General of Police of all states and in 1960 they recommended a committee for preparing the training courses. A high level committee recommended a training programme, and also establishment of an institute on the pattern of central forensic institute of Calcutta and on the pattern, a national institute was established in Delhi. Educational institutions like colleges and universities in India should conduct such course and seminars for these investigational staff to provide opportunities for participation of and discussion amongst police, judges, lawyers, social workers, etc. on their point of view regarding handling such a sensitive issue. Such seminars and courses whenever conducted, should be attended by the higher cadre of academic, judicial, and administrative wing and by the persons working in the field who have to deal with day-to-day situations. These seminars should aim at sensitization of all concerned at all levels so that real goes to concerned lot , i.e., the juvenile delinquents and the society as well. Such programmes are very necessary for spreading awareness and knowledge to the students and general public about causes and ways and means by which such delinquency may be controlled and reduced in the society. This subject should be included in the teaching curriculum at the school level.

The Juvenile Justice (Care and Protection of Children) Act, 2000 in Chapter IV titled "Rehabilitation and Social Reintegration" has taken some new and positive steps by inserting sections 40 to 43 in the Act. Section 40 deals with process of rehabilitation and social reintegration. It provides that the rehabilitation and social reintegration of a child shall begin during the stay of the child in a children home or special home and the rehabilitation and social reintegration of children shall be carried out alternatively by

(i) adoption,
(ii) foster care,
(iii) sponsorship, and
(iv) sending the child to an alter-care organisation.

Section 41 deals with 'adoption'. It envisages that the primary responsibility for providing care and protection to children shall be that of his family. Sub-section (2) provides that adoption shall be resorted to for the rehabilitation of such children as are orphaned, abandoned, neglected, and abused through institutional and non-institutional methods. According to sub-section (3) in keeping with the provisions of the various guidelines for adoption issued from time to time by the state government, the board shall be empowered to give children in adoption and carry out such investigations as are required or giving children in adoption in accordance with the guidelines issued by the state government from time to time in this regard. Sub-section (4) of the section provides that the children homes or the state government run institutions for orphans shall be recognized as an adoption agency both for security and placement of such children for adoption in accordance with guidelines issued under sub-section (3). Sub-section (5) has, however, put certain restrictions by inserting therein that no child shall be offered for adoption:

(a) until two members of the Committee declare the child legally free for placement in the case of abandoned children,
(b) till the two months period for reconsideration by the parents is over in the case of surrendered children,
(c) without his consent in the case of a child who can understand and express his consent.

Sub-section (6) further states that the Board may allow a child to be given in adoption:

(a) to a single parent, and
(b) to parents to adopt a child of same sex irrespective of the number of living biological sons or daughters.

It may be submitted that a balance is to be found between this Act and the said section and the Adoption and Guardianship Acts in this area and such conflicts may be ironed out in course of time by court decisions if some problem arises in this context. However, this provision is a pragmatic step in the right direction and empowering the board with such wide powers is appropriate. But such jurisdiction should be exercised transparently and with an open mind and not influenced by agents or institutions exploiting children for gains.

12

ALCOHOLISM

Alcoholism is the disease that makes you too selfish to see the havoc you created and care about the people you shattered.

—Anonymous

DEFINITION AND CONCEPT

Alcoholism is defined as an addiction to the consumption of alcoholic liquor or the mental illness and compulsive behaviour resulting from alcohol dependency. In simple terms, alcoholism is drinking alcohol to excess frequently. The term "alcoholism" itself was not coined until 1860, and the theory that it is a medical disease was only postulated in 1930. According to Johnson (1973), alcoholism is a condition in which an individual loses control over his alcohol intake in that he is constantly unable to refrain from drinking once he begins. According to Keller and Efron (1955), alcoholism is characterised by the repeated drinking of alcoholic beverages to an extent that exceeds customary use or compliance with the social customs of the community and that adversely affects the drinker's health or interferes with his social or economic functioning. An alcoholic is different from an 'occasional drinker'. Any person who takes alcohol is a 'drinker', while a 'compulsive drinker' who cannot live without taking alcohol is called 'alcoholic'. Clinebell (1956) has defined 'alcoholic' as one whose drinking interferes frequently or continuously with any of his important life adjustments and interpersonal relationships.

Generally, moderate drinking for people over 21 is two drinks per day for males and one drink per day for females. Binge drinking is having 5 or more drinks, and it is considered dangerous. Alcohol affects the brain directly, slowing down its activities as well as those of the spinal cord. It acts as a depressant, i.e., it slows down responses. It gives the false impression of being a stimulant because it lowers inhibition and makes people lively. Contrary to popular conceptions, alcohol contains only empty calories, without any nutritive value. Alcohol leads to dependence in the case of several people. This causes serious difficulties in occupational and family life. It also causes problems in financial areas, social interaction, and physical and mental health of the addict and his/ her family. The short-term effects of alcohol consumption in a small quantity can lead to a lowering of inhibition. It also leads to increased anger, forgetting of unpleasant events, and a feeling of relaxation. Regular, frequent, excessive, and inappropriate use of alcohol leads to moodiness and loss of judgment. It leads to lack of control over body movements, and absence of alertness. It also creates loss of clarity of speech, absence of judgment, and even chronic illness and death.

Signs and symptoms of alcoholism are:

- Not being able to quit drinking or control how much you drink
- Needing to drink more to feel the same effect
- Feeling sick to your stomach, sweaty, shaky, or anxious when you stop drinking
- Giving up other activities so you can drink
- Trying to quit drinking or cut back, but not being able to
- Continuing to drink even though drinking causes you problems
- Trying to hide your drinking from others
- Having blackouts, where you don't remember what happened while drinking
- Having friends and family being concerned about your drinking
- Keep alcohol in unlikely places at home, at work, or in your car
- Gulp drinks, order doubles, or become drunk intentionally to feel good, or drink to feel "normal"
- Have legal problems or problems with relationships, employment, or finances due to drinking
- Lose interest in activities and hobbies that used to bring you pleasure

Alcohol Use in India

Alcohol use is very uneven in India among different regions, population groups, and socio-economic strata. Overall, even though alcohol abuse among those who consume alcohol is high, the proportion of teetotallers in the general population is high among adult men and very high among adult women and children below 15 years. According to the 2003 World Health Survey (total sample size $n = 9540$, males $n = 4605$, and females $n = 4935$; sample population aged 18 years and above), the rate of lifetime abstainers was 89.6% (total), 80.2% (males), and 98.4% (females) are in India. Estimates from key alcohol experts show that in India, the proportion of adult males and females who had been abstaining (last year before the survey) was 75% (males) and 96% (females). Heavy and hazardous drinking was defined as average consumption of 40 g or more of pure alcohol a day for men and 20 g or more of pure alcohol a day for women. The mean value (in grams) of pure alcohol consumed per day among drinkers was 35.9 (total), 38.3

(males), and 12.9 (females). The rate of heavy episodic drinking among the total population was 1.4% (total), 2.9% (males), and 0.1% (females). Heavy episodic drinking was defined as at least once a week consumption of five standard drinks in one sitting.

CAUSES OF ALCOHOL ABUSE

A grave social evil like alcoholism is not due to any one single factor. It is the result of the operation of multifarious factors. In analysing the causes of alcoholism, the important factor to keep in mind is that, of those who use alcohol, about 90% do not become alcoholics. The key to alcoholism is in the motive for repeating the drinking. Therefore, explaining alcoholism only in terms of factors like personality structure will be inadequate. Alcoholic addiction is a complex phenomenon that research indicates is likely to be caused by a variety of factors rather than a single one. It was earlier believed that people who were of a certain type, viz. deviant were more likely to become addicted. There is no fixed type of personality which is addiction prone. Some factors may however, create a favourable environment or the development of addiction, while some factors may make it more difficult to give up addiction.

Factors of Addiction

Physiological Causes

It has been found that if both parents of a child are addicted, the child has greater chances of developing addiction. While this does not mean that children of all addicts will become addicts, it suggests a greater possibility. Alcoholism tends to run in the family, suggesting that the predisposition to be an addict may be inherited. Some physiological factors which are believed to contribute towards the development of addiction of alcoholism are nutritional deficiency, dysfunction of different body system, e.g., endocrine system, etc. However, none of these have been conclusively proved.

Individual or Psychological Causes

According to some scholars, there seems to be a definite connection between alcoholism and personality maladjustment. Initially, a person drinks to seek refuge for his problems of life or to find a temporary respite from his troubles. Gradually, he starts drinking more and more frequently until he becomes utterly dependent on it. However, psychologists maintain that only those people take to frequent drinking who are emotionally immature, emotionally deprived, lacking in self confidence, having a high level of anxiety in interpersonal relationships and those who have ambivalence towards authority, low frustration tolerance, low self-esteem, and feeling of isolation and guilt.

Sociocultural Causes

The sociological reasons for taking alcohol are essentially the same for taking drugs. Several theories are offered today which claim that addiction has sociocultural origins. People in societies that view that consumption of drugs and/or alcohol as acceptable, and where drugs are easily and cheaply available are likely to have high consumption of drugs/alcohol. In some tribal societies, the consumption of alcohol is a part of religious rituals and ceremonies. Such regular consumption may cause some people to become addicted. This does not mean that only availability and acceptance encourages addiction. In societies where this consumption is not accepted, some people turn to drugs/alcohol because they suffer normlessness. Youth often take drugs as a rebellion against adult norms and values. The cultural

In India, tradition has accepted the use of alcohol, bhang, or ganja on certain religious and social occasions like marriage, death, celebrations, etc. and more so among certain sociocultural groups.

defiance theory thus, indicates that drug addiction develops because of these emotional and social ties, with a non-conventional group. To add to this is the factor of social acceptance of alcohol and milder forms of drugs in certain sections of the society. In India, tradition has accepted the use of alcohol, bhang, or ganja on certain religious and social occasions like marriage, death, celebrations, etc. and more so among certain sociocultural groups. Today, the social consumption of alcohol in particular has risen in all sociocultural groups and it is considered to be a sign of social prestige to drink. In certain Western countries, taking alcohol is socially the norm and taking pills to reduce pain or improve performance is the regular practice. The legal status of the addicting substance is also an important factor in determining the incidence of addiction. Whether a culture accepts the consumption of a drug/alcohol or punishes it, is also believed to be closely related to the extent of addiction in that culture. Thus, both legal and cultural approval of drugs/alcohol are believed to increase rates of addiction. However, if milder forms of drugs/alcohol are legally permitted, the number of persons addicted to "hard" drugs/alcohol will reduce. Such persons hold that classifying all drugs/alcohol into one broad category has had a negative impact on attempts at preventing addiction. Among young people, growing up is a stage of proving oneself to one's peer, i.e., those in the same age group, who help to shape one's sense of identity. Since ability to tolerate alcohol is equated with one's manhood, boys often begin to consume alcohol and at times drugs at a young age, due to peer pressure. As in the case of age and cultural background, occupation too has been found to be related to addiction. Persons in jobs that create stress, physical and/ or mental, are known to become addicted.

Those prone to addiction thus include:

i) Persons in conservancy jobs, morticians, and morgue workers, ragpickers, etc. whose job is associated with unpleasant activities,
ii) Those performing excessively exhausting, monotonous, laborious work, e.g. load-carriers and porters, drivers, etc.
iii) Persons in competitive target-oriented jobs, where many deals may be struck around alcohol, like marketing and sales, etc.
iv) Persons who are induced by family members. Family influence is believed to be another important environmental factor in addiction. Imitation may occur if the family has an adult addict.

It is therefore clear that several sociocultural, psychological, and physical factors can contribute towards alcoholism, often in combination, rather than singly. However, a significant distinction can be made in the causes of drinking alcohol and taking illicit drugs. Since alcohol is more socially acceptable than drugs, drinking reduces a person's fear, worries, and anxieties. Besides, alcohol is more easily available and also cheaper than many costly drugs like heroin, cocaine, etc.

PROHIBITION IN INDIA

The 'World Health Organisation' recommends that member governments should begin to reduce per capita consumption of alcohol by reducing the availability of alcoholic beverages. Prohibition is incorporated in the Constitution of India among the Directive Principles of state policy. Article 47 says: "The state shall regard the raising of the level of nutrition and standard of living of its people as among its primary duties and in particular, the state shall endeavour to bring about prohibition of the use except for medicinal purposes of intoxicating drinks and of drugs which are injurious to health." Alcohol policy is under the legislative power of individual states. Prohibition, enshrined as an aspiration in the Constitution, was introduced and then withdrawn in Haryana and Andhra Pradesh in the mid-1990s, although it continues in Gujarat, (and now in Bihar) with partial restrictions in other states—Delhi, for example, has dry days. There was an earlier failure of prohibition in Tamil Nadu. The Excise department regulates and controls the sale of liquor in the NCT of Delhi. Retail supply of alcohol is regulated by Delhi Liquor License Rules, 1976. It prohibits consumption and service of liquor at public places. This also prohibits employment to any person (male under the age of 25 years or any female) at any licensed premises either with or without remuneration in part of such premises in which liquor or intoxicating drug is consumed by the public. Similarly, no individual should possess liquor at one time more than the prescribed limit without special permit. As per excise rules in Rajasthan, a person can possess maximum 3 litres of country liquor, 6 litres of IMFL, and 12 bottles of beer. The Bombay Prohibition Act, 1949, prohibits the production, manufacture, possession, exportation, importation, transportation, purchase, sale, consumption and use of all intoxicants. The Cable Television Network (Regulation) Amendment Bill, which came into force on September 8, 2000, completely prohibits cigarette and alcohol advertisements. The government controlled

Prohibition in Bihar

The Nitish Kumar government in Bihar has passed a stringent law to enforce its total prohibition policy. Prohibition on country-made liquor was imposed on April 1, 2016 and within days it was expanded to cover Indian-Made Foreign Liquor. The State has also come up with fresh legislation to supersede earlier Acts in a bid to ward off criticism that penal laws and administrative measures do not prevent alcohol consumption. The most draconian one allows action against all adult members of a family if liquor is found on their premises or one of them is suspected to have consumed it. The law presumes that all of them must be aware of the offence until proven otherwise, but essentially this amounts to collective punishment. Similarly, the owner of any premises in which liquor is stored or consumed is liable for prosecution. With the offences related to consumption, storage and possession of alcohol or any other intoxicant being cognisable, the sweeping provision could land anyone in jail because of the involvement of one family member, tenant or visitor. The authorities could seal or confiscate the property, and fine a group of people or a village, for repeated transgressions. The laws have faced criticism from many quarters for its sheer impracticability and inability to implement. The sheer confusion and social tensions it can cause has also been widely discussed. However, the move is seen to be more of a political gambit rather than a genuine attempt to resolve the issue.

Attempts to Enforce Prohibition

Drunkenness: Drunkenness is defined as the condition produced in a person who has taken alcohol in a quantity sufficient to cause him to lose control of his faculties to such an extent that he is unable to execute the occupation in which he is engaged at the material time. Section 84 of the Bombay Prohibition Act 1949 provides that any person, who is found drunk or drinking in a common drinking house or is found there present for the purpose of drinking, shall on conviction, be punished with fine which may extend to five hundred rupees. Section 85 provides that any person found drunk and incapable of controlling himself or behaves in a disorderly manner under the influence of drink in any street or thoroughfare or public place or in any place to which public have or are permitted to have access, shall on conviction, be punished with imprisonment for a term which may extend from one to three months and with fine which may extend from two hundred to five hundred rupees.

Drunken Driving: Across the world, governments have defined different acceptable blood alcohol levels. However, there is no minimum threshold below which alcohol can be consumed without risk. With rise in blood alcohol concentration, there is progressive loss of driving ability due to increased reaction time, overconfidence, impaired concentration, degraded muscle coordination, and decreased visual and auditory acuity. Though the laws to check the drunken driving do exist in India, there is need to effectively impose the same on the alcohol impaired drivers. The blood alcohol content (BAC) limits are fixed at 0.03%. Any person whose BAC values are detected more than this limit is booked under the first offense. He/she may be fined about 2000 and/or he or she may face a maximum of 6 months imprisonment. If he person commits a second offense within 3 years of the first, then he/she may be fined about 3000 and/or he or she may face a maximum of 2 years imprisonment. On 1 March 2012, the Union Cabinet approved proposed changes to the Motor Vehicle Act. According to The Motor Vehicles (Amendment) Act 2019, the maximum penalty for driving under the influence of alcohol or drugs has been increased from Rs 2,000 to Rs 10,000.

Alcohol Advertisements: Advertising alcoholic beverages has been banned in India as per the Cable Television Network (Regulation) Amendment Bill which came into effect on 8 September, 2000. Private channels often permit alcohol companies to advertise using surrogate means like selling the brand name for soda or water.

channel, Doordarshan, does not broadcast such advertisements but satellite channels however are replete with them.

WOMEN AND ANTI-LIQUOR MOVEMENTS

Women activists, women's organisations, and even ordinary housewives in rural areas have started struggling hard over the past several years to convince men against liquor consumption and force the government to introduce prohibition. They demanded that they will vote only for parties committed to prohibition in their poll manifestos. It was in 1993 that a small group of neo-literate women in Dabbagunta village in Nellore district in Andhra Pradesh, fed up with the drunkenness of their men, attacked a liquor shop, drove away its owners, and destroyed the stocks of arrack. The spark provided by the unorganized women of a small dusty village caught the imagination of the womenfolk all over Andhra Pradesh, from where the agitation spread to other states in the country. In 1996, 40 women from various states participated in a two day national workshop on "Anti-Arrack Struggles" jointly sponsored by the National Commission for women and Mahila Haat. The participants discussed the question of strengthening their struggles against this social evil. In Nellore district of Andhra Pradesh, before the anti-arrack struggle took off, 70% of men were drunkards and 70% of their daily wage was dissipated on arrack, but since the introduction of arrack prohibition, household disposal incomes have nearly doubled. The battle against arrack being not only an Andhra Pradesh women's movement but a general social movement, women in almost every state are fighting it tooth and nail. Chhatisgarh Mahila Mandal in Madhya Pradesh, Uttarakhand Mahila Manch, Pauri Garhwal Mandal in Madhyapradesh, and Mahila Mandals in Haryana, Punjab, Rajasthan, Kerala, Tamil Nadu, Gujarat, etc; are trying to make their anti-arrack agitation successful by attacking liquor shops and breaking the 'bhattis' where illicit liquor is produced.

CONTROL OF ALCOHOLISM

Alcoholism has been one of the earliest habits of man. Attempts have also been made from the times immemorial to control it. Over the years, this habit has grown into a social evil posing a big challenge to public health. With the failure of the prohibition model, state governmental control has come to be focused on the regulation of the liquor trade. The state governments, under the open licence system, leave the alcoholic beverage trade to private enterprise under licensing and regulation, the nominal public objectives being to eliminate people with criminal or questionable financial histories and to control the physical location of licensed liquor shops. Every state government earns crores of rupees every year when it auctions the contracts. Since the present social systems operating in Indian society produce more frustrations and deprivations, the rate of drinking would only accelerate in future. What is, therefore, needed is policies and programmes to produce more jobs, permit fair competition, and reduce corruption and nepotism in appointments and promotions. If the lives of people can made meaningful, rewarding, and satisfying, the need for alcohol would not exist in our society or it will be minimised. Parents can impart education on the dangers of becoming an alcoholic as well as punish the deviants and create the necessary fear. Parents education should be concerned with the shaping of the attitude and behaviour conducive to non-drinking. School and colleges can also educate young students about the psychological and sociological effects of alcohol and alcoholism. Gandhi could not think of an independent India without prohibition. For him, prohibition was an integral part of the freedom movement. He clearly declared that if he were to be appointed dictator of the country for one hour, his first action would be to close all the liquor shops without paying the compensation. For Gandhi, the evil of alcoholism was worse than theft and even prostitution, as it was the mother of both these evils. It may, thus, be concluded that the problem of alcoholism in India calls for a concerted attack which may embrace treatment, social and welfare measures, education, and research.

Nasha Mukt Bharat Annual Action Plan for 2020-21 would focus on 272 most affected districts and launch a three-pronged attack combining efforts of Narcotics Bureau, Outreach/Awareness by Social Justice and Treatment through the Health Dept.

The Action Plan has the following components: Awareness generation programmes; Focus on Higher Educational institutions, University Campuses and Schools; Community outreach and identification of dependent population; Focus on Treatment facilities in Hospital settings; and Capacity Building Programmes for Service Provider.

Based on the finding of the National Survey on Extent and Pattern of Substance Use in India and list of districts which are vulnerable from the supply point of view provided by Narcotics Control Bureau, the Ministry of Social Justice and Empowerment would undertake intervention programmes in vulnerable districts across the country with an aim to: Reach out to Children and Youth for awareness about ill effect of drug use; Increase community participation and public cooperation; Supporting Government Hospitals for opening up De- addiction Centers in addition to existing Ministry Supported De-addiction Centers (IRCAs); and Conducting Training programme for participants.

13

DRUG ABUSE AND DRUG ADDICTION

We realise that drug addiction is a sickness, but it's also a crime. —*Pam Bondi*

INTRODUCTION

Recent studies show that there is an increasing use of illicit drugs in India. The reported numbers reveal that over 3 million people of India are addicted to drugs. However, the World Health Organization does note that there is significant difficulty in estimating drug usage and addiction rates in the country due to poor enumeration processes. Cannabis, heroin, opium, and hashish are the most commonly used drugs in India. However, some evidence indicates that there is an increasing prevalence of methamphetamine as well. Drug addiction is a major problem for many families, communities, and law enforcement officials. Massive numbers of addicts are left to be treated by the families as financial costs, available services, and lack of appropriate care challenge the country. This is not only the case for drug addicts. HIV is a significant issue for drug addicts in India with over 2.4 million people being infected. This places India as the third-highest country in terms of rate of infection in the world. Injecting drug users make up nearly 10% of the affected groups. The increasing rate of HIV that spread throughout all communities of India alarmed the government which began to formulate policies to curb the menace. This included needle exchange programs and maintenance therapy.

ABERRANT BEHAVIOUR

Behaviours more likely to be associated with medication abuse/addiction:

- Selling medications or obtaining them from non-medical sources
- Falsification of prescription—forgery or alteration
- Injecting medications meant for oral use
- Resistance to changing medications despite deterioration in function or significant negative effects
- Loss of control over alcohol use
- Use of illegal drugs or controlled substances that are not prescribed for the patient

- Recurrent episodes of
  a. Prescription loss or theft
  b. Obtaining opioids from other providers in violation of treatment agreement
  c. Increases in dosing without provider's instruction
  d. Running short with medication supply, and requests for early refills

Behaviours that look aberrant but may be more a part of stabilizing a patient's pain condition, and less predictive of medication abuse/addiction:

- Asking for, or even demanding, more medication
- Asking for specific medications
- Stockpiling and use of medications during times when pain is less severe
- Use of the pain medication to treat other symptoms
- Reluctance to decrease opioid dosing once stable
- And, in the earlier stages of treatment:
  a. Increasing medication dosing without instruction to do so from the provider
  b. Obtaining prescriptions from sources other than the primary pain provider
  c. Sharing or borrowing similar medications from friends/family

BASIC STATISTICS

According to the data from the Narcotics Control Bureau (NCB), the number of people getting addicted to drugs has increased drastically. Currently, there are around 10 crore people in the country who are addicted to various narcotics substances. As per official estimates, More than 70% of the drugs are smuggled into the country through international sea routes, while 20% is by roadway and 10% by air.

What is alarming is the number of suicides due to drug abuse and alcohol addiction has more than doubled in the last decade in India. In the year 2010, 3,343 cases of suicides were reported, and the number increased to 7,860 suicides in 2019.

The United Nations Office on Drugs and Crime (UNODC), in its World Drug Report 2021, has highlighted that the lockdown restrictions during Covid-19 have accelerated drug trafficking using the Internet. By drugs, the Report refers to substances controlled under international drug control conventions, and their non-medical use.

The report has also revealed that between 2010-2019, the number of people using drugs increased by 22%, owing in part to an increase in the global population.

Around 275 million people used drugs worldwide last year, while over 36 million people suffered from drug use disorders. Opioids continue to account for the largest burden of disease attributed to drug use. A rise in the non-medical use of pharmaceutical drugs was also observed during the coronavirus pandemic.

Access to drugs has also become simpler than ever with online sales, and major drug markets on the dark web are now worth some $315 million annually. In Asia, China and India are mainly linked to shipment of drugs sold on the 19 major darknet markets analysed over 2011-2020. Cannabis dominates drug transactions on Dark web and on clear web involves sale of Narcotic Drugs and Psychotropic Substances (NDPS) and substances used in the manufacture of synthetic drugs.

India is vulnerable to the trafficking of narcotics as it is sandwiched between the 'Golden Crescent' and the 'Golden Triangle', the major opium production regions in the world. The Golden Crescent region of the South comprises Afghanistan, Iran and Pakistan. The Golden Triangle is the area where the borders of Thailand, and meet at the confluence of the Ruak and Mekong rivers.

NATURE AND IMPACT OF ABUSABLE DRUGS

Cannabis Addiction

Cannabis is an incredibly popular and widely used drug in India and is known as ganja, charas, or bhang. India has a long history of cannabis use, and the drug is one of the five sacred plants mentioned in the Hindu texts, the *Vedas*. It is typically associated with the Hindu deity Shiva, who is believed to like the hemp plant. The drug is often smoked or drunk as a beverage at Hindu ceremonies. Cannabis is combined with a mixture of milk or yoghurt and boiled with nuts and spices to make a refreshing beverage. This drink is consumed by many all over the country, especially by labour workers who find the relaxing properties beneficial. Despite its widespread and accepted use, cannabis is illegal to use and possess in any form. Some figures place regular cannabis users as high as 10 million in India, many of these among the working poor. Many of these heavy users are dependent on the drug and suffer from major health problems including respiratory disorders, memory impairment, mental disturbance, digestive tract problems, major weight loss, and problems with sleep.

Brown Sugar (Heroin)

India is known to be one of the primary consumers of heroin in the world along with China, Pakistan, and Iran. India is also the largest grower of illicit opium in the world, which is used to make a range of prescription medications including morphine and synthetic opium drugs. The geographical location of India is between two of the largest illicit opium growers, Myanmar and Afghanistan, and evidence shows that India is used as a major trafficking route between the two. Additionally, law enforcement has an increasing problem of dealing with illicit opium being diverted to illegal markets inside of India and being trafficked beyond its borders. A form of heroin known as brown sugar is commonly used in the country, which is made of a mixture of heroin which typically ranges between 20 to 60% purity, and adulterants in the form of chalk, zinc, or other chemicals. The drug is popular in India because it is cheap and readily available. However, the purity of the drug is questionable and can increase the risk of overdosing. Additionally, some users suffer serious adverse effects from taking the drug, as the adulterant substances can be toxic. Injecting drug users often suffer from cellulitis or other infections, and respiratory issues are common amongst users who smoke the substance. Evidence suggests that there is an increasing trend of Indian people using brown sugar (heroin) across all groups in society, from children as young as 13. It is not just a drug for the wealthy and elite. It is now taken by students and women, and is commonly used in slums, in wealthy enclaves, and by business people. Heroin is a drug that is easy to take but difficult to overcome. The addictive properties are well documented but access to rehabilitation services and medical treatments are

A form of heroin known as brown sugar is commonly used in the country, which is made of a mixture of heroin which typically ranges between 20 to 60% purity, and adulterants in the form of chalk, zinc, or other chemicals.

often not available to people in India. This is especially true for those who are from the poor communities. Accurate heroin addiction rates in India are unknown. However, there are over 1 million registered addicts, with estimates suggesting that the actual number may be as high as 5 million.

Methamphetamine

Methamphetamine is a major problem throughout the world and there are increasing reports of its use in India. The first clandestine methamphetamine laboratory was discovered by law enforcement in 2003, and many more have been found since then. India is a key producer of precursor chemicals for methamphetamine which include ephedrine and chemicals that are used in the processing. The majority of methamphetamine chemicals are trafficked to major manufacturing countries like China, Thailand, Mexico, and America. Methamphetamine use is linked to many serious physical and mental health concerns including violence, paranoia, insomnia, organ damage, and brain damage. Amphetamine drugs are often used by the working class poor as a stimulant to help them work harder, for longer, and with lesser requirement for food. Using drugs for this purpose is incredibly dangerous and can lead to major problems with families and communities. Not only are they highly addictive, but their use can damage motor skills, response times, problem solving skills, and cause sexual dysfunction.

OVERALL VIEW

The epidemic of substance abuse in the young generation has assumed alarming dimensions in India. Changing cultural values, increasing economic stress, and dwindling supportive bonds are leading to initiation

June 26 is celebrated as International Day against Drug Abuse and Illicit Trafficking every year. It is an exercise undertaken by the world community to sensitize the people in general and the youth in particular, to the menace of drugs.

into substance use. According to the World Health Organization (WHO), substance abuse is persistent or sporadic drug use inconsistent with or unrelated to acceptable medical practice. The picture is grim if the world statistics on the drugs scenario is taken into account. With a turnover of around $500 billions, it is the third largest business in the world, next to petroleum and arms trade. About 190 million people all over the world consume one drug or the other. Drug addiction causes immense human distress and the illegal production and distribution of drugs have spawned crime and violence worldwide. June 26 is celebrated as International Day against Drug Abuse and Illicit Trafficking every year. It is an exercise undertaken by the world community to sensitize the people in general and the youth in particular, to the menace of drugs. Today, there is no part of the world that is free from the curse of drug trafficking and drug addiction. Millions of drug addicts, all over the world, are leading miserable lives, between life and death. India too is caught in this vicious circle of drug abuse, and the numbers of drug addicts are increasing day by day. According to a

UN report, one million heroin addicts are registered in India, and unofficially there are as many as five million.

EXTENT AND NATURE OF DRUG ABUSE

Cannabis, heroin, and Indian-produced pharmaceutical drugs are the most frequently abused drugs in India. Cannabis products, often called charas, bhang, or ganja, are abused throughout the country because it has attained some amount of religious sanctity because of its association with some

Street Children and Drug Abuse

According to UNICEF, 100 million children live and work on the streets of the cities of the world: 40 million in Latin America, 25–30 million in Asia, and 10 million in Africa. India has the largest number of street children in the world. Though, India is largely still rural, urbanization is taking place rapidly, leading to fast growth of slums and shanty towns. All these factors have resulted in an explosion of street children in the country. 18 million children live and work in India's slums qualifying to be the street children. According to WHO estimates, up to 90% of the world's street children abuse some kind of drugs. There is no systematic data on the prevalence of drug abuse in street children in India and the published literature is available from the metropolitan cities only. The National Household Survey on Drug Abuse surveyed 40,697 males of whom 8,587 were children (aged 12–18 years). Of these, 3.8% were using alcohol, 0.6% cannabis, and 0.2% opiates. Though this survey looked into the substance use pattern of children living in houses, it provided a yardstick for comparing the substance use in street children.

Hindu deities. The International Narcotics Control Board in its 2002 report released in Vienna pointed out that in India, persons addicted to opiates are shifting their drug of choice from opium to heroin. The pharmaceutical products containing narcotic drugs are also increasingly being abused. The intravenous injections of analgesics like dextropropoxphene, etc. are also reported from many states, as it is easily available at 1/10th the cost of heroin. The codeine-based cough syrups continue to be diverted from the domestic market for abuse.

Drug abuse is a complex phenomenon, which has various social, cultural, biological, geographical, historical, and economic aspects. The disintegration of the old joint family system, absence of parental love and care in modern families where both parents are working, decline of old religious and moral values etc., lead to a rise in the number of drug addicts who take drugs to escape the hard realities of life. Drug use, misuse, or abuse is also primarily due to the nature of the drug abused, the personality of the individual, and the addict's immediate environment. The processes of industrialisation, urbanisation, and migration have led to loosening of the traditional methods of social control rendering an individual vulnerable to the stresses and strains of modern life. The introduction of synthetic drugs and intravenous drug use leading to HIV/AIDS has added a new dimension to the problem, especially in the Northeast states of the country. Drug abuse has led to a detrimental impact on the society. It has led to increase in the crime rate.

Adolescent drug abuse is one of the major areas of concern in adolescent and young people's behaviour. It is estimated that, in India, by the time most boys reach the ninth grade, about 50% of them have tried at least one of the substance of abuse nature. In the last three decades, many epidemiological surveys have been carried out in India to assess the prevalence of substance abuse. The important finding of these studies is that alcohol was the commonest substance used (60–98%) followed by cannabis use (4–20%). Epidemiological surveys also revealed that 20–40% of subjects above 15 years are current users of alcohol and 10% of them are regular or excessive users. Increase in incidences of HIV, hepatitis B and C, and tuberculosis due to addiction adds the reservoir of infection in the community burdening the health care system further. Women in India face greater problems from drug abuse. The consequences include domestic violence and infection with HIV, as well as the financial burden.

India has braced itself to face the menace of drug trafficking both at the national and international levels. Several measures involving innovative changes in enforcement, legal, and judicial systems have been brought into effect. The introduction of death penalty for drug-related offences has been a major deterrent. The Narcotic Drugs and Psychotropic Substances Act, 1985, were enacted with stringent provisions to curb this menace. The Act envisages a minimum term of 10 years imprisonment extendable to 20 years and fine of Rs. 1 lakh extendable up to Rs. 2 lakhs for the offenders. Comprehensive strategy involving specific programmes to bring about an overall reduction in use of drugs has been evolved by the various government agencies, and NGOs and is further supplemented by measures like education, counselling, treatment, and rehabilitation programmes. Substance abuse can be addressed at the individual level, at the local level (society, national, etc.), and at the cross-national level. At the individual level, there has to be a synthesis of biological understanding with the exploration of background sociocultural factors. At the national and cross-national level, there has to be a concerted effort of all the countries in managing the issue of substance abuse, taking into account the local sociocultural and political scenarios.

MOTIVATIONS IN DRUG USAGE

Social and cultural factors play an important role in initiation, maintenance, and therapeutic intervention of drug abuse. No single or generic set of variables explains the misuse of substances for every individual. Depending on an individual's biological makeup, developmental stage, and interaction with various environmental forces, individual risk, vulnerability, and resilience to substance abuse and addiction will vary for different factors at different times. Indian society, which enjoys cultural diversity, has a history of use of plant products, viz., cannabis, opium, and home brewed alcohol beverages within a defined sociocultural framework over five millennium. There are certain social groups which are more vulnerable to substance abuse. Local customs and traditions play significant role in the choice of drugs, their consumption, and their control in rural/semi-urban populations. Though some workers describe Indian society to be traditionally abstinent, the recent developments do not support this concept. In India, the numbers of drug addicts are increasing day by day. India also has a huge at-risk young population with 40% being below the age of 18 years.

According to UN Convention Reports on Narcotic Drugs and Psychotropic Substances in 1961, 1971, and 1988, it is estimated that, in India, by the time most boys reach the ninth grade, about 50% of them have tried at least one of the gateway drugs. Smokeless tobacco in the form of gutka is commonly used by children and adolescents in certain states. Every year, about 55,000 children take up to smoking, generally hailing from low socio-economic strata with poor social support, broken homes, and victims of deprivation and discrimination. This risky behaviour is often initiated during childhood and adolescence, as more than 70% of adult smokers report that they started smoking on a daily basis prior to age 18. One million heroin addicts are registered in India, and unofficially there are as many as five million.

ROLE OF FAMILY AND PEER GROUP AND MEDIA

There are various social and cultural factors associated with drug abuse, especially among children and adolescents.

1. Parental Influence

Parents have a tremendous influence on their children and the children of smoker parents are twice likely to become smokers. Parental disapproval of smoking makes an adolescent less likely to initiate smoking. Female adolescents are more likely to be smokers if both parents are smokers. There is a strong correlation between a mother smoking and the female youth becoming a smoker. When raised in a home where parents smoke exposes the young person to tobacco smoke. Parents who smoke may also give easy access to cigarettes and are less likely to oppose their children's smoking. The children are also more likely to smoke whose elder siblings are smokers. Cannabis, a traditional drug in Indian society is ritualized in social and religious gatherings. It is a socially sanctioned behaviour in certain cultural groups to use bhang and charas by adolescents and has parental approval for that. Parental attitude towards alcohol plays an important role in initiating the adolescent to drink alcohol.

2. Family Structure

Higher levels of parental education and socio-economic variables have an inverse relationship with tobacco use and use of other psychoactive substances among adolescents. Prevalence of smoking is more common in families which are with low socio-economic educational status of the society. Children using inhalants generally hail from low socio-economic status, engaged in menial work with unstable family income. Marital discord, divorces among parents, single parenting, etc. are associated with drug abuse among adolescents. Parents having poor monitoring of their children are likely to have their children abusing drugs.

3. Peer Influence

Friends have the greatest influence on the young smokers. The initiation of tobacco smokers generally occurs in the company of a friend who is a smoker. Female adolescents with a best friend who is a smoker are nine times more at risk to become smokers. Smoking is a shared activity with important socializing functions for the female youth. Peer smoking also predicts continued smoking among young people who have already begun to smoke. Cannabis abuse in school-going population has been associated with poor scholastic performance, school dropouts, and reinforcement of conduct symptoms. These adolescents form their own peer group.

4. Role Model Film and TV Stars

Pop stars and fashion models make smoking seem attractive. They leave a tremendous impact on the adolescent mind. The adolescents smoke to imitate their style.

5. Advertising and Promotion

Advertising is an effective weapon to influence the decision of the young to initiate smoking. Advertising bans have been found to be very effective in reducing cigarette smoking prevalence in youth. Indian Government has banned advertisement of cigarettes and other tobacco products through the Act called "The Cigarettes and other Tobacco Products Act 2003 (COTPA).

6. Socio-Economic Factors

Higher drug-abuse rates are observed in lower income groups. Adolescents from low socio-economic background are more likely to become smokers than the middle-class counterparts. In India, beedi smoking is more common in adolescents for the reasons of easy availability, low price, and convenience to use. Adolescents from low income families tend to use cheap and spurious country-made liquor prepared illegally. Use of inhalants is also common in the adolescents from poor families.

7. Availability

Availability and accessibility are important factors in initiation and maintenance of drug abuse among adolescent. An adolescent who has an easy access to drugs or alcohol because his parents or elder sibling is using, is more likely to use these drugs than those whose parents or anyone else is not using these in the family. Similarly, peer group members making the product available are likely to recruit new adolescents in the drug use behaviour.

8. Knowledge, Attitude, and Beliefs

Knowledge about the detrimental health effects has a preventive effect on drug use. Some believe that moderate alcohol consumption does not have adverse effects, tobacco cessation could lead to weight gain, and cannabis is a social and religious blessing of gods. These beliefs permit the adolescents to use drugs without hesitation or guilt. Positive attitude towards the drugs is likely to initiate drug use among the adolescents.

COMBATING DRUG TRAFFICKING, TREATING ADDICTS, AND PREVENTING DRUG ABUSE

The Narcotic Drugs and Psychotropic Substances Act, 1985 (NDPS)

India is a party to the three United Nations drug conventions—the 1961 Single Convention on Narcotic Drugs (1961 Convention), the 1971 Convention on Psychotropic Substances (1971 Convention), and the 1988 Convention against Illicit Traffic in Narcotic Drugs and Psychotropic

Substances (1988 Convention). Domestic legislation to give effect to these treaties was introduced only in the 1980s when the 'grace period' for abolishing non-medical use of cannabis and opium under the 1961 Convention expired. Exercising its powers to make law for the country for implementing "any treaty, agreement or convention or decision made at international conference", the Indian Parliament passed the Narcotic Drugs and Psychotropic Substances Act, 1985 (NDPS Act) hastily, without much debate. The NDPS Act came into force on 14 November 1985, replacing the Opium Acts and the Dangerous Drugs Act. The 1940 Drugs and Cosmetics Act, 1940, however, continue to apply.

The official record states that the NDPS Act was enacted in order to provide adequate penalties for drug trafficking, strengthen enforcement powers, implement international conventions to which India was a party, and enforce controls over psychotropic substances. The Act was amended in 1989, 2001, and more recently in 2014.

The NDPS Act prohibits cultivation, production, possession, sale, purchase, trade, import, export, use, and consumption of narcotic drugs and psychotropic substances except for medical and scientific purposes in accordance with the law. Preparation to commit certain offences is punishable as is attempt. Accessory crimes of aiding and abetting and criminal conspiracy attract the same punishment as the principal offence.

The Act covers three broad classes of substances:

1) narcotic drugs, that is, those covered under the 1961 Convention;
2) psychotropic substances or those covered under the 1971 Convention as well as other psychoactive substances such as ketamine which are not yet classified under international conventions; and
3) "controlled substances" that are used to manufacture narcotic drugs or psychotropic substances, for example precursor chemicals such as acetic anhydride, ephedrine, and pseudoephedrine.

Narcotic drugs include:

- *Cannabis*: plant; resin or charas and its concentrated variant called hashish; dried flowering or fruiting tops of the plant, that is, ganja and any mixture of charas or ganja. Importantly, bhang or the cannabis leaf is excluded (in accordance with the 1961 Convention) and regulated through state excise laws
- *Coca*: plant; leaf; derivatives include cocaine and any preparation containing 0.1% of cocaine
- *Opium*: poppy plant; poppy straw; concentrated poppy straw; juice of opium poppy; mixture of opium poppy juice; preparations with 0.2% morphine; derivatives include heroin, morphine, codeine, thebaine, etc.

The NDPS Act lays down the procedure for search, seizure, and arrest of persons in public and private places. Safeguards such as prior recording of information, notifying a superior, limiting powers of arrest to designated officers, informing the person being searched of her/his rights—have been scrupulously enforced by the courts, in light of the stringent punishments prescribed under the Act. At the same time, norms for investigation and evidence are permissive and have been interpreted in a manner that prejudices the accused.

While the NDPS Act is predominantly punitive, it also contains provisions to regulate drugs. The Act empowers the central and state governments to frame rules and authorize drug-related activities within the rubric of "medical and scientific purpose", a term which is neither defined nor described in the Act.

In 1988, the NDPS Act was supplemented by the Prevention of Illicit Traffic in Narcotic Drugs and Psychotropic Substances Act to provide for preventive detention of people suspected or accused of involvement in drug trafficking.

NDPS Amendments

NDPS Amendments, 1989

In 1989, the NDPS Act underwent the first set of amendments, after a Cabinet Sub Committee for combating drug trafficking and abuse recommended that the law be made more stringent. The 'tough on drugs' rhetoric led to the introduction of very harsh provisions such as mandatory minimum sentences of 10 years' imprisonment, restrictions on bail, bar on suspension and commutation of sentences, forfeiture of property, trial by special courts, and mandatory death sentence for certain repeat offenders. The changes, which came in less than four years after the law was initially passed, seem to have been influenced by international, regional, and domestic developments—namely, the signing of the 1988 Convention; deliberations at the South Asian Association for Regional Cooperation (SAARC) on the growing menace of drug trafficking, increasing political dissent and 'terrorist' activity in northern states, and the perception that terrorism is fuelled by drug trafficking.

NDPS Amendments, 2001

Criticism of the harsh and disproportionate sentencing structure created a momentum for reform. In 1998, the NDPS (Amendment) Bill, was introduced in Parliament and subsequently examined by the

Parliamentary Standing Committee on Finance. The amendments were finally adopted in 2001, to grade punishment on the basis of the quantity of drugs involved—that is, "small", "commercial", or "intermediate". Thresholds were specified by the central government through a notification dated 19 October, 2001.

NDPS Amendments, 2014

In early 2014, the NDPS Act was amended for the third time and the new provisions came into force on 1 May, 2014. The main features include:

- Creation of a new category of "essential narcotic drugs", which the central government can specify and regulate uniformly throughout the country
- Widening the objective of the law from containing illicit use to also promoting the medical and scientific use of narcotic drugs and psychotropic substances in keeping with the principle of 'balance' between control and availability of narcotic drugs that underpins the international drug control treaties
- Including the terms "management" of drug dependence and "recognition and approval" of treatment centers, thus allowing for the establishment of legally binding treatment standards and evidence-based medical interventions
- Making the death penalty discretionary for a subsequent offence involving a certain quantity of drugs under section 31A. The court will have the alternative to impose imprisonment for 30 years under section 31
- Enhanced punishment for small quantity offences from a maximum of six months to one year imprisonment.
- Allowing private sector involvement in the processing of opium and concentrated poppy straw
- Raising the rank of officers authorized to conduct search and arrest licence holders for alleged NDPS violations
- More elaborate provisions for forfeiture of property of persons arraigned on charges of drug trafficking.

14

COMMUNALISM, SECULARISM AND REGIONALISM

"Little pools of water tend to become stagnant and useless, but if they are joined together to form a big lake, the atmosphere is cooled and there is universal benefit."

—Sardar Vallabhbhai Patel on Communalism and Regionalism

CONCEPTIONAL BACKGROUND

Communalism

Communalism in the western concept is referred to as a "theory or system of government in which virtually autonomous local communities are loosely in federation". Communalism is a political philosophy, which proposes that market and money be abolished and that land and enterprises to be placed

Communalism is a political philosophy, which proposes that market and money be abolished and that land and enterprises to be placed in the custody of the community. But in the Indian sub-continent context, communalism has come to be associated with conflicts and clashes between different religious communities.

in the custody of the community. But in the Indian sub-continent context, communalism has come to be associated with conflicts and clashes between different religious communities.

Communalism as a political philosophy has its roots in the ethnic and cultural diversity of Africa. It was used to refer to the characteristics of different ethnic groups and the community's lack of interaction with each other. Communalism in South Asia is used to denote the differences between the various religious groups and communities. The term has been extensively used to denote conflicts between those groups.

Communalism as an ideology consists of three elements:

i. A belief that people who follow the same religion have common political, economic, and social interests.

ii. A notion that, in a multi religious society, these common interests of one religion are dissimilar and divergent from the interests of the followers of another religion.

iii. The interests of the followers of the different religions or of different 'communities' are seen to be completely incompatible, antagonist, and hostile.

The two other related concepts of communalism are Secularism and Regionalism.

Secularism

Secularism as a concept has its origin in western philosophy. It was initially used to refer to the separation of the church from the state, which gives the state a position of neutrality between different religions, while at the same time, it guarantees all citizens right to adhere to any religion. Holyoake has been regarded as the originator of the concept of secularism because of his important work, such as, 'Principles of Secularism' and 'The Origin and Nature of Secularism'. A secular state is defined as a state which recognises every citizen as equal and does not recognise any social or religious stratification for any political benefit. Secularism is tolerance of all religions with special emphasis on the protection of minorities and preservation of communal harmony. *However, in the words of Rizvi (2005), the essence of secularism rests on two basic principles:*

(i) Separation of religion from politics.

(ii) Acceptance of religion as purely and strictly private affairs of individuals and having nothing to do with the state.

Sometimes secularism is used as a concept opposite to religious dogmatism but in reality, rather than remaining opposed to religion, secularism takes a dispassionate view in running the affairs of the state.

Regionalism

Region is a geographical unit and is delimited from other regions. Region as a social system reflects the relation between different human beings and groups. Regions are an organised cooperation in cultural, economic, political, or military fields. Region acts as a subject with distinct identity, language, culture, and tradition. Regionalism is an ideology and political movement that seeks to advance the causes of regions. As a process, it plays a role within the nation as well as outside the nation, that is, on a transnational level. Both types of regionalism have different meaning and have positive as well as negative impact on society, polity, diplomacy, economy, security, culture, development, negotiations, etc.

At the transnational level, regionalism refers to international cooperation to meet a common goal or to resolve a shared problem or it refers to a group of countries such as—Western Europe, or Southeast Asia, linked by geography, history, or economic features. Used in this sense, regionalism connotes to the attempts to consolidate the economic links between these countries. Regionalism at the national level refers to a process in which sub-state actors become significant and power devolves from the central level to regional governments. These are the regions within a country, distinguished in culture, language, and other sociocultural factors.

COMMUNALISM IN INDIA

India from the ancient times has a traditional of religious coexistence. For example, from the ancient Indian history we know that Ashoka followed religious tolerance and focussed mainly on Dhamma. In the medieval period, we have the example of a great ruler like Akbar, who was the epitome of secular practices and believed in propagating such values by abolishing *Jajhiya* tax and starting of *Din-I-ilahi* and *Ibadat Khana*. Same acceptance for different cultures and tradition was practised in several other kingdoms throughout India, though examples of a few sectarian rulers like Aurangzeb are also present who were least tolerant for other religious practices. Such rulers expressed religious dogmatism by imposing taxes on religious practices of other communities, destructing other religious monuments, forced conversions, etc.

However, communalism in India as we know today, is believed to be of modern origin and a result of the emergence of modern politics. The roots can be traced to the partition of Bengal in 1905 and feature of separate electorate under Government of India Act, 1909. Later, British government also appeased various communities through Communal award in 1932 (by Communal award colonial government mandated that consensus over any issue among different communities—Hindu, Muslims, Sikhs, and others as a precondition for any further political development), which faced strong resistance from Mahatma Gandhi and others. The feeling of communalism has been heightened by these developments.

Chronology of Development of Communalism in India

India is a nation imbibed in diversity— lingual, ethnic, cultural, and racial diversity. The idea that is popularly propagated to contend the diversity is "Unity in Diversity". There have been instances in the history of the nation that have threatened to break this fabric of unity. Some of them can be accounted as:

First stage was rise of religious nationalism—Hinduism, Islam, Sikhism, etc. Roots of this can be surmised as the developments in the later part of 19th century with Hindu revivalist movement like Shuddhi movement of Arya Samaj and Cow protection riots of 1892. On the other hand, movements like Faraizi movement started by Haji Shariatullah in Bengal to bring the Bengali Muslims back on the true path of Islam also impacted the sense of communalism. Later, leaders like Syed Ahmed Khan projected Indian Muslims as a separate community (qaum) having interest different from others.

Second stage was of Liberal Communalism—it believed in communal politics but liberal in democratic, humanist, and nationalist values. This wave existed before 1937. For example, organisations like Hindu Mahasabha, Muslim League, and personalities like M.A. Jinnah, M M Malviya, and Lala Lajpat Rai had this approach.

Third was the stage of Extreme Communalism which had fascist features. It demanded a separate nation, based on fear and hatred. There was tendency to use violence of language and action, for example, the Muslim League and Hindu Mahasabha after 1937. It spread as a by-product of colonialism, economic stagnations, and absence of modern institutions of education and health. These factors caused competition, people started using nepotism (patronage bestowed or favouritism shown on the basis of family relationship, as in business and politics), etc. Short-term benefits from communalism started gaining grounds and this gave rise to communal politics.

After this period the spread of education amongst the peasant and small landlords gave rise to the new middle class. This class started demanding representation based on communal grounds and in this way the social base for communalism widened.

The Mughal rule and the 1857 Revolt made the colonial administration suspicious towards Muslims, hence they patronised the Hindus. Upper caste Hindus dominated colonial services as they adapted early to the colonial structure. This resulted in resentment in Muslims in the late 19th century and they then formed a pressure group under Sir Sayed Ahmed Khan to bargain as a separate community. In contrast, Congress focussed on 'rights and freedom of individual'. In several parts, religious distinction were layered by social and class distinction, causing communal distortion. In many instances, communal colour was induced by communal politics.

Communalism in many cases was crisscrossed by struggle for economic power. For example—in western Punjab at that time, Muslim landlords opposed Hindu moneylenders. In eastern Bengal, Muslim jotedars opposed Hindu zamindars. Later on, communalism developed as a weapon of economically and politically reactionary social classes and political forces.

Divide and Rule

Communalism was a channel for providing service to colonialism and the feudal lords. British authorities supported communal feelings and divided Indian society for their authoritative ruling. Through actions like official patronage of communal biasness, favouring communal press, and people and agitations, acceptance of communal demands by the British politically strengthened communal organisations. British started accepting communal organisations and leaders as the real spokesperson of communities and adopted a policy of non-action against communalism. Communal riots were not crushed. Separate electorate was introduced in 1909 and communal award in 1932. These fulfilled the agenda of the British authorities of ruling India by dividing the societies on communal lines.

These unprecedented developments in the administration of the Indian society gave rise to communal and sectarian facets in the political and sociocultural life of Indians.

COMMUNAL VIOLENCE

India has witnessed brutal communal violence in the pre and post Independence era. These have marred the achievements of the nation. Some of them are:

Partition of India, 1947

Independence for India came with a heavy price. The country was divided into India and Pakistan. After partition, millions of people were forced to move from both sides of the border. Hindus in Pakistan and Muslims in India were killed in masses, women were raped, and children and aged people were also not spared. Later, the problem of refugees and their rehabilitation became one of the biggest challenges for independent India.

Anti-Sikh Riots, 1984

This was one of the worst riots in the recent history of India. Sikhs in a large number were massacred by anti-Sikh mobs. This massacre took place in response to the assassination of Prime Minister Indira Gandhi by her own Sikh body guard in response to her actions authorising the military operation in the Golden Temple to curb terrorism.

Ethnic Cleansing of Kashmiri Hindu Pundits, 1989

Kashmir is known as the paradise of India and was known for its *Kashmiryat*, that is, the reflection of love, peace, and harmony through brotherhood and unity of Hindu, Muslims, and other communities living together. But, this perception faced a serious blow because of the extremist terrorism in the Kashmir valley. The terrorism believed to be inspired by Islamic nationalism has led to mass killing and large scale exodus of Kashmiri Pundits from the valley to the various regions and corners of the India, giving them the status of refugees in their own country. Since then, the valley is under the grip of communal violence and continues even till the present times.

Babri Masjid Demolition in Ayodhya, 1992

It is believed that in the medieval period, Mughal general Mir Baqi, destroyed the sacred temple of the Hindus that was built on the site of Hindu god Rama's birth place and in its place built a mosque, named after Mughal ruler Babur. In 1990, due to political mobilization, there was attempt to resurrect the temple in the place of the mosque. Hindu religious groups and "kar sevak" in large numbers visited Ayodhya from all parts of India, in support of demolishing Babri masjid and building Ram temple there. These movements caused a huge amount of bloodshed all over the country and since then it is a disputed matter.

Godhra Riots, 2002

"Kar sevaks" returning from Ayodhya in a Sabarmati Express were killed by torching the coaches of the train. This act was followed by the extended communal violence in Gujarat. Hindu and Muslim community became antagonists to each other.

Assam Communal Violence, 2012

Large scale illegal immigration from Bangladesh has threatened to change the demography of North eastern states. In 2012, there were ethnic clashes between Bodos' tribal extremist groups and immigrants from Bangladesh in the Bodoloand Terrotorial Autonomous District (BTAD) areas. Ethnic tensions between Bodos and mostly Bengali-speaking Muslims escalated into a riot in Kokrajhar in July 2012, when unidentified miscreants killed four Bodo youths at Joypur.

Muzaffarnagar Violence, 2013

The cause of this ethnic clash between the Jat and Muslim community still remains unconfirmed. According to some, it ensued after some suspicious post on social media platform Facebook and according to others, it was escalated after the eve teasing case in Shamli. Despite the cause and reason, the consequence and the brutality of this incidence left a scar on the face of the nation.

These and many other big and small violent incidents have disturbed the peace and communal harmony of the nation time and again. These have claimed the lives and property of innumerable innocent people untouched by communal feeling.

Besides the incidences mentioned earlier, Bombay bomb incident (1993), attack on Akshardham (2002), and Varanasi bomb (2006) are other instances when the peace and coexistence of the general public have been tarnished.

THEORIES REGARDING COMMUNALISM

Generally, communalism is understood as rivalry kept and practised by one community or religion towards another or each other. Communalism can be considered an ideology which states that society is divided into religious communities whose interests differ and are at times even opposed to each other. The antagonism practiced by members of one community against the people of another community and religion can be termed communalism. This antagonism goes to the extent of falsely accusing, harming, and deliberately insulting a particular community and extends to looting, burning down the homes and property, dishonouring women, and even killing people. Richard Lambert defines communalism as "something colours political behaviour and produces a community oriented outlook." Louis Dumont states that "communalism is an affirmation and assertion of the religious community as a political group." In the words of Satish Sabarwal, "communalism in our sense means the channelling of personal sentiments and actions primarily with reference to the ascriptive group whose boundaries are determined by the accident of one's birth". According to Bipan Chandra, "communalism is the belief that because a group of people follow a particular religion, they have as a result, common social, political, and economic interests".

Communalism is a modern phenomenon and its fundamental interests are secular, like competition for share in political power or economic benefits. Religion is not its fundamental cause but an instrument used to achieve these goals as it contains great mobilizing power. A significant example is Muhammad Ali Jinnah, the Father of Pakistan, who advocated the theory of a separate nation for Muslims (the Two Nation theory), was essentially a communalist but not essentially a man of religion. M.A. Jinnah did not represent the masses of the Muslim population. The conservative Ulamas, on the other hand, were closer to the masses and represented their aspirations. No wonder that Jinnah and the Deoband Ulemas never saw eye to eye on political matters. They were closer to the Indian National Congress than to the Muslim League, which was the party of the Muslim elite. They supported the composite nationalism than Muslim separation. Similarly, many religious people who are having deep rooted knowledge in religion do not engage in propagating divisive communal thoughts.

Jawaharlal Nehru while delivering a speech in Punjab Provincial Congress in 1928 clearly stated that the Hindu-Muslim antagonism was rooted in the economic exploitation stimulated by imperialism. The role of religion is too less in a communal issue and the economic and political aspirations of both the communities play the major role. "It is an outcome largely of anger and passion and when we regain our tempers, it will fade into nothingness. It is a myth with no connection with reality and it cannot endure. It is really the creation of our educated class in search of office and employment….. What does it matter to the Muslim peasant whether a Hindu or Muslim is a judge at Lahore? Economic issues run along different lines. There is a great deal in common between the Muslim, Sikh and Hindu (Landlords) and a great deal in common between the Muslim Sikh

Communal Violence

The Indian law defines communal violence as, "any act or series of acts, whether spontaneous or planned, resulting in injury or harm to the person and or property, knowingly directed against any person by virtue of his or her membership of any religious or linguistic minority, in any State in the Union of India, or Scheduled Castes and Scheduled Tribes within the meaning of clauses (24) and (25) of Article 366 of the Constitution of India". Though India is under the grip of communal violence, but till now, other than provisions under IPC and CrPC, there is no firm law to punish the originators of such violence, and no clear policy for relief and rehabilitation of victims. There is no regulation for security of witness, for accountability of public servants, etc.

and Hindu peasantry; but very little in common between a Muslim peasant and a Muslim landlord."

PRESCRIPTIVE MEASURES TO COMBAT COMMUNALISM

National Human Rights Commission (NHRC) in India fights for the causes of rights of the victims, but its recommendations are advisory in nature. From time to time, respective governments have constituted various committees, commissions, bills, and police force to give recommendations to solve the issue of communal violence.

Committees and Commissions

The Nanavati-Mehta Commission was set up by Gujarat government in 2002 to enquire about Gujarat violence. The Sachar Committee, appointed in 2005, was commissioned to prepare a report on the latest social, economic and educational conditions of the Mushin commissary in India. Equal Opportunity Commission (EOC) was set up in 2010. EOC was to set up a grievance redressal mechanism for all individual cases of discriminations—religion, caste, gender, and physical ability among others. The Ranganath Misra Commission was entrusted by the Government of India to suggest practical measures for the upliftment of the socially and economically backward sections among religious and linguistic minorities and to include the modalities of implementation for the same. The report of the National Commission for Religious and Linguistic Minorities, headed by former Chief Justice of India Rangnath Mishra, says that 10% should be reserved for Muslims and 5% for other minorities in central and state government jobs in all cadre and grades. The purpose of all the aforementioned committees is to give recommendations to find out the causes of backwardness of minorities and steps required to improve their conditions.

Prevention of Communal and Targeted Violence (Access to Justice and Reparations) Bill, 2011

This bill lapsed in the Parliament. The bill provided for a seven-member national authority for communal harmony, justice, and reparations. It attempted to safeguard the minority sections. It had provisions for ensuring accountability of the district administration. This has already been recommended by the Sachar Committee and Raganath Mishra Commission.

The Role of Police

The role of police in communal riots is highly controversial. Generally, riot victims complain that police did not come to the rescue, police forces were themselves instrumental in arresting the innocent people and harassing them inside the lockup, etc. But as we know, that police can act much better, if there is political will and if they are given a free hand along with the implementation of recommended police reforms. There are specialized battalions of Rapid Action force in India, which is a wing of CRPF, to deal with riots, riot like situations, crowd control, rescue and relief operations, and related unrest.

BIBLIOGRAPHY AND REFERENCES

- *The Study of Social Problems*. http://sociology.morrisville.edu/readings/SOCI201/SocialProblems-Intro-Pearson.pdf
- National Programme on Technology Enhanced Learning (NPTEL), Humanities and Social Sciences. *Indian Society: Issues and Problems.*
- Smrutisikha. *Social Problems in India*: Characteristics, Causes and Types.
- Farooq, Umar. *Social Problem: Definition, Effect, Characteristics, Classification and Causes*. Study Lecture Notes.
- Guerrero, Anna Leon. *Social Problems: Community, Policy, and Social Action*. Sage Publications. 2013.
- Barkan, Steven E. *Social Problems: Continuity and Change*. Saylor Foundation. 2013.
- Thio, Alex and Taylor, Jim D. Taylor. *Social Problems*. Jones & Bartlett Publishers. 2011.
- Theodorson and Theodorson. *Modern Dictionary of Sociology*. Crowell. 1969.
- Horton and Leslie. *The Sociology of Social Problems*. Appleton-Century-Crofts. 1970.
- Ahuja, Ram. *Society in India: Concepts, Theories and Recent Trends*. Rawat. 2002.
- Reinhardt, James H. *Social Problems and Social Policy*. American Book Co. 1952.
- Case, C. "A Definition of Social Problems". J. Gould and W.L. Kolb (eds.), *A Dictionary of Social Sciences*. The Free Press. 1964.
- Fuller, Richard C and Myers, Richard R. *The Natural History of Social Problem*. *American Sociological Review*. Vol. 6. 1941.
- Gupta Age: http://living-smartly.com/2015/01/guptas-dynasty-indian-heritage/.
- Mahajan, Gurpreet. *Negotiating Cultural Diversity and Minority Rights in India*
- Singh, K.S. *People of India*. New Delhi. Oxford University Press. 1992.

- Kulke, Hermann and Rothermund Dietmar. *A History of India*. Paperback. South Asia Books. 1991.
- Singh, Mahendra P and Deva Surya. *The Constitution of India: Symbols of Unity in Diversity* in *Yearbook of Public Law*. 2005.
- Gadgil, Madhav. *Biodiversity Profile of India*: http://ces.iisc.ernet.in/hpg/cesmg/
- Indian Geography: http://www.indiabook.com/india-information/indian-geography.html.
- Age Structure And Marital Status, Ministry of Home Affairs, Government of India, Census of India.
- Population Composition, Ministry of Home Affairs, Government of India, Census of India.
- *The Future Population of India: A Long-range Demographic View*. Population Foundation of India. Population Reference Bureau. 2007.
- National Planning Commission on Population, Ministry of Health and Family Welfare, Government of India: http://populationcommission.nic.in/.
- The Planning Commission: Approach to the 12th Plan. *The Challenges of Urbanisation in India.*
- "Report of the Steering Committee on Urbanization". *Planning Commission Government of India*. Twenty-fifth Year Plan. November 2012.
- Kadi, A.S., Halingali, B.I. and Ravishankar, P. *Problems of Urbanisation in Developing Countries: A Case Study of India*. International Journal of Science and Nature. Vol. 3(1) 2012.
- McKinsey and Company. *India's Urban Awakening: Building Inclusive Cities, Sustaining Economic Growth*. McKinsey Global Institute. 2010.
- Randhawa, Pritpal Singh. "Delhi Metro Rail: Beyond Mass Transit". *Economic and Political Weekly*. Vol. XLVII. No. 16. April 2012.
- Report of the Expert Group to Review the Methodology for Measurement of Poverty". Planning Commission, Government of India. June, 2014.
- "Poverty Alleviation Programmes". Planning Commission, Government of India.
- Mondol, Puja. "*Women: Essay on The Position of Women in India*
- Ministry of Women and Child Development, Government of India.
- Krishnan, Nandela. *Gandhi on Women's Empowerment*

- Singh, Savita (ed.). *Empowerment of Women: Miles to Go*. International Centre of Gandhian Studies and Research, Gandhi Smriti and Darshan Samiti. 2001.
- M, Suguna. *Education and Women Empowerment in India*. International Journal of Multidisciplinary Research.Vol.1 Issue 8. December 2011.
- Gull, Raashida Gull and Shafi, Aneesa. "Indian Women's Movement after Independence". *International Research Journal of Social Sciences*. Vol. 3, Issue 5. May 2014.
- Mishra, Manasee. "Gendered Vulnerabilities: Women's Health and Access to Healthcare in India". CEHAT. 2006.
- George A. *Sexual Behaviour and Sexual Negotiation among Poor Women and Men in Mumbai: An Explanatory Study*. SAHAJ: Society for Health Alternatives. 1997.
- "Public Health Statistics". Central Bureau of Health Insurance (CBHI). 2003.
- N. Lalitha and Nagaraj B.S. *Self Help Groups in Rural Development*. Dominant Publishers and Distributors. 2002.
- Chakrabarti, Shantanu and Chatterjee, Kingshuk (ed.). *Globalization and Development: Current Trends*. KW Publishers. 2012.
- Shrivastava, Aseem and Kothari, Ashish. *Churning the Earth: The Making of Global India*. Viking/Penguin, 2012.
- Buggi, C Reddy S and Gowda, G. "Impact of Globalization on Agrarian Class Structure: Its Implication on Indian Villages". *Third Concept*. January 2001.
- A. Maria Alphonsal and J. Delphine Prema Dhanaseeli. "Strategies against the Threat to Rural Poor". *Eubios Journal of Asian and International Bioethics*. Vol 13. 2003.
- Report on the Status of Elderly in Select States of India 2012,"Building a Knowledge Base on Population Ageing in India". United Nations Population Fund 2012.
- "Older women in India". Agewell Foundation.
- "Problems of the Elderly". Helpage India Programme.
- "Situation Analysis of the Elderly in India". Central Statistics Office. Ministry of Statistics & Programme Implementation. Government of India. June 2011.
- "Details of Welfare Schemes for the Aged Persons". Press Information Bureau. Government of India. Ministry of Social Justice and Empowerment.

- Prasad, S. "Deprivation and Vulnerability among Elderly in India". WP-2011-2013. Indira Gandhi Institute of Development, Mumbai. 2011.
- Singh Charan. "Aging Population in India: Select Economic Issues". Indian Institute of Management, Bangalore. 2013.
- Madhavan, M.C. "Indian Emigrants: Numbers, Characteristics, and Economic Impact". *Population and Development Review.* Vol. 11, No. 3. September 1985.
- Srivastava, Ravi and Sasikumar, S.K. "An Overview of Migration in India, Its Impacts and Key Issues". Conference paper on *Migration and Development Pro-Poor Policy Choices in Asia.* Refugee and Migratory Movements Research Unit, Bangladesh, and the Department for International Development, UK. June 2003.
- Skeldon, Ronald. "United Nations Department of Economic and Social Affairs Population Division Technical Paper". *Global Migration: Demographic Aspects and Its Relevance for Development.* 2013.
- Ratha, Dilip; Mohapatra, Sanket; Scheja, Elina. "Impact of Migration on Economic and Social Development: A Review of Evidence and Emerging Issues". Policy Research Working Paper. Vol. 1. 2001.
- "World Migration Report 2015". *International Organization for Migration, Geneva* 2015.
- "International Migration Policies". Government Views and Priorities. United Nations. New York, 2013.
- Seth, Rajeev. "Protection of Children from Abuse and Neglect in India". Special Feature: The 28th CMAAO General Assembly and 49th Council Meeting. Takemi Memorial Oration. *Japan Medical Association Journal.* Vol.56, No.5. September-October 2013.
- Child Abuse Prevention. http://www.nicwa.org/. Retrived 30 January 2016.
- "Study on Child Abuse: India 2007" Ministry of Women and Child Development, Government of India. 2007.
- "Guidelines for Prevention of Child Abuse". Delhi Commission for Protection of Child Rights, 2014.
- The *National Indian Child Welfare Association.* http://www.nicwa.org/.
- "It's everyone's job to make sure I'm alright". Report of the Child Protection Audit and Review. Education for Scotland. 2011.
- Sirpal, Suman Kakar. *Does Child Abuse Lead to Juvenile Delinquency or Crime? A Critical Examination of the Literature.* 1996.

- Haranath, S. And Prasad, Devi B. "Juvenile Home Inmates: Background Characteristics". *Indian Journal of Social Work*. Vol. 56. July 1995.
- "World Report on Violence and Health". World Health Organization. 2002.
- Corby, B. *Child Abuse: Towards a Knowledge Base*. Open University. 2000.
- Bowlby, J. *Maternal Care and Mental Health*. World Health Organization Monograph. 1951.
- Crittenden, Patricia M and Ainsworth. *Child Maltreatment and Attachment Theory*. University Press. 1989.
- Steele, B.J and Pollock, C.B. "A Psychiatric Study of Parents Who Abuse Infants and Small Children". Helfer, R. E and Kempe, C.H. (eds.), *The Battered Child*. University of Chicago. 1974.
- Buchachan, Ann. *Cycles of Child Maltreatment: Facts and Fallacies and Intervention*. Wiley, Chichester. 1996.
- Kempe, Ruth and Kempe, Henry C. *Child Abuse*. Havard University Press. 1978.
- Gil, David. *Violence against Children*. Havard University Press. 1970.
- Adenwalla, Maharukh. "The Juvenile Justice System in India and Children who commit serious offences –Reflections on the Way Forward". *Child Protection and Juvenile Justice System for Juvenile in Conflict with Law*. Childline India Foundation. 2006.
- Manoharan, Arlene and Raha, Swagata. "The Juvenile Justice System in India and Children who commit serious offences –Reflections on the Way Forward". Centre for Child and the Law, National Law School of India University, Bangalore. 2013.
- Juvenile Justice Board, Government of India, http://ecourts.gov.in/pithoragarh/juvenile-justice-board
- Johnson, Vernon E. *I will Quit Tomorrow A Practical Guide to Alcoholism Treatment*. HarperOne. 1990.
- Keller M and Efron V. "The Prevalence of Alcoholism". *Quarterly Journal of Studies on Alcohol*. Vol. 16. 1955.
- Clinebell, Howard J. *Understanding and Counseling the Alcoholic through Religion and Psychology*. Abingdon Press. 1956.
- Mondal, Puja. "Anti-Arrack Movements for Women in India". http://www.yourarticlelibrary.com/essay/anti-arrack-movements-for-women-in-india/32973/.

- Das, Subir Kumar, Balakrishnan and Vasudevan, D.M. "Alcohol: Its Health and Social Impact in India". *The National Medical Journal of India*. Vol. 19. No. 3. March-April 2006.
- "Aberrant Drug Taking Behaviors Information Sheet". http://www.drugabuse.gov/nidamed-medical-health-professionals
- Espejo, Roman (ed.). *Drug Abuse*. Greenhaven Press. 2002.
- Tandon, Tripti. "Drug Policy in India". *International Drug Policy Consortium*. Briefing Paper. February 2015.
- Ahmad Nadeem, Bano Rubeena, Agarwal V.K. and Kalakoti Piyush. Substance Abuse in India. *Pravara Medical Review*. Vol 1. No. 4. 2009.
- "Communalism –Meaning and Issues". *Insights*. November, 2014.
- "Communalism". *Essays on Human Rights and Law* hrln.org>Pdf>COMMUNALISM. Retrieved on 1 April 2015.
- Sengupta, Roshini. "Communal Violence in India: Perspectives on Causative Factors". *Economic and Political Weekly*. Vol. 40. No. 20. May 2005.